Jack Riepe

# CONVERSATIONS WITH A MOTORCYCLE

ZADIC &
DEVERELLE
SCRIBE NOBIS INOPINATUM

**Conversations With A Motorcycle**

For more information: contact the author at jackriepe.com

Zadfic & Deverelle, LLC

ISBN 978-0-9990287-0-4
ISBN 978-1-938022-24-1 (Previously Published)


First printed 2012

Second Revised Edition
Printed 2017

*This book is dedicated to the riders of the Mac-Pac Eating and Wrenching Society, the chartered BMW riding club of southeastern Pennsylvania. I can never repay this group for the camaraderie, confidence, respect, patience, and inspiration that they so generously share with me.*

# PREFACE

Revised for the 2nd edition

The caller's voice was abrupt and mysterious, as many calls from members of my motorcycle club tend to be. It's not that they have much to be mysterious about. They just assume everyone is connected by a kind of moto-telepathy. The caller said, "Not many people are getting an invitation to see this."

"What is it?" I asked.

"You'll see," I was told.

A cold rain was falling so we went by car. The two guys in the back had received the same briefing I had. They gave me the usual rolled eyes and blank smiles, indicating unbridled skepticism in the nature of our mission. The driver was a ranking club member, who bore the look of someone who had inside information. Every rider knows that look. It is a mask of smugness and mild conceit worn by those on the inside of things.

Our destination was a modest-looking garage, in a nicely appointed house, on a street in a staid neighborhood, in a Pennsylvania town that had six consonants and three "Y"s in its name. This town had originally been a WASP (White Anglo Saxon Protestant) bastion, but there were now more consonants in its name than WASPs in local residence. The door went up before we could knock and we stepped inside a darkened bay, cluttered by tool boxes and motorcycles lining the walls. But there was something parked in the center of the garage, with a soft cover on it.

The door came down, the lights came up, and the cover came off. I found myself standing less than three feet away from a 1952

Vincent Black Shadow. Three of the five men in that room caught their breath. I was one of them. For those unfamiliar with a Vincent Black Shadow motorcycle, this was the equivalent of venturing into the crypt at Saint Peter's in Rome, only to find Saint Peter there, ready to chat. This bike was museum quality.

The only Vincents I had ever seen were in books or on calendars. The design elements of this machine were as subtle as the motorcycle was sleek, fast, and seductive. There is an austere attraction to old BMW's and Velocettes that appeals to all riders. Yet nothing commands the attention of a Vincent Black Shadow.

There is an interesting story behind the acquisition of this bike that I will tell at some point (not now). As it turns out, I had been within 20 feet of this machine a dozen times (in another location) and just never asked what was beneath the cover. It was the best kept secret between two men in that room. (The bike was valued at over $100,000.) I was astounded to be this close to a bike of this distinction. It was then I felt, more than I heard, this classic motorcycle speaking to me. It spoke to my youth, to a sense of appreciation I didn't have in my youth, and to an acquired perception of mechanical perfection.

I asked the owner what possessed him to want to possess such a priceless thing.

He replied, "It spoke to me the second I saw it."

"What did it say?" I asked.

"Start me," said the Vincent's owner. "Ride me."

Shortly thereafter, that Vincent rode to a competitive vintage bike event, hitting 90 miles per hour in the first straight stretch, before taking first place. (It hadn't run in 40 years.) When I asked the owner if it spoke again, he replied, "Yeah. It said 'Aaaaaaaaaah' when the speedo tapped 90."

Many riders spend thousands of hours in the solitude of two wheels. They think of things they said; things they should have said; and things that got said by saying nothing at all; to lovers, to friends, and others, who no longer qualify as either. And sometimes, rather often actually, they get a different perspective colored by rising RPM, the thrum of the road, or the combination of the two. That's the motorcycle talking. Or the times they took a detour that added 1,200 miles onto the trip, that was the motorcycle's suggestion. Or when they headed into the garage to get a paintbrush and headed out the big door ten minutes later for a 12-hour run, that was in response to a whisper from the motorcycle.

I wrote this book from personal experience. I know the consequences of listening to the motorcycle too often, and the price you pay when you don't listen at all.

This book was initially written under another title. It was two-thirds complete when I noted the number of riders who gave me a variation of: "The bike just spoke to me." There were over a hundred of them and the messages from their machines varied. Among the most common were:

"Let's get the hell out of here."
"Just twist it and see what happens."
"How much can the ticket be?"
"So what if she is gone when you get back?"

One rider, who refers to his 1963 Triumph Bonneville as "The Trollop" because it screws him every chance it gets, said, "This bike lies to me. It calls me names. It makes fun of me in front of other bikes and refuses to start."

Another rider, who's owned many bikes, said, "By and large, my machines have been true and truthful to me. Then there was a Ducati I owned in the mid-seventies. Oh, how that bitch lied... But I loved to hear it."

In 1975, the motorcycle that is the focus of this book said to me, "You can have truth or you can have perspective. One never changes and is like getting a kick in the balls every fifteen minutes. The other changes whenever you lean the bike. Choose." I did.

I am cursed with a memory that records every last detail of my few successes and all of my failures. Two of the best years of my life were 1975 and 1976, and I remember them like they were yesterday. I remember the motorcycle that started a chain of events that continues to this day. I remember the odd ideas that popped into my head when I rode that bike any distance or speed. I understand now that it was the motorcycle talking. I changed the title of this book less than 2 months from it's scheduled publication date. I also rewrote a story that grew in the telling and shrank in the editing. My daughter, a brilliant communicator, led me through a process that changed my writing style forever. In honor of the great motorcycle that gave me this inspiration, I put the Vincent that was under the cover in the garage that day on the cover of this book. It belongs to one of the finest riders and classic gentlemen I have ever come to know. This revised cover is based on an incredibly beautiful image taken by Joseph Luppino, a man who understands the art and practical magic of photographing motorcycles. He is a specialist in bending color and light around sculpted steel, aluminum, chrome, and plastic. He has photographed hundreds of motorcycles in a special studio of his own specification. Getting your bike photographed by Joe Luppino is a privilege.

The book's cover design is the work of Brian Potash, the genius behind Devilfish Inc., a unique hi-fidelity design and screen printing shop in Philadelphia. Potash, and his staff, create the most incredible illustrations, covers, and posters, from kids' books to moto mags. Michele Leigh Cameron of pennyrich, LLC; Lori Zastrow, publisher of For The Love Of A Motorbike (blog); and Rogers George, publisher of The Writing Rag (blog) were instrumental in helping me salvage three critical months due to sickness. Rick Matz kept this project alive.

This book is dedicated to the Mac-Pac, whose collective adventures have given me unlimited moto horizons. Yet there are a handful of guys in this group who have no equal among mortal men. They are Peter Buchheit, Peter Frechie, Gerry Cavanaugh, Horst Oberst, David Hardgrove, Paul Pollio, and the late Ron Yee. Dick Bregstein is the best straight man I have ever had, and witness to my last great motorcycle crash.

This book references certain friends of mine from the 1970s: Cretin (pronounced "CREE-tin"), Stitches, Fast Freddie, Louie, Spider, and Weasel. Spider and Stitches are the only two still alive. The others lived fast, colorfully, and too briefly. None died in motorcycle accidents and none made it out of their early thirties. They were loyal, generous, funny, and genuine. All of the names of the characters in this book, other than mine, are utterly fictitious. Any resemblance to the street names, nicknames, or saloon names that anyone might remember from 1975 or 1976 is coincidental. While certain descriptions are accurate, they could apply to anyone in Jersey City at that time. I knew a lot of tough guys, and they all had names like these. So if you think you, or someone you know is a character in this book, then you're mistaken.

Dozens of women contributed to this story. Nearly all were intensely pretty. A number were incredibly sensuous. I learned something from all of them (mostly how to survive 3rd degree burns). I remember four of them 37 years after the fact. I still talk with one of them on a weekly basis. She called me this morning to tell me something about her new boyfriend. (She planted her foot in my balls when she was 17 and never took it out.) Three were brunettes who could have passed for sisters. They were all beautiful in that post-Woodstock sort of way. One was a blond who was as different as they get. All were unique. Some readers might think my tendency to refer to these ladies by their hair color is a sign of sexist disrespect. Nothing could be further from the truth. I have worked hard to conceal their identities. It is the least I can do for them now. I deeply regret that I was a horse's ass when I first fell in love with these ladies, especially "The Equestrian." I would be delighted if any of them would give me another shot. (One has already indicated that shot would be at point blank range.) I adored these women, and still do.

I am intensely proud of coming from Jersey City. (I don't have to put "N.J." after it as there is only one, and it is the absolute center of the universe.) If you can make it in New Jersey, then the world is your oyster. This book touches on certain New Jersey cultural issues like diners, Jersey big hair, accents, and douches. Famed for spontaneous breakfasts and the 3 a.m. "Cheeseburger Deluxe," the traditional New Jersey diner is a culinary marvel. If you want to visit a classic New Jersey diner, then hit the "Tick Tock" in Clifton, on Route 3. Diner waitresses in New Jersey should make $1 million per year. If elected officials were as efficient as New Jersey diner waitresses, we'd have fast, hot legislation, plus great coffee on Capitol Hill and in Trenton. New Jersey does not have more than its share of douches then California nor Illinois. But because the state is smaller and more compact, resident douches seem larger than normal and more numerous. There are five appendices dealing with douches in the Garden State and one on New Jersey facts toward the end of this book. Read them. They might save your life.

Locations in this book are approximate and may no longer exist. Certain saloons, diners, and county jails are now gone. Neighborhoods that were once cheap shit holes are now expensive shit holes. Towns or road names mentioned in these chapters may appear on a map, but unless they are major highways or state parks, they merely provide a backdrop for the action. I recently covered the territory listed in chapter 16 — Route 23 in New Jersey — and barely recognized it. Trust me, it has not been improved during the last 30 years. Please do not waste your time looking for the saloons I drank in nor folks who knew me. They are gone... Or dead... Or dead drunk.

Despite the cover, the motorcycle in this book is a Kawasaki H2. I have described this bike as being "a savage and primitive motorcycle." Compared to one of today's bikes, it was. But it was pretty special for its time and the bike has a substantial cult following now. The Kawasaki H2 was spawned in the era of raw power, primeval brakes, and temporary tires. It required no tinkering. It always started. It always ran like a prison riot for the first two or three minutes. It was a 750 two-stroke rig that would make clouds of blue smoke at the drop of a hat. If my gimpy leg would let me kick start one, I'd own a Kawasaki H2 today. Someone needs to restore a Kawasaki H2 in Jet Black. (I don't think it was ever issued in that color.) That stupid gas tank decal needs to be scrapped. That hideous chrome fender should be done in metallic red too. The shit chrome pipes should be replaced with custom ones, done in a jet black finish. An H2 bike like that would make an insidious statement.

I do not advocate riding while intoxicated nor under the influence of drugs. I did plenty of both when I was nineteen. I don't do it now. I do not advocate speeding, disregarding the regulations of state parks, nor operating a motorcycle like you are immortal. I do not advocate hitchhiking. I do not advocate stealing cars, wives, nor girlfriends. I no longer advocate gin for breakfast (though I still brush my teeth with it.) I do not advocate smoking cigars, especially the really pungent maduro ones, that remind you of all the pleasing things you can put in your mouth that will eventually kill you. I do not advocate disagreeing with women at the beginning of long holiday weekends for the same reason I do not advocate operating a toaster in the bathtub. (The results are identical.) I do not advocate lying to your wife, your girlfriend, nor that other one you met in the bar, unless you regain consciousness in the intensive care unit and all three are there. (This happened to me, once. I started the conversation with, "You're probably wondering why I asked all of you here today.") I do not advocate trying anything I have ever written about, or anything I have done. If you can honestly say, "This is something Riepe would do," then don't do it. Look where it got me.

Jack Riepe
June 24, 2017

# Chapter 1

# "THE SEDUCTION"

I'd had the bike less than two weeks and had yet to go beyond a ten-mile radius from the house. Shifting gears was a new thing to me, as was the potency and sudden effect of the front brake. The seat looked like it was designed for comfort but I soon discovered that this was an abstract concept among riders. I'd spent a good part of those first two weeks wiping micro-specs of grime from the bike and inspecting the chain for the proper tension and lubrication. On a day that was to realign my senses forever, I followed a friend on his bike into the next state (New Jersey into New York), to find adventure on old highways perched atop the cliffs of the Palisades, overlooking the Hudson River.

The trip would be 60 miles out and back, testing my ability to handle the new bike in traffic, around curves, and through changes in elevation. We took our time, stopping at vistas and to occasionally consult a map. I was pleased with the bike's performance and the way I had grown comfortable going through the gears. Yet it is growing comfortable with a thing that causes us to experiment with the parameters of the suddenly uncomfortable, or at least to sample circumstances that are less certain in the immediate outcome.

Our return trip called for crossing the Hudson River at the Bear Mountain Bridge, and heading south on US-9 through Peekskill, NY. Coming off the bridge, southbound traffic ascends a long hill that resembles the apex of an old-fashioned wooden roller coaster. I haven't been over this route lately, but the road was narrow, with an 18-inch gravel shoulder, lined by a short, jagged stone wall. The other side of the wall was a 400-foot drop onto railroad tracks. There was a little dimple at the top, before a sweeping descent that went on for a few miles.

I crested the hill and began the ride down.

Now there are all kinds of things to consider on endlessly sweeping, steep downhill runs, especially if you are new to a bike. For example, how does having a lot of the machine's weight on the front wheel affect its turning and braking capacity? Should you just coast, or should you add power to the equation? Is it enough to just enjoy the moment, or should you glory on the edge of the downhill twisties? It is important to remember that these were the days before the world had the benefit of so many safety regulations. I wasn't wearing a helmet nor protective gear, and rode in sneakers.

The speedometer read 60 miles per hour through curves and straight stretches posted at 45. I flashed by signs advising trucks to use a lower gear. The traffic around me became objects of delight, to be dodged or passed without touching the brakes. I zipped past several tractor-trailers by darting over the double yellow line and closed to within a few feet of cars in front of me, hesitating as I second guessed passing these as well. Never was raised the thought of how well the brakes would hold in a panic situation. I had never made a "panic" stop before anyway.

There was no accommodation for panic... Just pure euphoria.

The wind seduced me, moving about my face and whispering in my ears. It isolated me from the reality of my peril. I was astounded at how the bike responded to the slightest input to the handlebars! The merest suggestion of a touch leaned it in one direction or another, with the feeling that it was on rails. Instead of angling into curves, it was the sensation of conducting music with the slightest pressure of my hands. And what music it was! Deep and resonant. Compelling and urgent. Yet as silent as a dog whistle and audible only to a part of myself I didn't know existed.

I found myself leaning forward in the curves to lower a center of gravity that I sensed might suddenly work against me. There were no classes that taught this. I had no mentor to warn me of the euphoria. I had no prior experience with the lies of immortality the wind would tell me. How could I?

I was 14-years-old.

The bike was a ten-speed "racer" with paper-thin tires holding 90 pounds of air. The brakes were blocks of rubber activated by cables. There was no suspension system. I had no lights nor concern for signaling. Emboldened by my speed, I sliced through traffic. I started pedaling down that hill as hard as I could in 10th gear. The objective was to go as fast as I could, as long as I could, if for no other reason than to make it easier to get over the next rise.

There was no consideration for blowing tires that were thinner than commercial grade condoms. I never gave a second thought to the man-killing sewer grates designed to eat thin bicycle wheels. Since neither my friend nor I could yet drive, we had no idea how nearly invisible we were at that speed. Nor had we told our parents where we were going. Our combined financial resources didn't top $6.00. We were typical Jersey City punk kids who didn't give a damn about anything.

I was riding in the company of Steve Venner. Together, we were Huck Finn and young Albert Einstein, out for raw adventure. (I was never the smart one.) The ratcheting mechanism of the rear gear cluster, which gave a reassuring clicking sound when I coasted, buzzed like an enraged hornet's nest on that downhill run. Like most of life's exhilarating moments, this one ended abruptly: with a traffic light around a tight corner. I clenched the brake levers and felt the cables stretch as the center-pull binders converted forward motion into heat, noise, and an unsettling degree of vibration.

Steve and I dismounted at the bottom of that hill to exchange smirks and to exhale in safety. Though we had just shared an identical experience, it affected us in differently. Steve felt compelled to challenge inertia with the piston-like authority of his own legs by collecting more sophisticated bicycles designed to magnify the human effort well into his thirties. These included bikes that were made of exotic alloys, equipped with elliptical crank-sets and highly machined disc brakes. His last bike, purchased at age 35, cost more than my college education and weighed less than three sheets of paper. His love of bicycles was never compromised.

I felt otherwise. To me, the whispering of the wind in my ears carried the significance of my first French kiss. I wanted to savor it. To study it. To analyze it. To improve it. And I wanted to repeat it on demand. All I could remember of the music in my head that day was a single strain of a haunting lilt. I had to be sure I didn't imagine it and wanted to make it my personal anthem.

I took every downhill run as an opportunity to meet the vapory lady (the wind) who would again fondle my soul. I discovered that she was a fickle lover, when a year later I dropped a stitch on a Jersey City street corner at 45 miles per hour. The bicycle and I parted company when the curve tightened, and I spent the next five days in Saint Francis Hospital recovering from a nasty concussion. (My head was never the same.)

This was the seed planted in the barren wasteland of my adolescent mind. It would lie fallow for five years. But my next bike would come with a 70-horsepower engine. The wind would whistle in my ears from the time I left the driveway, and when going uphill as well as down. This was not an infatuation with speed, but an addiction to the lure of moto-motion. The motorcycle is the potter's wheel that shapes gravity and centrifugal force. I have since learned that you can encounter this sensation at any speed on a motorcycle, if you are among the cognoscenti.

I have flown in a Stearman open-cockpit biplane. I have taken flying lessons in a 1947 Aeronca Champ (on floats). I have boiled the alligator-choked St. John's River (Palatka, Florida ) in an open bass boat (going faster than 65 miles per hour). Nothing compares with the sensation of twisting the throttle on a hot motorcycle. Maybe one thing, and not always.

My first motorcycle was a viciously primitive 1975 Kawasaki H2, 750cc two-stroke street predator. I had the machine four days before I gave the engine a sustained jolt on an interstate. The wind whistled around my goggles with insistence and nuzzled my neck.

"Hey baby," I muttered. "Miss me?"

# Chapter 2

# "THE SUGGESTION"

**M**ost riders remember every bike they ever owned or ridden. I tend to remember the people I rode with the and conversations we had. There are one or two individuals who are impossible for me to forget. Some were tough and others were toughened in ways that were hard to fathom. One of these people nearly talked me into getting a Harley Davidson trike as my first bike.

He was as thin as a rail with a temper like a hand grenade. We grew up in the same city, and went to schools within a mile of each other. Yet he had a reputation for handling a machine gun at the same age that I was learning to drive. Most guys tend to say a bit more than usual when the whiskey flows, and he was no exception. Being in his company on those occasions was to risk hearing details that made you party to events better left without witnesses. You'd be sober in the morning, yet the images he painted would hang like tattered shrouds in the forefront of your consciousness.

So much of what guys tell each other is utter nonsense that won't stand close inspection even in the dim light that filters through a bottle. Still there was never any doubt as to the veracity of this guy's stories. When he spoke, it was was without unnecessary description and generally in response to a direct question. I pressed for details on the machine gun story. His first automatic weapon was a classic Thompson "Tommy" gun with a pancake magazine. What 18-year-old male wouldn't be thrilled to fire one of these? He described what was like shooting it from the back of a moving truck. This was simply the prelude to the main event: firing twin fifty caliber barrels at screaming Messerschmitts from the tail of a B-17G.

He was thirty years my senior because he was my father.

A professional fireman with a sense of adventure, my father was a rescue captain first and then a battalion chief in Jersey City (a municipality that burned like a Roman candle). He choose careers that had an edge to them. He came to the fire department after surviving 36-missions as a tail gunner in a B-17, a position that spawned a lot of corpses. As a kid, I used to love rummaging through my dad's stuff (in his dresser), but this had to be done when he wasn't around. Nevertheless, the day came when I got caught, examining the contents of a small box, the sort of thing that might contain a ring. But there was no ring; just a jagged piece of broken metal. When I asked my dad what it was, he replied, "Flack."

He also had a wicker basket of photographs. Among these was a picture of the Sphinx, guarding the pyramids in Egypt. One snapshot (in black and white) depicts this noble landmark taken at the statue's eye level.

"How did you come by this?" I asked. I had no idea he'd been to Egypt.

"Everybody in the plane's crew wanted a picture of the Sphinx," said my dad. "But the monument wasn't close to the base and none of us had access to a jeep nor a truck. So we asked the pilot to fly in front of it. He did. The wingtip cleared the face of the statue by about 50 feet." At the time, the B-17 was the largest four-engine bomber in the US-AAF's arsenal, carrying a crew of ten. The pilot was 21-years-old. He would have flown that plane through the Lincoln Tunnel if the crew had asked him.

My prized possession is my dad's old fireman's helmet. Known as the "New Yorker," it is the classic "fireman" style, in white, with the eagle on the front of it, holding a gold shield proclaiming him to be a chief of Jersey City. There is a hole burned through it. (These helmets were made of heavy duty leather.) I had to wonder what kind of situation my father had gotten into, where it was hot enough to burn through a quarter inch of leather.

There were three things my dad always wanted: a sailboat, an airplane, and a motorcycle. He got four kids instead, and put three of them through private schools. Had my father known me prior to my birth, I would have been the load shot into the sink. His pet name for me was "Shitbird," inspired by the fact that I had inherited all of the shortcomings of two ancient bloodlines, and none of the virtues.

There were many evenings when I'd get in around midnight, to find my dad sitting in a dimly lit kitchen, sipping incredibly cheap Scotch or drinking instant coffee. (I used to think he was training to be a hostage.) We'd sit and talk, sometimes for two or three hours. One night, the conversation turned to motorcycles. The Jersey City Police Department was selling off its aging fleet of Harley-Davidson trikes, and my father thought I should get one.

"Imagine the fun you could have with one of these things," said my dad. "You could throw all your camping gear in the back and take off for parts unknown without a care in the world."

My reply to this observation was a a nod and a smile, hoping he'd take this tacit agreement as an opportunity to offer me a drink too, though I never developed a taste for Scots Whisky in general, nor rot-gut Scotch in particular.

"The cops probably took good care of these trikes, and they can't be that hard to ride or keep running," he continued. "I bet you could get one really cheap. I'm sure one of our cop neighbors knows somebody who could take care of you downtown."

We lived in the Western Slope section of the city, overlooking the bogs and swamps that were known as the "Meadows." Virtually every other house on our block was owned by a cop or a fireman. We knew them all.

"Why don't you take a look at one of these things?" asked the old man.

My dad was already suffering the beginnings of the respiratory disease that would kill him. That he had had pneumonia as a kid, grew up in the era of tuberculosis, spent a good part of his adolescence at 25,000 feet (in an unheated bomber with open windows), ate smoke for a living, and smoked on top of all this, wasn't helping the situation. I was too stupid at the time to realize my dad's recommendation regarding the Harley trike was vocalizing one of his own fading dreams.

I did get an up-close look at the aging Harley-Davidson trikes the cops were unloading. Two, in fact. The first was broken down at the end of a quiet street, at the end of a quiet day, in Jersey City. A motorcycle cop, dressed in cop biker pants with a broad leather belt and knee-high, fascist storm-trooper boots was jumping on the kick-starter like it was a felon. He cursed and swore with practiced gusto. It was the end of his shift and this unexpected development meant waiting for the department wrecker to pick up the trike.

"Can I give you a hand?" I ventured. I was a helpful kid in a 1968 red Volkswagen Beetle.

The cop looked at the half-moon rear bumper on my car and asked if I could push him up to 20 miles per hour, at which point, he'd snick the trike into gear and get it started. We did this dance three times. The Harley popped in mechanical indignation, but made no sounds like an engine firing.

The cop shrugged and said "thanks," resigned to waiting for the wrecker.

"Does this happen often with these?" I asked.

"Often enough," said the cop. "We're getting rid of them."

The second Harley-Davidson trike I inspected was prominently parked by the classic fountain in the center of Lincoln Park. The legend, "Jersey City Police Department," in gold lettering on the Harley's white trunk, had been replaced with a timeless illustration of an ice cream pop, from which a bite had been taken. The picture was bracketed by the words "Good Humor Ice Cream." As with the other trike, this machine was also under the command of a man in a uniform, albeit it was white, with a matching hat and gloves.

"What can I get you?" the ice cream man courteously asked.

"A vanilla pop."

He started whistling to himself as he rummaged around in cardboard boxes nestled among scraps of dry ice, stowed in the back. He gave me the pop and I gave him a quarter.

"Have you had this trike a long time?" I asked. "How does it run?"

"This is mostly for promotional purposes," said the Good Humor man. "I use it during the week to carry less product as the park crowds are smaller. On weekends, I rely on the white truck. I don't run it far, just a few blocks each way. I don't like to push it."

Even though he was speaking figuratively, I had no problem catching his drift.

"You're leaking oil," I noted, pointing to a black puddle the size of a saucer under the engine."

"It's been doing that for 20 years," he replied.

I'd come across two Harley-Davidson trikes in a week and neither one had a sterling endorsement. Yet my dad got me thinking along certain lines that appealed to my imagination, though not for the same reasons that stirred his. I was approaching my 18th year and I had still to experience the benefit of sexual congress. I'd either read or heard someplace that if a man hadn't been laid by his 18th year, the most unused part of his anatomy would turn to salt and fall off in the shower. I expected this to happen momentarily. Naturally, I couldn't discuss this crisis with my friends because then I'd have to admit that I had yet to seen a totally naked woman (in person).

It's not that my friends wouldn't be sympathetic. But they were typical guys and they'd turn on me like wolves before providing pack support. I had managed to get to second base with a girl, if that means lifting up a blouse and getting through the treble hooks so popular on brassieres in those days. My sole success was with a sweet thing in the stairwell of an all-girl's academy, during a school dance. She had eyes like delft saucers and a smile bereft of better judgement. I was under the impression that breasts were hermetically sealed in brassieres for freshness, as the damn treble hook fasteners seemed permanent. I was about to go out to the car for wire cutters when the "booby traps" released with a loud "twang," like a bungee cord suddenly free of its moorings. In an instant, I was staring at two, perfectly round bunnies with little pink noses.

"Wow," I said. "Tits."

I regained consciousness with the now deflated brassiere wrapped around my head like a python. (For a moment, I thought that first glimpse of heaven had rendered me blind.) It certainly left me blacklisted as no girl in that school would ever talk to me again. (Do adolescent women transmit this stuff by drums or what?)

Bikers always seemed to have hot women clinging to the backs of their machines, or so I thought. (I would learn that the second half of the seat is called the "pillion.") I couldn't imagine a biker going through this degree of personal torment just to get a look at hooters. I was slowly convincing myself that the acquisition of a motorcycle as the ultimate prop was essential in attracting a more agreeable class of women. I would have been delighted if "women" was actually "one woman," on a one-woman-crusade to prevent shower drains from getting clogged by salt. In answer to that question, a pride of Harley-Davidson motorcycles roared by the next day. Each of the twenty (or so) bikes was adorned by mouth-watering pillion candy (women wearing skin-tight denim jackets and leather chaps that framed their derrieres like artwork.)

I envisioned myself bringing up the rear of that assembly, like the Great Khan, dressed in rough hides, with a horned helmet, accompanied by a steaming hot, leather-wrapped honey, astride a wheezing Harley-Davidson trike, that had "Good Humor Ice Cream" emblazoned across the back.

I knew my answer lay elsewhere.

This was not a wasted exercise, however. I was onto something with the motorcycle gambit. It was the summer of the "Seventies" and bikes were everywhere. Ninety-nine percent of them were black Harley's, with an occasional red or green Triumph (splashed with white trim) thrown into the mix. It was the last hurrah for the British contingent, as Triumphs, Nortons, and "Beeza's" (BSA - Birmingham Small Arms) had reached their final stages of mechanical evolution.

Several truths seemed evident:
• Every motorcycle rider had a girlfriend.
• All of these women were hot.
• And all of them looked like the kind of women who did the kind of things that I wanted to have done to me so I could write about the experience 35 years later.

I challenged anyone to fault these conclusions. I knew I was destined to become a biker, though how this would happen was still murky. Unbeknown to me, stars and planets were aligning that would seal my two-wheel fate, yet in a way that would guarantee nothing.

*Author's note — I became acquainted with full frontal female nudity when I was 12 years old. A classmate, Bennett Lanzetti, found some naked Polaroids of his older cousin Frank's girlfriend. He sold one to me for a dollar. She was a tanned brunette with huge hooters and a muskrat at the top her legs. I was amazed. (These were the days when Playboy showed only breasts, and these seemed to be on women as old as the substitute teachers in my school.)*

"Wow," I said to Bennett. "That thing looks like it should have teeth."

"I hear they do," Bennett replied.

Truer words were never spoken.

# Chapter 3

# "THE PUSH"

**A**rocketing bicycle introduced me to the sensation of "flying four feet above the ground." My father planted the suggestion that freedom and reckless abandon would accompany a motorcycle, specifically a used Harley-Davidson trike. A perceived awareness of the kind of women most commonly associated with motorcycle pillions fermented a lust in my soul. Yet it was my mother who forced the circumstances that made the acquisition of my first bike possible. Had she known the outcome, she'd have sold me into slavery first.

My mother was half Irish and half nuclear reactor. In a previous life, she was the percussionist who beat the drum while Roman galley slaves rowed from Sicily to Argentina. She worked full time; ran a house; raised four kids; monitored piano lessons; supervised dancing school; managed Cub Scout events; perfected science fair projects; and baked a cake every other morning before leaving for work. This regimen was accomplished without her driving a car until she was in her forties. She believed in God, the natural supremacy of the Irish, and two weeks off each summer at the Jersey Shore.

Mom also had some notion that constant employment was good for her adolescent son.

So from the time I was a sophomore in high school through my freshman year in college, I worked part-time as a stock clerk in a local supermarket. It was here I had my first taste of the organized labor movement. The store's management ruefully explained that all employees had to join a union, for which dues and membership fees would be automatically deducted. A union representative blathered on about my benefits, which included something that was "retroactive." To my thinking, anything retroactive would touch off a Geiger counter. The union rep had explained that a substantial raise had been negotiated on my behalf, but since management had cried their eyes out (from the comfort of their limousine), this sum would be paid at some point in the future.

Paychecks were dutifully turned over to my mom for saving. These covered the expenses of my first car and costs associated with school. She'd give me $20 out of the $100 I earned as "walking around" money. I was content to pound register keys or stock shelves in exchange for an occasional night out with my friends, with the added thrill of a little cash in my pocket. I never gave another thought to the retroactive aspects of my employment.

Nearing the end of my 3rd year with the supermarket, I was informed that I would be receiving five extra paychecks. Each of these checks was more than $500. An honest boy, I told my mom about two of them, creating a secret slush fund of epic proportions (for a kid at that time).

A more gifted and visionary youth might have used that cash to fund a computer company in his garage... Or to float an initial public offering that launched an empire... Or to finance a recording company. I yielded to a far more compelling and primal need.

Part of the money sponsored a college  dorm party in which the women of four floors were invited to attend a catered affair — with an open bar — provided they came alone and wore skirts. Aside from a DJ flipping records and a handful of my friends from the fencing team, I was the only guy there. I met more than forty women in one fell swoop, and got a look a good look at their legs as they danced.

It was the sale of my aging Volkswagen Beetle that created a need for immediate transportation. I found myself with cash in hand, trudging along the sidewalk, when a black Triumph Bonneville flashed by, with a hottie clinging to the rider like a sexual bandage. She waved. In that instant, I wanted that bike, that girl, and that rider's life. All of this occurred on the sidewalk in front of a motorcycle shop, in Union City, NJ.

The plate glass windows were lined with brand-new motorcycles. Each was a variation of an established British design in that they were straight-up frames with no-nonsense handlebars. Several sported placards proclaiming some previously unheard of technical enhancement.

Not one was black. They were colors you'd find by ripping open a bag of M&Ms. They all bore manufacturers' names that had blackened the skies over Pearl Harbor.

On impulse, I pressed against the glass to get a closer look, and found myself staring face-to face with a salesman, who grinned, and gestured for me to come inside.

There are two kinds of motorcycle sales people. The first has the smile of a game show host with a personality as shallow as a petri dish. I was in the presence of the second kind, and the most deadly. He had penetrating eyes and a gravely voice like the famous radio personality "Wolfman Jack." He worn an earring at a time when only Barbary Coast pirates had gold loops dangling from their ears. And he had the smile of a man who got the joke, and who didn't hesitate to make a few of his own. The trick was not to find yourself the punch line.

"The bikes look much better from in here," he said to me, extending his hand. "They call me Fabulous Sam."

If anyone was looking to cast the role of the Gypsy King, here was their man. "What can I show you today?" asked Fabulous Sam.

I explained that I was just looking, and that while I had the money for a bike, I had other priorities.

"Well, if you were looking for a bike, how much would you be willing to spend?" asked Sam.

"About $1600 bucks."

I told him I had a few questions, and he smiled, like an alligator taking a bead on a slow-moving pork loin.

"Of course," said Fabulous Sam. "I'm here to assist you."

Now in his confidence, I asked a question that marked me as a real dope; as a clay pigeon in flight; as a country rube on the carnival midway: "What's the difference between a two-stroke and a four-stroke engine?"

Had I looked around, I would have noticed steel shutters slowly closing over the dealership's windows and doors. There would be no escape until I had been savagely drained of cash and left for dead, bleeding from the ass.

Fabulous Sam looked me right in the eye and said, "There really isn't much difference. Some gentlemen prefer blondes and others like brunettes. What do you like?"

"Brunettes."

"We've got a hot little brunette right here," replied Sam. He steered me to a green Kawasaki H2, the fastest stock 750cc street-bike of its day, and one of the most primitive two-stroke motorcycles to ever curse the pavement. "Sit on it. See how it feels."

The bike's forks and shocks compressed slightly under my adolescent fighting weight as I settled into the seat, which felt kind of plush. I didn't know it at the time, but all new motorcycle seats feel great in the shop. I had no problem flat-footing the machine and it balanced easily between my legs.

"You look like a man who's comfortable on a brunette," Sam wryly observed.

I simply nodded, but thought, "You bet your ass."

He pointed out the Spartan features of the instrument cluster, and I noticed that the speedometer went up to 160 miles per hour.

"Will it go that fast?" I asked in childish wonder.

"It might. That depends on the rider," said Sam.

The bike would go that fast, but only if it were launched into space at the top of a rocket.

"This is a special motorcycle for a special rider," continued Sam. "It's very fast, very powerful, and very light. It requires a steady hand, a good eye, and fast reflexes. You might prefer a slower, less aggressive one."

I was determined to own that motorcycle. I didn't dicker. I didn't look at any of the other bikes on the showroom floor. I didn't even ask if it came in another color. I was afraid the dealer would produce an amusement park-type sign that said, "Your Dick Must Be This Big To Ride This Motorcycle." (If he had, I was prepared to say that I had left mine at home, returning with a roll of quarters in my pocket.)

"Do you want a sissy bar for the pillion, so your girl can ride in comfort?" asked Sam, writing up the sales order.

I had only been sitting on this bike for 10 minutes, and here was a seasoned motorcycle professional who automatically assumed I had a hot girlfriend.

"Yeah, I want the sissy bar."

"You want the deluxe pad for the sissy bar?" asked Sam, with pen poised in midair.

"Gotta keep the ladies happy," I shrugged. "I'll take it."

Sam just smiled and added another $75 to the growing total.

"I can have it ready the day after tomorrow," said Sam. "How do you want to pay for it?"

"Cash," I stuttered.

"Want to leave a deposit?"

"No... I'll pay for it now," I said.

"It's a pleasure doing business with a man who knows his mind," said Sam, handing me a bill of sale. I shook his hand again, and staggered out in the street, $1600 dollars lighter. The entire transaction had taken 20 minutes. I bought my first motorcycle in less time than I would have spent buying a motorcycle magazine.

Fabulous Sam got me for an additional $120 two days later, when I bought two metal-flaked, green helmets that seemed to go with the bike. The dealer never flinched when I explaincd that I had never ridden a motorcycle before. He had a mechanic ride the bike over to a parking lot across the street, where I got 30 minutes of instruction.

"Want a lift back to the showroom?" I asked the instructor, eager to show him what I'd learned. The blood drained from his face at my suggestion.

"No thanks," he said.

With that, I pulled out into rush-hour traffic and rode the three miles home.

Rush-hour traffic on Kennedy Boulevard, in Hudson County, New Jersey is the ultimate oxymoronic statement. There is no "rush" about it. About 2.5 million drivers were making a left turn out of the Lincoln Tunnel (from New York City) and heading into Jersey City — all at the same time. There were some 30-yard stretches on that ride where I got the motorcycle into third gear. The miserably congested traffic probably saved my life. I had to work the clutch 452,765 times to get from traffic light to traffic light, and my feet were on the ground more often than they were on the pegs. The heat from the engine added to the wilting vapor of thousands of running car motors, though the peculiar, guttural twang of the bike's two-stroke motor rose like a courtroom objection whenever I twisted the throttle.

I was giving it too much gas, as new riders will do, and slipping the clutch to find the "friction zone." I was also throttling down once I got moving, another beginner's mistake. (This played hell with the spark plugs, a condition common to two-stroke "brunettes," not shared by the new four-stroke Honda 750 "blondes.") Here I was, caught in the middle of a shuffling steel vise, sitting on a three-cylinder powerhouse, attempting to synchronize the unfamiliar activity of hands and feet, while balancing on a seat that was narrower than a bar stool (but about as high) — when the magic happened.

The motorcycle felt great.

While incredibly novel, it failed to intimidate me. It never occurred to me that I could easily drop it. My only concern was in stalling, something that wouldn't happen until I was in the driveway. Ahead of me was my first left turn into opposing traffic, and a three-block descent on one of the steepest hills in Jersey City. I gave neither one the slightest consideration.

I had no fear of the traffic. Years of riding bicycles among columns of moving cars, buses and trucks had inured me to the immediate dangers of being run over or crushed. (I was always aware of the threat... I just never let it dictate my course of action.)

The left turn was nothing. By reflex or by luck, I looked "through" the maneuver, and up-shifted by "listening" to the RPM. The hill was another nonevent. Compared to the rubber-block brakes on my last ten-speed bike, the binders on the Kawasaki were as smooth and as powerful as retrorockets. The third nonevent of the day was my triumphant arrival with the new motorcycle at my folks' house. Not a neighbor was out as I slowly cruised our block. A stunningly beautiful girl, Karen, lived across the street. She was the kind of woman who invariably ended up on magazine covers. (Karen had made it clear she'd rather chew through her own throat than go out with me.)

It was in looking for her that I made my first mistake of the day. Coming up on the driveway, I downshifted into first without jazzing the throttle. This had the effect of riding into wet cement — about four-feet deep. The bike shuddered and my first instinct was to cut the throttle. The front wheel bumped up the driveway's raised lip and the engine stalled. With the front wheel above the curb and the back tire in the street, there was an inch of open air between my extended toes and the ground. This is usually the recipe for the first drop. In that split second, the bike rolled backwards. I grabbed the front brake and held the machine upright, balancing on my left leg. Without movement (and in this odd stance), the motorcycle suddenly weighed a ton. Barely able to twist my butt around in the seat, I got the kick starter unfolded and gave it a feeble shove. The next few years would reveal the many faults of that Kawasaki, but starting wasn't one of them.

It fired on one cylinder, and I ran it into the driveway.

My father regarded this metallic green motorcycle with amazement. He was speechless for a bit, then asked, "Does this look like a used Harley-Davidson trike to you?"

There wasn't a good answer to that question, so I said nothing in the famous "Shitbird" tradition of adolescent males.

"When did you learn to ride one of these?"

"Today," I shrugged. "It's not that hard." If the bike had been a saddled dragon in a fantasy novel, it would have looked at me and snorted fire.

"Did you have any problems with it?" my dad pressed. I hesitated, which spoke volumes to my pop, and I almost said, "Karen-Across-The-Street nearly made me drop it." Yet I just shook my head and smiled. I'd been a biker less than an hour and learned the first rule: "If you almost drop a motorcycle and there is no one to witness it, then it never happened."

His last comment was, "Whatever the hell you paid for it, tell your mother it was half that."

My mother regarded the motorcycle as an exotic toy and assumed I'd grow out of it in three months. Since no one in my family (going back 16 generations) had ever owned a motorcycle, neither she nor my father were aware of the risks and the dangers of riding. She'd met the mother of a grammar school friend of mine later that week, and shared the news of my acquisition. The other kid's mom explained her son (also age 18) had gotten the neighbor's daughter pregnant, and was getting married. I later heard my mother say to the old man, "Some things are far more dangerous than motorcycles." Little did she know I was aiming to get the worst of both worlds.

*Author's note — Let the record show that I grew to like and admire "Fabulous Sam" and would buy a redish-purple Kawasaki H2 from the Gypsy King two years later, when the green one got smashed by a car. The guy was an absolute pisser, and I hope he reads these lines and laughs. I would meet him again, a decade later, at the bar of a famous eatery (the Red Apple Rest) on NYS-17. He was riding a Harley then and had some doll on the pillion.*

# Chapter 4

# "ONE IS COMPANY"

A bicycle moves in comparative silence, with unmatched economy, leaving a near-invisible footprint on the environment. It converts a simple, pumping action of the legs into forward motion, magnifying the human capability to move faster than the average person can run. The bicycle is the vehicle of choice for millions of people looking to reconcile a need for physical exercise with an activity that helps clear the mind. For many, it is the primary means of transportation in cities choked with traffic or in economies choked by reality.

My motivation for riding a bicycle brought greater clarity to one of the reasons I started riding a motorcycle: escape. Escape means getting away from something in the nick of time, and an 11-year-old can't drive. My bicycle was a knotted rope leading to freedom. I wanted to escape from parental supervision; to escape from the gray confines of Jersey City; and to escape from the horrors of baseball.

There must have been forty kids in my immediate neighborhood, who played for various Little League teams. When they were not competing in some Lilliputian World Series, they were playing "stick ball" in the street. (Stick ball is a variation of baseball in which urchins attempt to whack a "Spalding High Bouncer" with a broomstick.) I hated baseball. I hated stick ball. And I hated most of those kids, who were equally good at both.

Baseball is one of those sports that must be played in the misery of summer heat. To me, it meant standing for hours (sometimes days) in an open field, with the sun in your eyes, waiting for someone to hit a ball (that was the size of a muffin with the density of a hand grenade) in your direction. The logic of this game was as fleeting as any personal gratification I may have derived from it. However, my mother determined that a boy's interest and skill in baseball was the most accurate measure of his future success as a man. By her reckoning, I was a mutant.

Nothing brought this woman to a boil faster then to see a gang of kids embroiled in a raging baseball game, with me orphaned on the sidelines. (I sucked so badly at the game that any team who chose me got a 12-hit advantage — and still they usually lost.) My mother once threatened to raise me in a barrel, locked away in the attic, unless I played ball. My response was, "Can I see the barrel?" (To this day, my left eye is larger than my right, from staring out of the barrel's bunghole. The sad truth is that my vision is poorer on the left side from my mom jamming a stick ball bat into the hole.)

A shiny, three-speed "English Racer" bicycle solved the problem.

I got on it and rode away from baseball, stick ball, and the proponents of both. Furthermore, my mother didn't have to endure the shame of seeing me scorned as the athletic kids picked teams "sans Riepe." I had reached the age when I was expected to ask permission of one parent or another, before attempting anything that was obviously stupid or dangerous. My folks assumed I understood that asking permission to do something stupid or dangerous was part of the process by which I would learn "responsible" behavior. Naturally, their answer would always be, "No."

I quickly learned there was no percentage in asking permission to play on the tracks, to break windows in the abandoned gunpowder factory, or to zing rats with homemade sling shots (down at the dump). Yet all of these things could easily be covered under the blanket request of, "Hey Mom, is it okay to ride my bike?" I could then ride over the horizon, where it would be impractical or impossible to interrupt the fun stuff by seeking permission.

There were a couple of other kids who liked to ride as well. One was a girl who lived on the next block. She was a trifle older than me and cute in a tom boy sort of way. We'd sometimes pack sandwiches and soda, then ride to a wooded area a mile or two distant. Usually we'd discuss books that we were reading, stuff we learned in school, or things that typically appealed to kids whose worlds precluded the intrusion of adults. Then came the day when she asked if she could put her hand in my jeans. (I sure as hell knew better than to ask my Mom for permission for something like this.) As new as I was to this sort of thing, I quickly brokered a trade.

Riding back that day, we passed the stick ball crowd. One of the guys yelled out, "Creepy Reepy plays with girls! Creepy Reepy plays with girls!"

"Yup," I thought, "And you're playing with balls."

The true measure of escape came the following year, when grammar school classmate Steve Venner and I started riding 20 and 30 miles out, trading the tar and cement confines of Jersey City for the wooded cliffs of the Palisades, bigger parks in a neighboring state, and historic points of interest mentioned in books of history and fiction. A new ten-speed bike dramatically increased the range to places like "Sleepy Hollow" the home of the headless horseman (40 miles), and to "Sunnyside," the home of The Legend Of Sleepy Hollow's author Washington Irving (50 miles). Jersey City was always a cool place, but it had all the appeal of a black and white Ingmar Bergman movie. These other places we pedaled to were fascinating.

The declaration, "I'm going riding on Saturday," was now code for: "I'll be eating my lunch on the edge of a cliff 400 feet above the Hudson River." Or, "I'll be riding my bike on the George Washington Bridge's walkway, headed into New York City." (My mother wouldn't let me take the subway into New York City at age 12. But she never said anything about riding a bicycle through death-defying traffic.) As long as I didn't fall off anything high, crash, or come home in the company of the police, I could do whatever I wanted. Quite frankly, I got used to this level of freedom. My parents got used to me being gone for 12-hours at a stretch — and these were the days long before cell phones.

Bicycle riding was an activity that I always did in the company of a friend, but the social aspects dwindled as the distances mounted. Gone was the conversation that ensued when riding side-by-side. Traffic mandated riding single file and frequent changes in elevation added a more exhausting aspect to the pedaling. Distance became a prerequisite as the more interesting places were always farther away. We might pull over for a fast break every 90 minutes or so, but these were usually taken in silence. We were seldom more than an hour or two at our final destination (somewhat longer if it was a historic site or a nature museum), but were always conscious of the need to start back.

Never would we call a parent to get picked up.

Little by little, our bicycle rides became days of shared silence, mutual respect for the run, and an appreciation for the character of the towns and communities we passed through. Steve and I began to take note of architecture, geographic characteristics, and even the locations of historic events (heady stuff for a couple of 12-year-olds). Yet we might not discuss any of these aspects until days after the actual ride. It was through thousands of miles of pedaling in my early adolescent years that I learned the value of being alone with my thoughts on a two-wheeled machine, even in the company of my best friend.

This worked out well because a motorcycle is a vehicle for personal solitude.

The solitude aspect of the motorcycle slowly began to manifest itself as I rode around, showing the new Kawasaki to my friends. I was the only one in this circle who had a motorcycle. Consequently, all of my initial rides were alone. Came the first Saturday when Steve headed north alone, pedaling at his usual cadence (which was steady and impressive as he was now an 18-year-old in peak shape). I left two hours later and caught up to him in no time at all. Amazed to see me, there was the flash of a grin, and a laugh at the bag with the can of soda and peanut butter sandwich on the sissy bar. (He had the same in saddle bag behind his seat.) I rode behind him, on the shoulder for a mile or two, before jazzing the engine and pulling away. The plan was to meet him 30-miles distant, at Bear Mountain State Park, where we'd have lunch at the usual spot.

The highway was State Route 9W, known as the "Old Road" north to the Catskills. This road runs from Fort Lee, New Jersey to Rensselaer, New York (just short of the state's capital). I had been up and down it dozens of times on a bicycle (as far as Bear Mountain). I knew every pothole, every blind spot, every hill, and every curve. I was familiar with every smudge of gravel and the places where sewer grates would eat bicycle tires. On this day, I twisted the Kawasaki's throttle, and became Alice stepping through the looking glass. None of it would ever be the same.

The highway has some heavily wooded spots, incredible river vistas, and endless hills. There is a nice little dip, with a curve, right around the state line. On a bicycle, this entails taking the first rise leaning into the pedals to clear the top at speed, then charging through the drop, and leaning into the crank set again to get up the other side. The Kawasaki only required me to flex my left foot a couple of times, and to twist my right hand, to experience escape in it's purest form. No longer would I regard any stretch of this ride as "soul hardening."

One ball-bust of an uphill climb dissolved into the growl of the engine as I made a sweeping turn to the right, feeling absorbed by the land-scape and released by the bike. The anticipation of the view at the top wasn't diminished. I just got there sooner. The climb was as exhilarat-ing as the downhill stretch that followed. That was certainly different. Best of all, I didn't have to yield the road to other vehicles. Another surprise was the power of the brakes. No longer was I at the mercy of little rubber blocks that overheated in hard stops that invariably came at the bottom of the better hills.

I always divided this route into stretches, like the "high curve to the right," or the "18-inch shoulder stretch," and the "screwed up traffic light at the bottom of the hill." This information was now significant only in terms of measuring progress. The "high curve to the right" be-came 45 seconds out of an hour. The "18-inch" shoulder was of no con-cern to me any longer. Getting stuck at the traffic light at the bottom of the hill now represented an opportunity to put my feet down without pulling over. With 19-year-old knees and a bladder like a llama's, the need to pull over was nonexistent.

I was thoroughly familiar with my surroundings, yet free from the lim-itations by which I had come to experience them. I was still out in the elements — the hot summer breeze, the gritty backwash of trucks, and the assault of sound — but found myself absorbing my surroundings on a level never before imagined. I was as exposed to my environment as I would have been on a bicycle, but the bicycle ran me through it like a car wash, at 10 or 15 miles per hour. The motorcycle powder-coated me in sensation. It magnified the magic of the curves and seamlessly tagged each visual experience with a new level of awareness.

This did not happen all at once like the sudden illumination of Edison's lamp nor the elation that follows orgasm. It began with the gradual realization that I always returned home slightly different from the per-son who'd left. This metamorphosis would continue whenever I threw a leg over the saddle.

I made dozens of mistakes on that first foray, lugging the engine from time to time, or downshifting too enthusiastically and sliding onto the gas tank. I made lousy, hesitant, left turns, and stalled several times. I put my foot down in gravel, nearly dropping things before shifting my weight to the other side. The Kawasaki overlooked my transgressions like a coconspirator. I never felt so much the master of my own destiny; nor so at the mercy of every little decision I made; nor so alone.

This two-stroke engine was alleged to be a questionable performer at low RPM, but I didn't know that. This was the era of bikes that ran like shit as a matter or course, and I thought that jiggling the throttle was what bikers did, like biplane pilots blipping the engine on landing. There were a couple of times where I got caught at a traffic light at the top of a hill, and struggled to get things moving again when the signal turned green. I over-revved the engine as I slipped the clutch. (Had I let that clutch go, that H2 would have thrown me like an enraged mustang.) Some things were not improved. On a bicycle, you could easily pull over just about anyplace to take in the view. Taking long glances at the scenery was a benefit of a bicycle ride. Taking a long glance to the side on the Kawasaki turned the bike in that direction; right quickly too. The shifting of my weight or a change in the placement of my hands on the grips produced a dramatic change in the bike's attitude, especially at slower speeds.

The Kawasaki covered the 30 additional miles to Bear Mountain State Park like a paint roller in a small bathroom, and I had a two-and a half-hour wait for my friend. I used that time to cover many of the interior roads in the park. I hadn't felt a need to pull over for a break in 65 miles. I wasn't compelled to stop and sip water, as I wasn't drenched in sweat. But I was close to breathless just the same. My love of bicycles had forever faded in the arc of a kick starter.

I buzzed into the picnic area where my buddy would come looking for me. Pulling up to a weathered wooden table (covered with carved initials and with benches attached), I cut the ignition and flipped down the kickstand. Two women (about my age) were having lunch at an adjacent table. Their bicycles leaned against the nearest tree. They had their water bottles and little bags of trail mix in hand, as they looked for some particular point on a map that doubled as a tablecloth.

Feigning an indifference that I assumed was the genuine mark of a real biker, I put my goggles in my helmet and sat on a table top, with my feet on a bench. I pulled a park map out of my back pocket and pretended to trace a route with my finger. I was thin (with the physique of a varsity fencer), had long hair (with a classically-defiant chin), and had arrived on a gleaming motorcycle. I assumed these were all good things. Both of these ladies appeared to regard me as an enormous roach. (There were 20 empty tables in this particular picnic area of the park, and I took one directly next to theirs. That may have been somewhat obvious.)

I looked around, in an attempt to align the map with the road, then asked "Excuse me, do you guys know this park well? I'm looking for the haunted graveyard."

Now I had no idea if there was a haunted graveyard in either Harriman or Bear Mountain State Park, but I knew that nothing dispels the aroma of a questionable overture like a really good story-line. I also knew where there was a solitary headstone, standing in a copse of trees by a road, in this very state park. This could have been the troubled resting place of some early nineteenth century serial killer, especially if it served my purposes.

The ladies hadn't heard of the cursed cemetery, though there was an old churchyard marked on their map. I concocted an appropriate tale, adding an unusual twist. I claimed that my great-grandmother's diary told of how she'd had an assignation in her youth with a man from a small Dutch settlement up here. The man had died under a cloud. Specifically, he was hung (though this can be said of nearly all Riepe men).

I limited the details of the story to the fewest possible facts, claiming that I'd ridden up that way, to see if there was any truth in the old diary. My grandmother didn't give a name, just that grave was now lost in the woods of a state park in neighboring New York.

I had them.

While both suspected they were being handed a line, it was one hell of a good story. (And I have it on good authority that I had laughing blue eyes when I was a kid.) They were Cheryl and Doreen, up from Manhattan, visiting Doreen's brother, who was a cadet at West Point, the US Military Academy, about 15 miles to the north. They showed me their route through the park, and where they were going. Their ride would swing west in a loop that brought them close to NYS-17.

The road they were following led past the hidden tombstone.

I figured Cheryl had designs on Doreen's brother, but Doreen was the better looking one anyway. She had a soft smile, a sweet voice, and the kind of body that could set the rulers of neighboring Greek city states at each others throats. They packed up their lunch things, folded the map, and mounted their ten speeds. I watched Doreen's derrière guide the bicycle onto the road and head out at a sedate pace, where it was still possible to hear the individual clicks of its ratcheting cassette. A glance at how badly their seat posts were adjusted gave a clear indication that they were just out for a few hours diversion and not at all serious about speed nor riding. I had time to formulate a plan.

Steve arrived shortly thereafter and found me dozing next to my parked bike.

"So how was it?" he asked.

"I'm sorry it wasn't another 50 miles farther," I said truthfully.

What I didn't tell him was that I didn't mind riding alone, and that I was damn-near overwhelmed trying to process the other sensations I'd experienced, including several relating to two good-looking women I'd just met. For him, the escape was in the act of pedaling somewhat faster than the last time. For me, the escape was in the getting away, and in feeling a sense of having arrived at someplace or something. This happens every time I straddle a motorcycle, regardless of whether I'm riding thirty miles to a club breakfast or the first of 300 miles through West Virginia. My escape begins when I hit the starter button. It is complete when I have both feet on the pegs. In later years, when I'd ride with a select group of guys, I discovered that each of them felt exactly the same way, though this sentiment is not common to all riders. There was no one to tell me about this aspect of riding in 1975. The motorcycle would have teach it to me, and not every lesson would be a delight.

Steve and I ate our sandwiches together in the customary silence. Yet the aura of our individual rides had changed. His ten-speed was silent when it wasn't moving. The Kawasaki ticked and clicked as it cooled off. There was a breeze from a nearby lake, but my end of the table also carried the slightly sweet scent of gasoline. (These may not seem like positives, but I still remember them fondly.) Other changes regarded our immediate objectives. Had we had both arrived on bicycles when the ladies were present, we'd have taken a table as far away from them as possible. (Because to us, cycling was not a social pursuit and they would have been annoying.) Now I was the one pushing to get moving, though reserving ample time for the ride home was no longer a consideration.

"Are you going back on 9W?" Steve asked.

"Nope," I said. "That was fun but I am going to head over to US-6 and go south on Route 17."

"There's a lot more traffic on Route 17."

"But now I drift in and out of it," I replied, laughing.

We parted company exiting the picnic area. It was the last time I'd ride with him where a bicycle was involved.

The Kawasaki's strong point was not on the twisty, hilly roads of Harriman State Park. I didn't take it over 45 miles per hour in the confines of the park as there were stretches where even that speed was foolhardy, considering my limited experience. I took roads parallel to the direction the ladies had taken, with the intent of getting in front of them — without having to ride past them. This was a perfectly silly idea but one that appealed to my sense of illusion. It took me 20 minutes to get to the little copse of trees in which the tombstone stands. I u-turned on the road and parked the bike on a bit of shoulder. Then I made myself comfortable, waiting in the trees, leaning on the mysterious tombstone.

Cheryl and Doreen appeared right on cue. I could hear them chatting, above the audible clatter of their bikes, and then their silence, as they saw the Kawasaki parked on the side of the road — their side of the road.

"Isn't that the bike that guy was riding?" I heard Cheryl ask.

"It looks like it," Doreen said. And then she called out my name.

"Doreen... Cheryl?" I yelled back, stepping out of the trees with a puzzled look on my face.

"How did you get past us?" Cheryl asked, noticing my bike was pointed in the direction in which they were traveling.

"I wasn't aware that I had."

"That's creepy," she said.

"Even creepier... I found the tombstone."

"No way," Doreen gasped.

"Way," I said. "It's right here."

She laid her bike against the embankment and followed me into the trees.

The tombstone was a bit of an anomaly. It was of a design common to the 1950's, but the dates went back to the mid-1800's. Somebody traced this grave to an ancestor and wanted it properly marked.

"Your great grandmother's story was true," said Cheryl, in amazement. (What she meant was, "Your story was true!")

"Little comfort in that... That means my great grandfather was a murderer," I lied. For all I knew the guy buried there could have been a kindly old cuckoo clock-maker, beloved by all in the community. (He was actually a farmer named James Lewis, whose plot of land is now covered by a lake.)

"Why is this place supposed to be haunted?" asked Doreen.

"People who come here doubting my great-grandmother are alleged to be cursed."

"By a guy on a green motorcycle?" asked Cheryl.

Some women are as perceptive as they are suspicious.

"Did your great-grandmother really leave a diary with that story in it?" asked Doreen.

"It was more like a cookbook," I said, with a shrug. The magician should never show the audience what happens to the rabbit when it goes back into the hat. My green motorcycle and laughing blue eyes weren't enough to carry the day.

*Author's note —The tombstone is still in the park, though someone has toppled it. I sincerely hope the gentle reader forgives me for not pinpointing the location of this monument. I prefer to find fewer footprints there on my next visit. But to those who know this park well, you are looking for stand of trees by a trail that wraps around a lake. Parking is much harder now, but not impossible — especially before the park is fully open for the summer season.*

I returned to this spot several years later in the company of a close friend who is an archeologist. Pointing to the toppled tombstone, I asked, "Isn't that odd?" He looked at me, raised an eyebrow, and said, "You are an idiot."

Then he paced off three steps to the left of the stone and kicked up the forest duff. There was a stump of rock, like a broken tooth. Three steps to left of that one, was another broken piece of stone. It turned out there was a row of these things. And about seven feet below the first row, there was a second line of jagged stone stumps.

"There's at least 20 bodies buried here," said my friend. "What does that tell you?"

"That the Mafia was active in small Dutch communities before the American Revolution," I suggested.

"You really are a horse's ass," he replied.

# Chapter 5

# "LE RAISON D'ETRE"

There are thousands of compelling reasons to get a motorcycle and none of them are good. The only acceptable premise for acquiring a motorcycle is because you want one. No one expressed this better than the late Hunter S. Thompson in his legendary piece *The Song Of The Sausage Creature*. He wrote:

*"There are some things nobody needs in this world, and a bright red, hunchback, warp-speed 900cc café racer is one of them — but I want one anyway, and on some days I actually believe I need one. That is why they are dangerous."*

While Thompson was writing specifically of a Ducati, this sentiment applies to all motorcycles. A motorcycle can be one thing or many things. It can become a substitute for the lover you always wanted. Or the time machine you've needed. Or the metaphor for which your soul has been searching. Or the last chance to inject a little magma into your life. Things only get dangerous when you think, "I need this machine now." But this is all nonsense. A friend of mine down in New Orleans once told me that every motorcycle he ever owned reminded him of the first Creole lover he ever had. "She was trouble from the word go," he said. "And nobody could talk me out of her."

Look at all the different motorcycles sitting in showroom windows: cruisers, sport bikes, dirt bikes, custom bikes, touring motorcycles, and racing bikes. For some new rider, one of these will appear as the answer to a cosmic question. It is the sad truth that a motorcycle is the wrong answer for so many of them. Yet there is no other way to tell if you can hear what the bike has to say, unless you ride one. It is the ultimate "Catch 22."

I admire those first-time riders who claim to have purchased their motorcycle after researching machines, exploring the market, and speaking with dozens of bikers. But there is no guarantee that this process will be any less painful nor spare them the agony of discovering that there is more to riding a motorcycle than the alleged freedom of the road. You can sit on a thousand bikes for fit. You can evaluate 25 brands for reliability. You can conduct a comprehensive maintenance comparison of different marques. And in the final analysis, you are most likely to buy the bike that you think makes your ass look the coolest. My reasons for wanting and getting a motorcycle were the absolute worst, which in the long run, were just as good as any.

In 1975, I was Jersey City's last remaining unlaid, 19-year-old male. A sign on the city-line read, "Welcome To Jersey City. Population: 260,545 — With one sexually bereft 19-year-old male, who lives in The Heights." This was not because I didn't have girlfriends, and not because I didn't try. The sexual revolution had long since evolved into a series of skirmishes, and while I got myself to the front lines time and time again, it was only to be left for dead.

All that was about to change. I was reinventing myself from the ground up, starting with a screaming Japanese motorcycle. Bikers rode around with red-hot, pillion candy clinging to them like pythons. I envisioned what it would be like the first time I picked up a leather-clad blond lollipop, or a brunette in grease-smudged denim, whose burning ambition would be to ride like hell on my bike, before riding me to sexual nirvana. I was focusing on one of the least significant aspects of riding a motorcycle, but I didn't know that at the time.

I never imagined that meeting pillion candy could be a test of strength, cunning, and masculine dexterity, such as one would encounter in an ancient Visigoth encampment. My plan was to fire an intoxicating look at one of the hotter babes in some bar and leave with her clinging tightly to the pillion. What could be easier? I would discover there were rituals governing every aspect of this part of the riding experience.

The Jersey City of my youth was a loose confederation of neighborhoods (Bergen, Downtown, Greenville, The Heights, Lafayette, Marion, the Western Slope, and the Westside). These charming enclaves had their own collection of neighborhood bars. There was at least one gin mill in each neighborhood that attracted the lowest conceivable element. "The Bucket of Blood" (not the saloon's real name) was the seediest joint in the section where I lived. It was the social nucleus of street bawlers, petty thieves, bookies, corner pharmaceutical brokers, and hot bar women.

While I never actually saw anyone get their throat cut in this place, it was obvious that one false move, or one poorly-chosen word, could easily produce that result. It was less of a bar and more of a club for those whose portfolio was life on the street. The door was always open to the occasional stranger but the sense of welcome was highly selective. It was not a biker's bar per se, though some of the more colorful patrons rode motorcycles.

One of these was "Cretin," (pronounced CREE-tin).

Cretin was the ultimate Jersey City anomaly. A street legend with a prep school education, he could quote the great Roman philosophers — in Latin. He could also cite Shakespeare, Shelley, Keats, or Mussolini when drunk. He romanced some of the best-looking women and laid some of the skeeviest hose bags I have ever seen. He rode a motorcycle (usually a Norton) like an animal. He was a flash of light in the urban miasma. I was proud to call him my friend, and prouder still that he thought of me as his. Cretin had introduced me to the substrata of Jersey City café society and branded me with his seal of approval. Consequently, I was welcome in this bar, though somewhat of an anomaly in my own right.

"Reep," said Cretin. "You are the writer in a gin mill where no one can read. You are Toulouse- Lautrec in a society that has yet to discover art. Make the best of it. Limit yourself to words of two syllables, or these guys will think you're making fun of them and beat the shit out of you."

I never envisioned myself as a tough guy. I lacked the tattoos, the scars, and the missing teeth that marked others as brawlers or curbside negotiators. I never carried a knife, a blackjack, nor brass knuckles... Though I saw them on occasion. To be sure, not everyone in this joint qualified as a potential thug. These guys were roofers, truck drivers, dock workers, and laborers in a dozen professions. A good number were urban entrepreneurs on the side... Bookies, pharmacists, and brokers of goods that traded without receipts. If you wanted something, you could discretely inquire. Inquiring indiscreetly could earn you scars or cost you teeth. It was a fine line.

I have always had a thing for hot, tough, bar women... And there were women in this bar who drove me crazy.

There were some whose clothing seemed like a second skin, outlining every curve or barely covering the places you wanted uncovered anyway. They moved with the sensuous ease one associates with leopards and panthers. They could look at you or through you. Their eyes registering instant appraisal, scoring acceptance or dismissal. They were pre-tuned to the Visigoth gene.

Teri had a flawless face with hypnotic eyes and full lips that could coax a sigh into a gasp. She also had a mouth like a longshoreman and said the word "fuck" every thirty seconds. I used to close my eyes and imagine her saying that word to me, preceded by "Let's."

There were ladies whose tattoos would dance around on their bodies under the filmy atmosphere of cigarette smoke. They'd laugh and kiss with their mouths visibly open, thrusting their hips against the guys as they gyrated to the honkey tonk beat of the juke box. Angie was one of the first women I ever knew to have a tattoo. It was a praying mantis, whose head peeked out of low- cut jeans against her bare, tanned midriff. Cretin pointed out to me that the female praying mantis rips off the male's head before they mate. I would have made the sacrifice.

Then there were the others: women hardened by years of a social life that started and ended in saloons like this one. They had Jersey City accents that could shatter a clay pigeon at 40 yards. (The Jersey City accent is the equivalent of British "Cockney" and fingernails on a blackboard.) Christina was a brunette whose accent had a head like a badly poured beer. She once used the word "bahhtdroom," and I asked to hear it in a whole sentence. She replied, "The bahhtdroom in this dump is so filthy, I pissed in the sink." She had a tragic allure that transcended sexuality. You could read an untold story in her eyes. But I was just another penis with a kick-starter at the time, who simply wanted to look at the pictures without becoming part of the text. I was sorry I didn't get a glimpse of her pissing in the sink.

The sad truth was that none of these ladies had the slightest interest in me. I was a non-entity around a tribal fire that flared for others. I complained to Cretin that I wasn't having much luck, and that these women were cock teasers.

"These women are saints," said Cretin. "Have you seen the guys in this bar? You need five to get a full set of teeth and ten to get a lucid idea. These are the guys H.G. Wells had in mind when he envisioned the Morlocks eating the Eloi."

"I am the only guy in this bar not getting eaten by somebody," I said.

"Reep, you're missing the point. Look at these guys. They are all tough, strong, made of steel tempered by circumstance," said Cretin. "The steel may be twisted, but it endures. Look at you. You're a 19-year-old eclair who smokes cigars. You're the freak in this place. When you turn on your charm, these ladies just take in the show."

"So how do I beat that?"

"Do something dramatically out of character... And do it convincingly," said Cretin.

So I showed up on a motorcycle.

There were six bikes parked outside the bar that afternoon: three Harley's, a Triumph, a BSA, and a Norton. All were black and bore the correct degree of lustrous chrome. All had the look of motorcycles ridden by road warriors: rainbow tinted pipes, well-creased leather seats, oil smudges burned into the appropriate places, road-scuffed pegs, and the occasional temporary repair (wired or taped to the frame). My Kawasaki H2 looked like a new sneaker just taken out of the box; a green sneaker that smoked from three cheaply chromed exhaust pipes.

The other bikes were parked at identical angles to the curb, with virtually the same space between machines. It took me three tries to squeeze in, and I finally just parked my bike at the end of the line, closest to the fire hydrant. I swaggered into the bar with my helmet under my arm, grinning like an idiot. The response was not what I anticipated. It was as if a monkey had walked in wearing a top hat.

One of the Harley riders looked at me and asked, "Did they cut $500 bucks off the price to get you to take that color?"

Cretin, who owned the Norton, was almost speechless. "I told you to do something out of character. You got a douche's motorcycle. What's out of character about that?"

He pulled a lime wedge off a gin and tonic on the bar and asked, "Do you see any other motorcycles painted in this shade of fruit?" The guys at least had the courtesy to go out and look at the bike, and all wished me luck. But none invited me to ride with them. My disappointment must have been obvious. Later, Vinnie the bartender said to me, "Buying a pistol doesn't make you a gunslinger. But sometimes it makes you a target." Then he poured me a rum and Coke, and wished me luck with my douchebag, green, Japanese motorcycle.

I took a good deal of shit over my choice of a helmet too. I bought two metallic green brain buckets, with black stripes down the center, flowing back from the black edging around the face. The black edging was rich with faceted metal flakes. Each helmet had a cheap, clear-plastic windscreen snapped across the front.

Cretin held one up in amazement.

"What possessed you to buy this?" he asked. It was then I noticed that all the other guys had simple flat-black, open-face helmets, most of which were chipped or scratched. "Did they tell you that Vincent Price wore this when he made that movie The Fly?" Cretin slipped my helmet on, and it did, in fact, look like the head of a giant horsefly. "Did you give any thought to how you would look on a green bike, that leaves a smoke screen, wearing the head of a giant fly?"

I was suddenly fearful that my nickname in this bar would become *"The Fly."*

We were looking out the sole window of the bar at that moment, when a woman came down the street walking some big, stupid-looking mutt. The dog paused to piss on the fire hydrant, and then in a salute to Japanese technology, included the back tire of the Kawasaki in the stream. The bar exploded in laughter. I inwardly seethed.

The Harley riders pulled out shortly, leaving me in the company of Cretin and the other two Brit bikers. I let the dust settle and made my move on Teri, buying her a drink and asking if she wanted to ride on the back of my new bike.

Her response was predictable, especially after my entrance. "I don't want to ride with 'The fucking Fly' on that fucking green bike," she said. "Besides, Cretin asked me to ride with him."

The smirk on Cretin's face burned into my soul like a glowing brand. "Come with us," said Cretin. "We're gonna ride someplace where we can see the sunset. Maybe Teri's got a friend."

"I'll pass. I want to get some open highway time on my new rig."

We all left the bar together. Cretin straddled the Norton, and told Teri not to mount until he'd started it. He unfolded the kick starter and gave it a good shot. The bike coughed, and Cretin kicked it again. He kicked it ten more times. The aroma of unburned gas wafted from the Norton's carbs. I thumbed the handlebar-mounted choke on the Kawasaki, and kicked the starter once. The H2's engine roared into life, albeit with some bluish-white smoke.

"It's the dog piss," I yelled over the noise of the engine. Snicking the bike into gear, I pulled away from the curb laughing. My turn would come when a pretty woman would stand expectantly by the side of road while I tried to get a bike to start. But it wouldn't be that day. I headed north, to the Palisades Interstate Parkway (PIP), for a short, 50-mile ride out of the city. It was a route I would take a thousand times. The first ten miles were grimy, traffic-infested, truck-choked arteries to I-95 and the George Washington Bridge. But it got nice after that, and the summer air seemed less humid under the trees on the tops of the cliffs. The speed limit was 55 mph, but I found myself hitting 70 in the straight stretches. There are three vistas along this highway, which are great make-out points, and I pulled into one to take a leak.

There, parked by itself, closest to the trees, was a purple, 1975 Kawasaki H2.

The rider came out of the woods, in the process of hitching up the first skin-tight leather pants I had ever seen. The pants went over black riding boots. She had a matching black leather jacket that complimented the black hair framing her Asian face. (These were the days when Asians in New Jersey were as rare as silver dollars in the church collection plate and this one was as exotic as a bird of paradise.) The fact that she had her own bike, and that it was the same bike that I had, was mind-blowing.

She flipped me a glimmer of a smile and said, "Nice bike. Traditional Kawasaki green. Curious choice of a helmet though." Hers was jet black.

"It was free with the bike," I lied.

"Still," she said, wincing over the smile.

"Had your bike long?" I asked.

"Long enough," she replied.

"I'm Jack."

"Im going," she replied.

She reached down and extended the purple H2's kick starter. Then in one fluid motion, she straddled the seat, fired up the bike, and rolled it off the side-stand. That may have been my invitation. But if so, I missed it. I have often wondered what might have happened if I had been a seasoned rider and took off after her, matching her every move with perfect synchronicity.

But I was not a seasoned rider. I'd had the bike for three days and rode it like I had palsy.

The whole scenario hadn't taken 90 seconds. The Japanese have a name for mystical, divine beings that suddenly appear and disappear. They call them "kamis." I wondered if this woman was a kami whose purpose was to torture me with an image I still vividly recall. There was no comparison between her and any of the ladies in the bar. Just as there was no valid comparison between the Harleys, the Brit bikes, and machine I was riding. Then again, no comparison could be valid.

I thought there would be more of an exchange between me and this rider, as we had the same bike, which could have been the basis of a conversation, if not a bond. My disappointment was palpable. It would be six months before the Kawasaki taught me that the perfect number for most rides is one. And that the longest ride you will ever have is in the company of someone who has an incongruous riding style. The hardest lesson that I would learn was that worse than an empty pillion is one that you wish was empty.

Chapter 6

# "THE MOTORCYCLE SPEAKS"

I had the Kawasaki a month before it spoke to me. Its message was so utterly stark and unexpected that I almost missed it. So far, the bike was a miserable failure in jump-starting my career of sexual exploration. I thought that having a motorcycle would make me cool and somewhat exotic to the hot local bar women. I was going to be the sensitive writer/poet, who rode a screaming Japanese street bike. Instead I was the "dweeb" who rode a lime-green, odd-sounding, smoke-generating two-stroke motorcycle. Not only did the bike fail to compensate for my peculiar dweebiness, it emphasized it.

I loved tough neighborhood bar women. And I could do this with impunity because I was invisible to them. From the cut of their hair (falling around some of the most beautiful faces I have ever seen) to the cut of their jeans (defining some of the hottest asses I have ever desired), the women at the bar of The Bucket of Blood were tantalizingly close, yet always just beyond reach. I couldn't understand it. Most of the guys who took them home looked like "Jason" in the "Friday the 13th" horror classics.

There was one blond who moved through the bar like a breeze in the aspens, smiling through lips that were miniature love pillows. She was part of the bar, but appeared to be less touched by it. She seemed softer than the other women, which made me think I might have a chance with her. She was prettier than she was hot, and affected my DNA like the moon draws the tides. Yet her movements were calculated for maximum effect, followed by a cursory glance to see who noticed, and who might be succumbing to her subliminal messages. I thought she might have been sending a message to me. I imagined the scenario that would bring the two of us together: a ride to the shore for the weekend, a run to the mountains, or anyplace far from the bar where her heat could ignite my passion.

The opportunity presented itself on a summer afternoon, when the saloon was deserted, except for the blond, the bartender, and a couple of vapid barflies. I had popped in looking for my pal Cretin, and found the ideal conditions for making my pitch. The blonde looked especially attractive and I felt lucky.

"Hey Vinnie... Hey Tina...," I said, in a forced casual tone that could have gotten me an academy award. "Cretin been in here today?"

"Not yet," replied Vinnie, with the smile that was the trademark of his profession. "Unless you mean 3am this morning, when Neil found him passed out under the pool table."

"That would explain why he's not answering his phone," I said. "I'm headed to the shore for clams and rum on the boardwalk, and I'm looking for company. Wanna come?" This last question was directed at Tina, the blond.

Something was different about her today. There was no audience. There was no adoring crowd. There was just me and my potential date face. Under these circumstances, I might just as well have been a bale of prison laundry. She shook her head.

"C'mon," I said. "It'll be fun."

"Only for you," she replied, with a look of finality that indicated the conversation was at an end.

"Don't you like motorcycles?" I pressed.

"I love motorcycles," she said. "But I'm not getting on the back of yours. What's the point in getting on a guy's bike if you know you'll never sleep with him?"

"Ooooooh," winced Vinnie. "Instant crash and burn."

I flashed Vinnie a grin and rode out. A handful of words from a blond had torpedoed my buoyant mood. I had planned on riding 90 miles to Seaside Heights, NJ, getting a couple dozen clams, and hoisting a few

Cuba Libres at a boardwalk bar. But now the joy was suddenly gone from the whole idea. I went anyway.

Traffic on the New Jersey Turnpike was fairly light. I brought the bike up to the speed limit, then cranked it 20 miles per hour beyond that. You could never describe the engine on a Kawasaki H2 as "smooth running." But it seemed to run smoother and sound better the faster I pushed it. The New Jersey Turnpike is as straight as a telegraph line, with only one or two gentle twists, between Newark International Airport and Exit 11 (the Shore Points). The bike tracked well (going straight) and I began to dance from lane to lane.

The engine settled into that throaty yowl, peculiar to two-strokes, with a steady buzz coming through the handgrips like the pulse of a huge wasp. That was when I first detected a near-musical cadence between the sound of the engine and the hum of the road. At first, it was like trying to remember he lyrics to a long-forgotten song. I would eventually realize the motorcycle spins new lyrics with each ride; and that nothing has to rhyme when the lyrics of the road set the mood for the run.

My mood was foul. I had wanted that woman to ride on the back of my bike. Actually, I wanted her to ride me, with a wild-eyed look in her eyes like a deer caught in destiny's headlights. I wanted her to scream my name in passion and claw my back in wild desire. Instead, she was back at there bar, waiting for some grunting man-meat.

It was then that the bike distinctly said, *"Fuck the blond. She's sitting in the sweltering heat of the dog shit and broken glass capital of the universe, and you're gonna see the sun set on Barnegat Bay."*

"What the hell?" I thought.

*"You heard me,"* said the bike. *"Fuck her. Quick... Look to the right... There's a plane taking off at Newark. Wanna race it to the end of the runway?"*

I did.

The New Jersey Turnpike parallels the longest runway at one of the country's busiest airports and there was a big jet rolling into its takeoff. Without thinking, I twisted the throttle wide open. The plane pulled ahead, left the ground, and banked to the left. The bike climbed a rise and I banked right, rocketing through the next curve. The Kawasaki felt light in the steering and I throttled back to a more confident speed.

*"Pussy,"* the bike said.

"What did you say?" I asked.

*"Nothing,"* said the bike. *"Don't think of women tonight. Think of the ride. Think of those rose-colored clouds over there. Think of the road. Think of where you're going to be in an hour."*

It would seem odd if a piece of furniture started talking; or if the washing machine suddenly voiced an opinion. (The average guy would have to keep a pistol handy to shoot the living room sofa if it was capable of spouting inconvenient details.) But it seems perfectly natural the first time a motorcycle weighs in with a remark. Motorcycles are not held to the rules that govern other inanimate objects, as motorcycles are the most animated inanimate objects on earth.

I heard the bike in my mind. I would learn that the language of the motorcycle can be strong and meaningful, or the rawest of innuendos, or faint to obscurity. The present tense is the sound of the engine, the guttural thunder of the exhaust, and the change in pitch (speed) when twisting the throttle. The future tense is the sound of the engine, combined with the noise of the road, as interpreted by the tires. At 85 miles per hour, the bike was defining the future at 124.6 feet per second. There is no past tense on a motorcycle. The past is behind you and that die is cast.

*"What is that blond bitch compared to 124.6 feet per second?"* asked the bike. *"Had she been on the back right now, she'd have wanted to take a piss already. And what is the fun of that unless you can watch?"*

It is impossible to refute the logic of a motorcycle. I started to compose my thoughts for a reply and the bike added, *"Questions posed by a motorcycle are rhetorical. You can only answer them by riding."*

"If she was my girlfriend," I started to think...

*"If she was your girlfriend, you'd still be headed to the shore tonight, you'd still be alone, and she'd be blowing somebody else,"* said the bike.

"How do you know that?" I demanded.

*"I don't,"* said the bike. *But you do. You're just pissed it's not you."*

Exit 11 popped up like bread from a toaster. I banked right, following the signs for US-9.

*"Take the Parkway,"* said the bike.

"The Garden State Parkway is closed to motorcycle traffic," I said. (The Garden State Parkway would be closed to motorcycle traffic for two more years.)

*"Take it anyway,"* said the bike. *"Fuck them too. They'll never take us alive."*

I then realized that this bike had attitude. They all do. Never rely on one for advice.

Riding to the shore on US-9 then, as now, is a lot like getting a root canal in a Turkish prison. The pace grinds from stoplight to stoplight, and aside from a few glimpses of open water and an increase in boat dealerships, there is little indication you are nearing the beach. State Routes 35, 36, and 71 all run through shore towns but require replacing the speedometer with a calendar. Shore-town cops fed on bikers who pushed the speed limit. Yet the aroma of salt eventually gets heavy in the air and the cry of gulls belies the presence of the sea.

The machine grew quieter as we reached Seaside Heights. This honky-tonk, painted lady is my favorite among New Jersey shore towns. In high school, my peers preferred saloons in Belmar. Bruce Springsteen immortalized Asbury Park. But my first love remains Seaside Heights. It is the epitome of the Jersey shore without pretension. I like authentic shore bars and there is one I have been frequenting for years. Located right on the boardwalk (surrounded by the light and noise of tinny thrill rides), this joint makes it possible to tongue raw clams out of their shells, sip rum and Cokes, and gaze at an array of scantily-clad girl flesh on endless parade. I am not a shore person and have never hooked up with a woman in a shore bar... But I didn't know that in 1975. Watching these women in an implied intimacy with guys who had arms around their waists, or hands on their asses, just put a sharper edge on my own unfulfilled desires.

I ate two dozen sweet, icy-cold clams on the half-shell (kissed by Tabasco sauce), and a dozen ice-cold, steamed jumbo shrimp (swirled in a fiery mixture ketchup and horseradish). I had three sassy rum and Cokes as big as my ass (doubles) and watched dozens of hot women sashay past me. The sun went down on Barnegat bay and the flashing neon came up on the boardwalk. That's when I made the first bad decision of the day: to return to the Bucket of Blood to get another look at Tina.

It was around 10pm. I headed back a slightly different way, cutting across New Jersey's fabled Pine Barrens to the Turnpike at Exit 7A. New Jersey has a reputation for being crowded and compact. Yet the state has some of the most extraordinary topography to be found anywhere. The Pine Barrens are a one million-acre expanse of twisted and tortured evergreens, covering seven counties. Despite their proximity to major traffic arteries and places like Trenton, Philadelphia, and Atlantic City, the Pinelands are incredibly rural and sit atop the purest, natural aquifer in the country. In 1975, it was also the least densely populated part of the state, with straight roads leading through haunting nighttime darkness.

My experience with riding a motorcycle at night was limited. I found myself exhilarated chasing down the narrow beam of the bike's headlamp through the blackness of the Barrens. I felt like I was riding the tip of a rocket, yet the speedo indicated I was barely clipping 55 miles per hour. Aside from one or two sets of headlights that passed me coming the other way, the only other illumination I encountered was the glow of the Kawasaki's instrument cluster. And that was cool too.

This way back was longer, but a greater percentage of it was on the Turnpike, where I could go like bloody hell.

Civilization clings to the New Jersey Turnpike and I was soon surging through a sea of headlights. The allure of the slab that night was speed, and feeling the cool night air in my face, while holding 80 miles per hour, had a strange calming effect. Once again, I heard the hypnotic strains of the engine and the road, and once again, the bike spoke.

*"I am never going to get you laid,"* said the Kawasaki.

"Never," I thought, almost in a panic. The motorcycle had been my last resort.

*"Never,"* said the bike. *"Only you can get yourself laid. But I can fix it so that the first time will be utterly memorable."*

"Swell," I thought. "Fucking swell."

*"You know that going back to the bar tonight is a mistake,"* said the bike. *"But if you can't remove yourself from the bar, then remove yourself from the situation. The biker you'd like to be wouldn't give a shit about any of this. And when you truly don't give a shit about stuff like this, then you can't be held down by anything some blond says. Not that blond anyway."*

"Then what matters?" I asked.

*"The only thing that matters right now is that you are covering 124.6 feet per second, in the dark, and that your balls are filled with rum,"* said the bike.

I pulled up to the bar 90 minutes later. I could hear the juke box over the engine when I was still 100 yards away. The joint was packed and the noise was as dense as the cigarette smoke. The blond was at the bar, surrounded by the usual beef and the lesser beauties, who hovered around her like pilotfish. Cretin was chatting up some local talent and Vinnie the bartender was slamming drinks on the scarred mahogany bar as fast as he could pour. He laughed when he saw me and handed me a rum and Coke.

"Jack is back," he yelled.

Rum and Coke is one of the world's most underrated summer drinks. I was halfway through this one when I found myself blinded by a blond light. Tina was standing next to me, sharing a half smile and half smirk with two pilotfish girlfriends.

"I have something to say to you," she shouted into the music. The other two girls started to laugh, and I suspected I was about to become a punch line. It was at this point the music stopped as the juke box changed gears. "I have to whisper it," she yelled again.

With her mouth an inch away, she spit in my ear.

It wasn't a real loogie or a nasal oyster. Just a mouthful of gin-flavored saliva and nothing more than I would have sampled if I had kissed her good and proper. But it stung as if it had been flaming cobra venom. In that sudden vacuum of sound, it seemed as if a hundred people witnessed the exchange. I was being consumed by the red flush of humiliation, and felt as if I was shrinking. Yet with the resolve of a man who just covered 124 feet per second for 3600 seconds, I smiled.

It wasn't the smile of an embarrassed idiot either. It was the smile of a rider/poet who just didn't give a shit anymore.

I wiped the dripping saliva into my hand, and without taking my eyes off the blond, tasted it with the tip of my tongue. Then I wiped my hand on the crotch of my jeans. "This will hold your place for you," I said.

Cretin exploded in laughter, two seconds before the juke box shattered the moment with Led Zeppelin. I don't known what the blond's reaction was. I never looked at her again. What's more, I never looked at any of those women in quite the same light again either. Despite the blond's allure, there was a hard edge to the satin fabric that could cut steel. I also realized that the woman I wanted probably didn't exist in this bar. I'd have to find one someplace else. How hard could that be?

*"Well I think you finally impressed her,"* said the Kawasaki.

"I'm still leaving alone."

*"But you're leaving like Clint Eastwood in High Plains Drifter,"* replied the bike.

"Yeah," I said, kicking down on the starter. "There is that."

Chapter 7

# "FLAWED VISION"

I made two fundamental mistakes in the acquisition of my first motorcycle. One was assuming a bike would make me more attractive to the dangerous kind of women I craved. (These women wouldn't jump into my arms if they were on fire and I was standing in a jacuzzi.) The other mistake was attempting to substitute the motorcycle for a car without realizing the elemental differences between the two. I saw both in terms of basic transportation, unaware that I was swapping out a shopping cart for a Komodo dragon.

Cars were far along the road in reliability and predictability by the mid-seventies. They always started and the driver had few surprises hitting the brakes. Tires routinely lasted 20,000 miles and rarely did you ever see anyone changing a flat. The automatic transmission made it possible for a generation of young males to enter the motoring population without knowing how to work a clutch (myself included). And aside from a rudimentary familiarity with changing a tire, many young drivers were strangers to tools.

I replaced a 1968 Volkswagen Beetle (semi-automatic) with a 1975 Kawasaki H2. The Beetle had 250,000 miles when I sold it, and aside from rust on the pan, the car ran like the day it was new, which is to say, "oddly." It was initially thought I'd share the car with my mother, hence the appeal of the "semi- automatic," a uniquely German concept. This was a transmission that allowed you to drive in one gear, up to about 30 miles per hour, before shifting into a second gear. There was no clutch. You could drive it in either gear, but there was no real acceleration from a stop in "second." Technically, there was an electric clutch that activated whenever the "stick" shift lever was touched. The clutch bumped and made an odd noise if the driver rested a hand on the stick or hesitated in the process of changing gears.

My mother never quite got the hang of this. The Beetle would "conga" down the road as she'd hesitantly grab the shift lever, trying to get it into that second gear. Mom learned to hate the Beetle before she learned to shift it and the car became mine exclusively.

For the most part, the Volkswagen started the same way everyday. It had lousy heat in the winter and shitty defrosters under the best of circumstances. Yet the AM radio worked and I had wheels in my senior year of high school, when the other kids were still taking public transportation. I smoked my first cigar in that Volkswagen (at age 17). It was the first vehicle I ever drove to the Adirondack Mountains of New York (at 400 miles, the farthest I had ever been from home). It was also the first vehicle I drove to a bar and ordered a legal drink like a man. (The drinking age in New York City was 18-years-old then.) The vehicle had the character of a Disney cartoon, but it also had the predictability of a German appliance.

All this changed with the advent of the Kawasaki.

The only reliable thing about motorcycles in the early-seventies was that a huge percentage of them wouldn't start if the weather was slightly damp, soaking wet, too cold, too hot, too dry, or just perfect. Then if they did start, a lot of them would leak oil. Two-stroke street bikes burned oil. So did many of the others. Tires might have lasted all of 4,000 miles. No one ever mentioned the joys of synchronizing multiple carburetors. Brakes were a constant compromise between poor performance and hopeful expectation. Motorcycle suspensions in those days rivaled those of early suspension bridges. Most bikes of the period transmitted vibration from the engine and the road directly to the frame and the handlebars, then to whatever bolts that could loosen over a reasonably short period of time, like a month (or a week, in some cases).

Coming around a corner one day, I tried to downshift and found the shift lever missing. It was dangling about an inch above the pavement. A "C" clip had vibrated off its stem and the shifter followed. I used a wire tie from a sandwich bag to hold the shifter in place until I could find a gas station. A new clip cost a quarter. I bought a dollar's worth. When they'd all vibrated off (over the course of a summer), I carried a supply of sandwich ties. It is almost impossible today to find a gas station that has any kind of useful hardware, let alone a mechanic in the bay. You can find plenty of places that sell gas — plus lousy sandwiches, mediocre smoothies, bad pizza, old donuts, beer, and beach chairs — but nothing like rubber tubing, "C" clips, nuts and bolts, nor cotter pins — all common items in a 1970s service station.

My vision of owning and riding a motorcycle precluded the pre- and post-ride rituals. The truth was as abrupt and eye-opening as a kick in the balls from a ballerina.

I apologize to the gentle reader if I gave the impression that I was a natural rider. I found "false neutrals" often, then stalled the bike trying to start off in third gear. It was not uncommon for me to miss a shift every now and again, lugging the engine like it was a steamer trunk. All this played hell with the spark plugs, which would foul, resulting in peculiar starts and odd backfires that sounded like robotic farts.

There was a spare set of plugs under the seat. I thought this was very thoughtful of the folks at Kawasaki. I would soon learn the ghastly truth and popping these in and out became second nature. This meant carrying a thin pair of leather gloves to keep from burning my hands on the hot engine. (I certainly didn't wear the gloves when I rode.) This also meant carrying a gapping tool and piece of emery paper to clean the old set as it became impractical to buy brand new plugs on a week-ly basis. I learned the hard way that a flashlight and fuses were critical additions to the tool kit. And the drive chain had to be lubed often and adjusted on a near weekly basis.

I am not now nor have I ever been mechanically inclined. I never changed a tire on the Kawasaki. I never figured out how to synchro-nize the three carburetors. I never touched steering head bearings nor fooled around with anything other than light bulbs. But the standard day-to-day operation of a motorcycle in1975 required about 1,300 per-cent more fiddling around with things than did the average car of the period. You would no more mount a bike without a screwdriver and a pliers than you would without your boots. And every bike was different. Other riders I knew had similar rituals that incorporated a greater number of tools and a lot more cursing. I saw the Harley guys on the ground with their tools as often I saw them in the saddle. The Brit bike riders swore in metric and they hated somebody named "Lucas" with a mad passion. There was no way an individual could ride a motorcycle in 1975 without becoming committed to a much higher operator/ma-chine relationship level than one would ever need with a car. (Honda would change this.) Dealing with the mechanical quirks of the motorcycle became part of the biker qualification process. Each of these rituals separated me from the blank-eyed sheep in the cars around me.

I rode the bike every day, sometimes leaving for work an hour earlier just to get some fun time on the road before loading trucks at night. I took the "scenic route" everyplace. And I began to crave the long straight stretches in which I'd stampede the machine's 71 horses with enthusiasm. I'd ride for four or five hours every Saturday or Sunday morning, always covering familiar terrain, learning to handle the bike in traffic, in the rain, and in the heat. Throughout all this, I learned the "normal" operating sounds of a Kawasaki H2. These included the "ring, ding, ping" noises of the engine when ramping up and when cruising at various speeds, plus the different "thrum" of the tires on asphalt, concrete, and steel grate surfaces.

These were the days when just getting a motorcycle started could be an adventure. There were a dozen urban legends of Harleys that "kicked back" through kick starters armed with huge clockwork springs, allegedly throwing riders over the handlebars or even breaking someone's leg. (I never saw this happen, nor met someone it happened to. But everybody I knew at the time knew someone who'd been "kicked" by a Harley.) I remember beautiful, clear afternoons that were instantly clouded by motorcycles that refused to fire. On one such occasion, my friend Cretin jumped up and down on the starter of his beloved Norton Commando about 20 times, muttering mystical (and presumably helpful) incantations like, "This fucking British bitch of a motorcycle," between efforts.

"What's wrong," I asked.

He looked at me like I was a moron, and asked "What's today's date?"

"June 6th."

"The fucking Norton has its period," he replied, going back into the saloon. It would start on the third kick 20 minutes later. There was no explanation and it was pointless to look for one.

The Kawasaki always started. There were plenty of days when that three-cylinder mill ran like a barroom brawl, but the bike always idled. One of the early characteristics (and visionary aspects) of Japanese motorcycles was the notion that they should start and run a lot more often than not. If this was a drawback, then it was one I was willing to accept.

Within five months of acquiring the H2, I didn't give a shit if no one liked the bike. I liked it. I liked the way I felt when riding it. And I liked the way I had started to think when riding it too. I was developing an attitude that was more in keeping with my new personal preferences. For example, while I desperately wanted to hook up with a hot, tough bar chick, I found myself wondering what the hell would I do with her after a week? What would we talk about? My interests were history, poetry, and literature of the 1930's. (I was in speech therapy to lose a Jersey City accent.) Now it would be short-sighted of me to assume that any of the ladies in that bar had limited personal ambitions, nor was incapable of appreciating art and literature, but I could only deal with the evidence at hand. It was the kind of place where the ladies said "deeze" for "these;" and "doze" for "those," and while most would take the toothpick or the cigarette out of their mouth before kissing, there were no guarantees.

I gradually understood that I was not like the other bikers in the bar. They grew up in a biker culture. I was attempting to buy into one for a limited personal advantage. I was the poser.

But then I also started to realize that there is no greater myth than the horse shit of the "two-wheeled" brotherhood. While there were plenty of riders who nodded and smiled at each other in the liberation of soul and spirit, there was an equal number who preferred the sanctity, tradition, and mystery of their own marque. I noticed the Harley guys seldom rode with the Brit bike crowd. Some of these guys (of both marques) were great riders and purists of the road in every sense. Yet they practiced the total buy-in of a "higher" form of the legend. To the real leather-men, there was no point to riding a motorcycle if it wasn't a Harley. The Brit bikers were no less committed, but less discriminating as their own standing on the totem pole positioned them to receive a certain amount of shit too. They were delighted when I arrived on a fine hunk of Japanese scrap metal, standing at the bottom of the shitter, looking up.

I also learned that many elements of the ride were not to be discussed, but merely acknowledged by a certain look in a rider's eyes. The windburn and sunburn on a rider's face; the oil smudges on his pants; the toxic aroma of his gear lashed to the back; the millions of dead bugs on the bike; and the "I'm-not-going-another-fucking-mile-on-that-fucking-motorcycle" look on the face of the rider's girlfriend (which I was apparently never going to have) said it all. The experience was private and holy, akin to weightlessness shared by those who travel in space. It was assumed by the bikers in the bar that I would do something stupid and crash; or just do something stupid and scare the living shit out of myself — prior to getting rid of the bike. Since no one ever spoke about close calls in the bar, no one ever knew that I had already scared the living shit out of myself on a number of occasions, and never once thought about giving up the bike. (It would be two years before my first crash, and two weeks later before I replaced the H2 with the same make and model.)

I was on my way to becoming the biker poet and writer who already existed in my mind, but it was necessary to first construct that image as I wanted it to be, and not merely perceived. I told myself I didn't give a shit if I ever got laid, if getting laid meant eating shit at the hands of cruel and vicious women. The truth is I was resolved to never getting laid and was resigned to being the "Unlaid Night Rider — Who Saved Himself For Death." (I wisely decided not to have this embroidered on the back of a jacket.) I also realized that most riders who mocked Japanese motorcycles in 1975 only saw the taillight of the Rising Sun. So I stopped giving a shit about their opinions too.

I looked the part of a rider.

My favorite jeans were grease-smudged and my left boot was scored where it came into contact with the shifter. I carried a screwdriver and pliers in my jacket pocket, and had a slightly sunburned/windburned mask where the elements branded my face around my goggles. My stops on the bike had long since lost that wobbly beginner stance and my take-offs were smooth, accompanied by the rising crescendo of an engine held to the power curve. I drank my whisky straight and bit the ends off my cigars. I was 19-years-old and the closest I ever came to being able to say I legitimately didn't give a shit about anything.

I learned to ride the bike in a very half-assed way, experimenting with hard stops, tight turns, and swerves as I felt like it, accumulating two bad riding habits for every good one. I discovered the rider is the point of an arrow that is self-guided through traffic, the countryside, life, and the most personal of thoughts. It was on one of hundreds of solo rides that I discovered the auto-pilot: the capability to get lost in my own thoughts and still keep track of everything that was going on around me. It became second nature to change direction by leaning, by shifting my weight in the saddle, by extending my knee in a curve — or by doing everything at once. Driving a car, which I still did occasionally, became boring.

I was burdened by the impatience of youthful disappointment and the short-fuse of anticipation regarding my stalled adolescence (at the point when it was almost over). The motorcycle fed these volatile emotions, compelling me to move (weave) through traffic and "line dance" at the higher end of the tach, empowered by the immortality of being 19-years-old. I had no two-wheel mentor nor moto-guru to advise me of when I had passed from borderline foolhardy to genuinely stupid. For me, riding a motorcycle in 1975 was the ultimate proof of social Darwinism: "That which does not kill me will make my sperm highly sought-after-by-the-hottest-of-women;" even if the second part of the equation had yet to present itself. (I believed in this principle the way physicists bet their careers on the existence of quarks, and other invisible marvels.)

Not only did the bike affect the way I moved through traffic, but it also altered the manner in which I passed through the bar. Not quite a swagger (which would have gotten my ass kicked in certain circles), my walk hinted at the first steps of something that was cool beyond belief. I was finding out something about myself every day, while viewing life though piss-colored glasses. The differences between me and the other riders were becoming undeniable.

I would never own a leather biker's jacket. They cost as much as two sets of tires in 1975 and looked as uncomfortable as hell. (Unlike the classic leather "bomber" jacket, which I did like, the typical biker's jacket seemed carved out of a solid cowhide block.) Biker boots back then were apparently designed by the Waffen SS, and equally effective at kicking the shit out of prisoners as they were for basic foot protection. I wore my Dad's army fatigue jacket from WWII, and got my boots from Sears. I rode in grease-smudged Levi's and a tee-shirt during the heat of the day. My hair was halfway down to my shoulders, and despite the biker mannerisms I was attempting to display, I had a distinct scrubbed "preppie" look about me. Absolutely genuine was my preference to be out riding and a constant desire to get lost among my thoughts as I rode. It was acknowledging my own individuality that hastened my acceptance with the group.

The turning point came mid-summer in 1975.

I was spooning my way through a bowl of Manhattan clam chowder at the bar of the "Bucket of Blood," when I discovered a whole, fat clam bobbing the bright red broth.

"Hey Vinnie," I yelled to the bartender. "I got the clam. Do I win a prize?"

The bartender, who was stirring a huge pot of the stuff in the kitchen, walked over and looked down at the clam with interest.

"I wondered what the hell happened to it," Vinnie replied. Then he grabbed the clam with a spoon and tossed it back in the pot. "Thanks, I've got to make five more gallons."

The place exploded in laughter and he poured me a rum and Coke on the house. I chugged it, looked at the clock and said, "I gotta go. There's someplace I gotta be."

"Where do you go every Saturday about this time?" asked Cretin, who'd popped in to place a bet on something or to sniff up a skirt.

"I head up the Hudson."

"Up the Hudson?" asked Cretin. "What does that mean? Montreal? Hudson's Bay? Sing Sing?"

"There's a topless joint west of the Tappan Zee Bridge," I said, in the most offhand tone I could muster. "There's a dancer there I like. I think she likes me too. She fed me a French fry from her "G" string last week."

This scenario was so damned unlikely that it caught Cretin completely off guard. To be sure, there was a topless joint around Nanuet, NY, that I had ridden past a dozen times. I had just never stopped there.

"You ride to Nanuet to make time with a dancer at a topless joint every Saturday?" asked Cretin.

"Yup... I like looking at tits without all the bullshit. I'm never gonna see any in here," I said, rolling my eyes at a handful of dollies in for lunch.

"How far is this place?"

"Forty miles or so, but I like the ride too."

"You want company?"

This was the first time any of the Brit bike guys had expressed an interest in riding with me.

Concealing a smile that barely covered the falsehood I was perpetrating, I answered with a shrug. Fifteen minutes later I found myself riding north, leading Cretin and Spider over a road I have covered dozens of times. I did this run the way I like my chili: hot. Yet I felt myself growing anxious. What if the strip joint was closed? Suppose the dancers were porkers from the "porcine ballet?"

I envisioned the necessity of having to get friendly with some forty-year-old bar sow in her underwear just to support my stupid story. The joint was jumping and nearly pitch black inside. The dancers were hot and varied in their technique. We weren't sitting at the bar five minutes when a skinny young beauty came up to me and asked if I wanted a lap dance. I nodded and let her lead me off by the hand. I turned to the other two guys and indicated that she was "the one." I would not have minded a bit if that's how things turned out.

We ended up in a dimly lit booth where this woman shimmied around me, thrusting the subtle curves of her naked breasts within an inch of my face. She had a stunner of a face and was as flat as a board. There was a grace to her movements that suggested she could really move to music of her own choice. I was thoroughly captivated. Her heady perfume conquered the aroma of beer and cigarette smoke. In the absence of any real light, she had an exquisite light of her own. Dancers in places like this are either very pretty or pretty jaded. This might have been the first week for this one. It was certainly the first time for me. I held out a $20 bill for a $10 buck dance and she took it all. I wanted to talk to her, but I couldn't think of anything that would sound clever to a pretty woman who was standing there, naked, except for a "G" string. I didn't realize that there is nothing a man can say to a woman in place like this that she hasn't heard before.

Her name was "Lou." She brought me back to my place at the bar, touched my face, and left.

"When does she get off?" asked Cretin.

"No one's getting off. It's over," I said. "She wants nothing more to do with me." Spider and Cretin just looked at each other.

"What happened back there?" asked Spider.

"I made her feel the roll of quarters I've got in my pocket and she told me she was a lesbian."

"You came to a joint like this with a roll of quarters in your pocket?" asked Cretin, rolling his eyes.

"Will she do a lesbian lap dance with another woman?" asked Spider. "I'd love to be on the inside of a veal sandwich."

I attempted to shrug and hold a straight face at the same time.

"You asshole," said Spider. "You didn't know that dancer. You've never been here before, have you?"

"Nope."

"Let's get out of here," said Cretin. "I could have taken you to 50 places closer than this, where you might have gotten a little action. We thought you were coming up here to knock off a piece. Falling for a topless dancer is a sucker's bet for jerks like you."

Cretin occasionally said something that should have been carved into the base of a monument. Regarding my character and penchant for hopeless romance, truer words were never spoken. I had known that beautiful young lap dancer for all of 11 minutes, and I was already planning on coming back to this place the following weekend.

"You are probably thinking about coming back here tomorrow," said Cretin. "Believe me, you're not ready for any of this."

"What makes you say that?"

"Because you are looking for a Hollywood set that only exists in your mind," said Cretin. "For you, riding a motorcycle to places like this is vindication that you are tough, and capable of blending into a culture that is not even remotely parallel to anything in your experience. You aren't blending into anything. You're like a loose moon that has been accepted into orbit around a dark planet. You're not tough. You'd last thirty seconds on the street. You couldn't talk to that dancer without sounding like a douche."

There were times when Cretin's assessment of a situation was painfully accurate. What pissed me off was that he could easily blend into the same conflicting cultural structure that was offering me an insular orbit, even though we came from similar backgrounds. He had a Christian Brothers Prep School education with a strong emphasis on the classics. I had four years of a Jesuit Prep School, with an equally strong focus on literature. (Both of us studied Latin. He could speak it like Caesar.) Cretin was viciously tough, and fought like a wolverine. He thought nothing of beating an opponent into the sidewalk. In most conflicts, my initial strategy was to block a kick with my balls. Cretin knew the vernacular of the street. I spoke in the dialect of the crosswalk. He had a tremendous command of "cool." No one ever accused me of being cool. (I once asked if "The Dead" and "The Grateful Dead" were the same group.) Cretin first got laid when he was 13-years-old, by his 17-year-old former babysitter, who used her babysitting money to buy him cigarettes, beer, and Playboy magazines on Valentine's Day. I was 19 and still unlaid and unblown. According to Jersey City law, I would have to register as an involuntary eunuch the following year.

"That beautiful stripper has a story that led her to your lap. And whatever that story is, you'd be compelled to rewrite it. You'd feel funny introducing her to some of your other friends as a topless dancer," said Cretin, preparing to mount his bike. "And yet she is much prettier than most of the women those same friends are hooked up with. Wouldn't you rather have a gorgeous firecracker of a girlfriend, who ran around topless, than some pedigreed skirt who jerked you off every time she jerked you off?"

I had no immediate answer for this last one. But there only was one answer. And the fact that I hesitated just made Cretin's point.

"You're not quite Toulouse Lautrec yet," said Cretin. "But you ride better than I expected."

What Cretin didn't realize was that I had been over this route so often that I knew it as a practiced course. There was a question in my mind at how I'd ride over unfamiliar routes. Then again, this entire conversation with Cretin had been about unfamiliar routes.

Each topless place is much the same as another, but no two rides are ever alike. It was past dusk when we fired up the bikes. We took turns on the point, taking our own lap dances with the wind, and getting caught in a vortex of darkness and speed. I watched the headlights of the other two machines expand and shrink in the convex mirrors of the Kawasaki. I had waited months to be asked to ride with these guys, to be part of a formation of motorcycles, and to share in the biker identity. They were just making sure I wasn't an asshole with a new motorcycle.

The ride back became something of an intrusion, especially when riding in the middle. Maintaining my position in line meant carefully monitoring the movement of the bike in front of me, which was easy enough to do in daylight, but still something of a challenge for a new rider at night. It was fun, but required a much higher level of concentration as Cretin and Spider carved through urban traffic like it was a roast turkey. I would go on hundreds of rides of these guys in the ensuing years. Yet they tended to be short on miles (inner city stuff) and big on trouble. They didn't feel the urge to ride 150 miles when 25 would do. Then again, they weren't looking for anything in particular. I was still looking to escape. But this time, I was escaping from the kind of man I didn't want to be; running from fears and hesitation that could define vicious limitations later.

Chapter 8

# "SENSATION"

The motorcycle was born in the 19th century, in the choking renaissance of the industrial age, when men sought liberation from the horse, but not from the mad excitement of the gallop. The motorcycle replaces the thrill of the gallop with the lure of the lean. Motorcycles were conceived when all methods of transportation were high risk. Ships disappeared into the fog. Trains blew up or wrecked for want of brakes or signals. Automobiles were built like watches, and were about as fragile. Roads were largely conceptional and just arriving at a destination was an accomplishment. Early twentieth century travelers were more accustomed to rain, mud, sleet, washouts, days of fog, the absence of roads, and the kind of mechanical challenges that would break a modern motorist's heart.

Transportation evolved. Trains became reliable; then cushy; then threadbare. Cars became plush and insular, to soothe the cager stuck in endless lines of them. The airplane surfaced as a flying squeeze tube of instant gratification for those who were above the mire; until everyone was above it, and the mire followed them. But the basic premise of the motorcycle has never changed, even though many bikes now rival space vehicles for sophistication. They start. They have antilock brakes that work like retro-rockets. They have self-adjusting suspensions and traction control. They accelerate like bullets. They have tires that last for an unbelievable 13,000 miles and you can sometimes get 3 years out of a battery.

But the motorcycle is grounded in the early 20th Century. The rider is still open way to the influence of the elements, engine heat and vibration, and the cumulative way these things spawn poor judgement. And therein lies the motorcycle's charm.

Riding a motorcycle is one of the most hedonistic pleasures on earth. Every cell in the rider's body touches the environment, as he (or she) is bombarded by millions of sensory impulses per mile. Automobile manufacturers pride themselves on building machines that screen the occupants from the environment. The motorcycle catapults the rider into it. Initially, cars and airplanes were open. Even when the passenger compartments of early commercial aircraft were closed (and heated), the pilots sat out in the breeze. One school of lost thought maintained you had to be out in the elements to feel them, to sense them, and to properly defy them. Modern Visigothic riders understand and embrace this principle, though many feel it to a different extent.

The barflies I knew primarily used their motorcycles to traverse the inner city, to skirt the periphery of polite society, to seek out the female of the species, and to conduct the kind of business that demanded twilight. These were city guys, who needed the gray atmosphere of flat roofs, narrow streets, and dimly lit alleys to give their world definition. I desperately needed to get away from all this, and I had the kind of bike that ran best in a straight line, at 90 miles per hour. I started out seeking a certain kind of sensation. And then I began to find it.

I was carving through rural New Jersey when I first blew through fields where tractors were cutting hay. This is the most common scent experienced by riders in their epiphany. The aroma of cut grass was as tangible as smoke from a rubbish fire. I couldn't get over it. And since it was the season for cutting hay, I kept running into it, and delighting in the sensation. To be truthful, this is one that can be experienced by the sheep in the rolling cages too. But there are aromas that are far more subtle. Cornfields have a rich scent of their own, as do wildflowers. I have detected cigar smoke, cigarette smoke, and the perfume of women in cars around me — even when cruising at high speed. The rotting fragrance of a dead deer off in the brush is unmistakable, both for its pungency, and its unspoken warning. Streams, lakes, and little rivers in my native New Jersey had a cool scent that could be sensed by the rider before the bike paralleled or crossed them. (It was only after I found 1,200 lakes and streams in upstate New York that I realized fresh, flowing water has no definitive smell.)

There scent of cut hay was replaced by an aroma of fish and salt in the marshes, of balsams in the mountains, and by fresh manure in farm fields. The fragrant bite of ripening horse and cow shit was highly objectionable to the senses of a city boy, who eventually understood that the smell of manure was the basis of fresh life and an element of the pastoral scenery I craved. (I had no idea just how endearing the perfume of the barn was shortly to become to me.)

Then on a day that started out as sunny and as bright as pork belly futures at a barbecue, the air was filled with something else: ozone.

*"Today is going to be a little different,"* said the Kawasaki. *"You better be at the top of your game."*

I could smell the approaching thunderstorm as the sky darkened. I was cruising the pine barrens in southern New Jersey, on roads that ran as straight as an arrow for miles, without an overpass or a gas station for cover. The trees in the pine barrens are scrub pine that seldom get taller than 15 or 20 feet, occasionally punctuated by stands of hardwoods. The atmosphere ahead turned black.

I pulled over to assess the situation.

The wind swept through the hardwoods, revealing the pale silver-green underside of their leaves. The thunder began as fusillade that echoed inside my helmet as the rain fell in horizontal sheets: sheets of water as dense as drywall. I was soaked through in about 10 seconds. More than a downpour, this was an outrage of a summer storm, and the water pooled to a depth of an inch or two on the nearly flat roads. Lightening flashed to the ground someplace off to the right, and I realized it was getting the range.

I got moving again. The bike handled as if the wheels were covered with margarine. I barely hit 30 miles per hour, before dropping back to 20 on the deserted road. The engine snorted as I lugged it in third gear. (I was afraid second gear would spin the back wheel when I hit the throttle.) The stream of water coming out from the front fender was impressive and managed to soak the one place on my crotch that the deluge had missed.

Nothing is as wet as a thunderstorm on a motorcycle. You might just as well be scuba diving. The rain was in my helmet, my eyes, my ears, my boots, my pockets, and in every recess on the bike. Coming up on an intersection that led to a town, I cut right onto a divided highway. The spray from other traffic was intimidating and the teeming rain thickened into churned truck-tire mist.

Do you remember the panic you first felt when a speeding vehicle in an opposite lane threw a wall of water over the divider? Do you remember how it hit the windshield of the car, overwhelming the wipers as 20 or 30 gallons crashed up against the glass? (I was always amazed it didn't break.) Sure enough, a bus or something went by and raised a tsunami of rainwater.

*"You are so fucked,"* yelled the bike.

It is amazing how objects hurtling toward you at the speed of light (i.e. large stones, huge bees, cigarettes, cups half-full of soda, and half-eaten burgers) suddenly slow enough so your eye can record every twist and turn as they pivot in the air. And then, when they are about three feet away, they accelerate and improve their aim. I watched the water rise like a science fiction bitch-slap, and pause, before slamming into me.

The initial shock was overcome by a desperate instinct to keep the bike upright.

I had a cheap, plastic, snap-on windscreen wrapped around the open faced- helmet, and I swear that if I had been riding in sunglasses, the water would have used the brain bucket as a fulcrum, knocking me out of the saddle. The water was as warm as if it had been heated, as indeed it was, by the road surface baked in the July heat. My vision was a blurred distortion of steel boxes moving around me, as I tried to bleed off speed through attrition — as opposed to skill.

*"I can't believe you didn't screw that up,"* said the bike.

"Eat shit," I agreed.

Then I applied the brakes as the car in front of me came to a dead stop. Not a damn thing happened. The brakes were so wet salmon had spawned in them. The brakes took exactly eighty-three feet and two inches to bite. The car was 80 feet in front of me.

*"Don't aggressively downshift on a wet road like this,"* screamed the Kawasaki. But it was yelling in Japanese. I thought it wanted me to attack someplace at dawn.

I downshifted.

There are moments in life when you just know that whatever the hell you just did just wasn't right. The back wheel slid for about 30 feet as it turned much slower than the bike's forward speed. The ass-end veered right and I executed an "Oh shit" swerve to catch it. The bike left the road, right were the curb was pierced for a diner's driveway. I came to a really cool "Steve McQueen-type" stop, instead of being high-sided through the diner's plate glass window. No one was more surprised than I.

A waitress about my age, wearing one of those little waitress skirts, was getting out of a two-tone Chevy Impala, where one tone was faded blue paint and the other was rust.

"Wow, you sure know how to handle a motorcycle," she said.

*"Like a fucking golf-club,"* said the Kawasaki.

I ignored the bike and gave her a modest shrug and a grin.

"But I swear I heard you yell, 'Oh shit,' out there," she said, laughing.

"That's the bike's name in Japanese," I replied. "You pouring coffee soon?"

"Soon enough."

But the motorcycle gods giveth, and the motorcycle gods taketh away. She wasn't my waitress when I got inside. Mine looked like Medusa minus the snakes. My waitress had a face that curdled the fake cream product in those little plastic containers. And she was pushing a mop and a pail to capture the puddle that was seeping out of my jeans. The bucket was one of those industrial strength units with a huge wringer on it (the sort of thing you'd expect to use when mopping a feed lot).

"You could raise cranberries in the swamp coming out of your boots," she said.

"I came in here for coffee and a cheeseburger... Not the farm report," I replied.

"You want secret sauce on that burger?" she asked. And before I could answer, she hocked a throat oyster into the bucket.

"Never mind," I said. I resolved to leave her a buck for a tip, after rubbing it on my balls under the table. "Hold the secret sauce and send the cute one over here."

"You mean my daughter."

I examined that cheeseburger for secret sauce very carefully.

Twenty-five minutes later, the rain had stopped and I was outside again.

The Kawasaki was as wet as it I had ridden it into a lake and still it started without fail. New Jersey is famous for summer thunderstorms. The temperature before a storm might be 92°, and could easily drop to 71° as the contents of a watershed fell in a ten-minute microburst. Then the sun turns the wet roadways into lateral saunas. Clouds of mist rise to a height of six feet, as drivers cautiously probe the road clouds with the front of their cars at 80 miles per hour. I pulled into a little park and smoked a rope of a Italian cigar (a DeNobili, I think), until the mist dissipated. Riding in the mist struck me as unbelievably dangerous, though I must be in the minority as I have read damn little about it from other riders. It can only be compared to cruising through a vegetable steamer. I could find no positives. But the temptation to ride through a dense fog, even at night, was overpowering.

The mist was always humid. The fog was always cool. The mist followed violent storms. The fog was tranquil, silent, and soothing. The mist was malevolent in nature, hiding certain death behind a gauzy, table-skirt of a cover. The fog was the gentler side of certain death, telling the lie that there was nothing to fear in the soft, white reality filter.

On one occasion, I rode down Route 23 from High Point, NJ, in a dense fog on an early Sunday morning. I hadn't known about the fog when I left my point of origin, but it wouldn't have stopped me, not like a driving rain. It was as if the cloud cover had mated with the pavement, and I was moving through it by invitation, displacing the droplets in suspension as opposed to colliding with them. There was no sense of going up nor down on the steeply pitched roadway in the soothing murk. Just a peculiar state of detachment in which the world was me, the bike, and the eerie illumination of the instrument cluster. I found solace in a universe where I was my own sun and the only intelligent life. And that is the essence of the lie. Fog is the great outer space in which the asteroids are merely invisible, as opposed to non-existent. No fog in my experience is totally seamless, and puffs of wind would usher the cloud into denser concentrations, leaving some stretches of road completely shrouded, while others would be virtually clear, like cylindrical rooms illuminated by translucent walls and a ceiling.

The ride would have been holy, except I was still half in the bag from three days of solid partying. Twice, I saw the blurred orbs of headlights creeping up behind me, only to have them fade again, as the driver hit the brakes. The turn signals on the Kawasaki were bright, and I alternated between left and right, to create a flashing warning that augmented the red taillight. I careened through a turn, following the double yellow line as the line of my curve, and went from a densely shrouded stretch into a clear patch of road. There, just to right of dead center, stood a whitetail doe, posed with all the grace, beauty, and abject stupidity of her species. I shot by her — taking no evasive action — with two feet to spare, and was again swallowed up by the fog a second later.

*"Someday, there is going to be a bullet in the chamber when you point the pistol at your head,"* said the Kawasaki, with a sigh.

I cut the throttle a split second later, thinking there might be two or three equally stupid deer standing on the road, which lowered the crescendo of the motor to a mere buzz. The muted idle of the engine created just enough quiet to hear a vicious, slamming "boom" go off behind me. Not two seconds had passed. That car was really close and that deer was in hell.

Hitting the deer could have easily killed me. And all I could think of was I would have died unloved and unlaid. The mind of a 19-year-old is focused on limited absolutes.

I have never experienced the great pea-soup fogs of London, where reading a street sign is difficult. But fog occasionally descends over the lower Hudson Valley, and clings to the mighty Palisades like the ghost of an airborne tide. For those of you who have never seen the great "Palisades," these are the cliffs that overlook New York City from New Jersey. They stand about 400 feet high and run from Jersey City to the state line, past West Point, and nearly to the Catskills. It was etherial to ride along the edge of those cliffs, flitting from streetlight to street-light — along Boulevard East — with the whole of Manhattan rendered invisible. River traffic (tugs, barges, and ferries) moaned at each other in the white stillness, while my bike would snarl through wisps of cloud, fifty-stories above its greatest concentration.

On just such a night I found myself pulled over on a little side street, in Weehawken, NJ, a community famous for the last view of New York City unbroken by high-rises. The fog covered the skyline of Manhattan, less than a mile away, and all that could be seen was a gray blanket, dimly illuminated from within. I was atop the cliffs at one of their sheerest points, standing by a monument where two of the greatest men in early American history — Arron Burr and Alexander Hamilton — ended their political careers and Hamilton's life, in a duel. It was 2am on a Sunday morning, and on impulse, I switched off the idling Kawasaki.

The rise and fall of a motorcycle's RPM is the most reassuring sound a biker will ever hear. It means the dragon is awake, with fire in its heart, ready for the twist of the throttle. For all that, there are those moments when the loudest commentary on the ride is delivered by the silence that occurs when the engine is switched off. And in the fog, that silence was magnified ten-fold. It was a moment for reflection. I would have reflected if I had had some thing to reflect on. Instead, I looked down from my eyrie and imagined what it would be like to ride across the mighty Hudson had the fog been a thing of substance, capable of carrying me and the bike. I wondered if the fog was a metaphor for the stories I was already thinking of writing, or my expectations for becoming a rider, or anything. I realized this was one of those moments that qualified as unbelievably romantic, and I was here alone.

I wondered what it would be like to stand on the very point of this cliff, with fog all around me, and the head of a woman on my shoulder. I had a woman in mind but she had become my dark secret. The trouble with reflection is that you never know what's going to stare back at you from hell's mirror.

*"Don't give it a second's thought, Ace,"* said the Kawasaki. *"You'll be on her mind forty years from now."*

I was touched by the motorcycle's sense of delicacy.

"Do you really think so?" I asked.

"No," said the bike. *"But you looked like such a sap standing there that it was the only thing to say."*

"Well, I wish she was here tonight."

*"Why? It's you and me, and the fog. She'd just be a pain in the ass."*

"You don't know her..."

*"Neither do you,"* replied the Kawasaki with a laugh. *"You don't know any of them."*

"How come you're being so nice to me?" I asked. Usually you're as sarcastic as hell."

*"Because the fog is my lover too tonight,"* said the bike, *"And if we give her half the chance, she'll kill us both."*

"Still, it would be nice to have a woman tonight," I said.

*"It certainly is nice to think so, isn't it?"*

I kicked the starter... And nothing happened. The same thing occurred a second time. I glanced at the "kill" switch and the "pet cock" from the gas tank. Everything was in order. I switched off the ignition and switched it on again. The headlight and gauges came right up. I kicked it a third time, jumping on the starter with unaccustomed gusto. Still nothing.

"What the hell?" I hissed. I was two miles from home and the idea of pushing this motorcycle along the boulevard held no appeal for me.

*"Just kidding,"* said the Kawasaki. *I thought you might appreciate a little silence of mine."* It started on the fourth kick.

"Asshole Japanese motorcycle," I thought.

The bike stalled when I put it in gear.

"Sorry," I thought. It started on the next kick, and we headed home.

The silence that ensues when the engine is switched off is not limited to the fog. The same effect can be experienced when killing the motor in a remote campsite, on a deserted beach, or at the road's end on a mountain top. Ride your bike to the top of Whiteface Mountain in New York, or the top of Mount Washington in New Hampshire. Do it early in the morning, before the tourists arrive. Park away from everyone else, if you can, and kill the engine. The silence is penetrating. The heartbeat you hear is the mountain's.

Chapter 9

# "A TALE OF TWO PRETTIES"

**M**y motorcycle education continued throughout the summer of 1975. For the most part, the motorcycle gods were kind, broadening my biking experiences, with injury only to my pride. I learned the list of potential hazards were varied and multi-phased. Just when I thought I saw the threat, the threat within the threat would reveal itself. One of these was a cattle crossing on a back road in Branchville, New Jersey. In the mid-70's, Branchville could have been the model town for Norman Rockwell paintings. A more traditional American-style small town would have been hard to find in New Jersey, or anywhere. There were cornfields hosting pheasants, pastures filled with cows, streams loaded with smart trout, and forests teeming with stupid deer.

It was here the Hudson County kid found himself behind another kind of deer, a John Deere tractor pulling farm equipment on a public road. I had never before seen anything like this. Then I saw the sign for the cattle crossing. Cattle and tractors are as common as horse-flies and cheap beer in the midwest. To an inmate of Jersey City, the concept of a cattle crossing was like an advertisement for a miniature rodeo.

Branchville did not have the same cattle-town reputation as Dodge City or Abilene. There would never be cowboys in chaps, boots, and Stetsons driving a herd of longhorns to the railhead. It would be more like a farmer and his son opening gates in fences on opposite sides of the road, so twenty or thirty dairy cows could head to the barn. In my mind, I conjured up a scenario of cows drifting across the road, while a redheaded beauty (about 19, with freckles, in overalls and a tank top) tried to keep them moving (by whistling and slapping her hip with a straw hat or whatever the hell one does to hustle cattle). I'd stop the bike and look on with frank appraisal. She'd shoot me a smile with pouty lips.

Then one of the cows would get loose and head off down the road, which would start the redhead yelling. (This cow, whose name was "Essie," would have a reputation for bolting.) The redhead would be faced with a tough decision: to chase "Essie" or to get the rest of the herd through the other gate. This would be the point where I'd say, "I'll get her."

A running cow would be no match for the Kawasaki.

I'd get ahead of the wayward Holstein in a minute or two, and get her turned around. Then I'd chat with the redhead, whose name would be something like "Penny" (for the copper color of her hair). Her experience with green Japanese motorcycles would be minimal, so her interest in me would be high. That was the scenario I developed in my mind within 15 seconds of first reading the cattle crossing sign. (This is a clear indication of how I thought then and how I think now, though the age of the women in my daydreams has increased from 19 to 42.) So vivid was that daydream, that I would go miles out of my way whenever I was in that part of northwest New Jersey, just to go past that sign, though I never found any cattle crossing the road.

A light drizzle was falling on the day I last rode through Branchville on the loop that brought me past the cattle crossing sign. I'd been riding for three hours and my focus was on a little diner where I could get liver and onions for an early lunch. The air was heavy with the fragrance of fresh rain, cut hay, and cow manure, with the added aroma of damp clothing, as even a light drizzle gets into your soul when riding a motorcycle.

To my left was cut hay... To my right were cows in the field... Ahead of me was heavier drizzle... And on me was the damp clothing. Every fragrance was accounted for and all was right with the world. The day was gray, with a bit of wind, but not anything that would depress a rider's soul. I wondered about the people in the houses I passed. What did they do? What did they talk about? Were any of them looking out the window as I went by on the bike and wondering about me? I wondered if today was the day I'd meet that redhead at the cattle crossing? Maybe she'd be a waitress at the diner. Or wouldn't it be cool if she was working the pumps at the gas station?

My mind was not entirely on the business at hand.

Cattle are creatures of habit. On any given day, thirty bovines would cross this road to go from the barn to the upper field at 7am, and line up to make the return trip at 3:15pm. Like politicians, they shit wherever they can get away with it. For the many in the immediate field, that was as they crossed the road. Cow manure is not nearly as objectionable (nor as long-lasting) as special interest legislation, and it baked into a fine odorless crust on the hot asphalt road, where it was ground into particles by 120 hooves twice daily. I had ridden over it a few dozen times without glancing down once — but those days were always hot and sunny.

I saw a cattle-free crossing in the gray mist and gave the throttle an aggressive twist, not realizing the threat within the threat.

The gentle drizzle had mixed with the fine layer of ground cow shit, producing a surface like polished glass. (Note: I do not recommend polishing a glass surface with cow manure if other stuff is available.) The bike fishtailed and nearly got away from me. I was all over the road in my fight to keep the Kawasaki upright, and successfully resisted the urge to hit the brakes or to downshift. But I ended up bouncing the bike against the split rail fence that held the cows in check. It was a hard stop and the weight of the bike violently shook 20-feet of fence.

"Muthafuka," I muttered to myself.

"*Smooth,*" said the Kawasaki. "*Very smooth.*"

The bike had come to a stop against the fence. I took a few seconds to catch my breath and to regain my composure. (I was going to have one hell of a bruise on my right arm.) Then I tried inching the bike back onto the pavement. The fence was in bad shape and didn't seem like it would deter a cow bent on escape. I didn't want to knock the damn thing over, thereby releasing the bovines to the road.

It was then I planted my foot in a pile of cow shit, slipped, and dropped the bike onto the fence for the second time. On the inside of the top rail was strung a bare strand of wire. This was connected to a switch at the headquarters of the Syrian Secret Police. What really kept the cows from challenging the integrity of the fence was the 20,000-volt charge in this wire, which was now firmly pressed against the bare skin of my right hand. My eyes flashed three times as every light in Branchville dimmed. I shoved the fence away, and the bike gracefully fell to the left, pinning me to the damp, cow shit-veneered road. Now I would have a hell of a bruise on my left arm too. At least I was no longer connected to the agrarian power grid.

*"I could have done this by myself,"* said the Kawasaki, *"with less suspense. Why do you always have us in some kind of shit?"*

I laid on the road thinking about my next move. I wanted to get out from under the bike but not at the risk of grinding the paint on the pavement. My thought was to raise it just high enough without causing the machine to slide, so I could squirm free.

"Are you okay?" asked a feminine voice.

"This is not happening to me," I thought. "I'll scream if she has red hair."

She wasn't a redhead, but about 19, wearing jeans and a plaid shirt. The difference in her build and that of the cows on the other side of the fence was marginal. She picked up the Kawasaki like it weighed no more than the morning newspaper, and leaned it on the fence one more time.

*"Woooo Weeeeeeeee,"* said the bike. *"She did that with one hand."*

Then she pulled me to my feet.

*"Don't let her pull anything important,"* said the Kawasaki.

"That cow dung is slicker than shit, which I guess is what it is," she said. Her name was Cassie, and she had been looking out the window of a nearby house, apparently watching me when the bike started sliding. These were her dad's cows. "We don't get much biker traffic back here."

The left front turn signal was bent at an angle, but it was still attached and unbroken. The end of the left handgrip was scraped and the mirror was askew. The gas tank was undamaged as was the end of the steering damper (my real concern). A continuous smudge of dampened cow manure ran from the left shoulder of my fatigue jacket to the knee of my jeans. There was no mistaking the khaki smudge for anything other than what it was, as it carried an air of the barnyard about it. "Want to come up to the house and get cleaned off?" Cassie was looking at me like I looked at the women in the bar. Her eyes were the color of male deprivation.

"Thanks," I said. "I'm okay. I don't think I damaged the fence any. The rain is picking up and I've got about 70 miles to go. My arm is gonna' get stiff and I wanna get back before it hurts to move it."

"You didn't break it or anything?" she asked, gently rubbing my elbow. "Does it hurt anywhere else?"

"I'm fine."

"I can see that. Are you sure I can't make you a cup off coffee or something?"

*"Go on,"* said the Kawasaki. *"Go back to the house with her. Ask for the 'or something.' Throw her a pop. What a great story this will make... The first time you ever got laid —covered in cow shit — in the arms of a corn-fed, farm girl. I promise I won't tell anyone."*

"Thanks for coming to help me," I told her, unfolding the kick starter. "It was nice meeting you."

The bike started on the third kick, as the gas had spilled from the carbs. I pulled away with both feet down, until I was free of the bovine leech-field. The diner was a few miles away, and I carefully pulled into its hard-packed gravel driveway 20 minutes later. The manure smudge had merely been diluted, not erased, by the light rain and I left the jacket on the bike. I took a seat at the counter and asked for the liver and onions, with a hot cup of coffee, to be followed by a slice of blueberry pie.

"No pie," said the waitress, a cute brunette, with a slight build and great eyes. She used those eyes to peer over the counter at my rugged condition and asked, "Did you have to get under the tractor this morning or something, Honey?"

"I laid my motorcycle down on a curve earlier today," I said through the blue of my eyes, "dodging a lightning strike. I was under the bike for a while."

"Lightning," she said, rolling her eyes. "I never even heard thunder today. You didn't get hurt, did'ja? Take your time with the liver, we're expecting a pie delivery any time now."

"I banged my arm up pretty good, getting pinned under the bike."

"You were pinned under your Harley?" she asked, looking at me with new respect.

"Something like that," I said.

"How did you get it upright by yourself, with a banged up arm to boot?" the waitress (who went by "Cookie") asked.

"There's a trick to it," I shrugged.

I was on my second cup of coffee and had been regaling the waitress with the morning's exploits, when she said, "Here's Cassie with the pies." My blood ran cold. I turned, and watched the woman who'd picked up my bike without missing a beat, walk in with a rack of fresh-baked pies in each hand.

"Jack," giggled Cassie. "You decided to stop anyway!"

"You two know each other?" asked the waitress with some surprise.

"Jack dumped his bike on the manure slick between our two fields, this morning," said Cassie. "I picked it off him like it was a tick."

"The manure slick?" asked the waitress, raising her eyebrows. "And you pulled it off him?"

"Yeah, Jack here tried some fancy footwork but ended up on his ass anyway."

"Do you name your cows?" the waitress asked Cassie, refilling my cup with coffee.

"Every one."

"You got one named Lightning?" asked the waitress, looking me right in the eye. She then cut me a slice of the blueberry pie.

"I don't think so..." Cassie shrugged. "Get a mouthful of my pie! You could have had a piece right in the kitchen, while it was still hot."

The waitress was moving down the counter, pouring coffee for others, when she turned and asked Cassie, "So you picked up Jack's Harley by yourself?"

"It's not a Harley," said Cassie.

I could hear an invisible umpire yell, "Strike three!" I have never been back to Branchville since.

Fate had me cruising Henry Hudson Drive (the road that runs along the Hudson River in Palisades Interstate Park), when I found a living ad for designer jeans pulled over on a little two-stroke Suzuki 250GT. She was blond, cute, and baffled by the gradual loss of power on her bike. I had lately become an authority on fouled spark plugs, which I suspected was the extent of her problem. She had a smile like a laser and accepted my offer to look at her bike. It would take about 30 seconds to pop the plug. Still, it wouldn't do make this look too easy.

I checked the gas in the "Suzi's" tank, twisted the ignition key to make sure the battery juice was freshly squeezed, and then tried to kick-start the bike. It fired, but only on one cylinder. (The Suzuki 250GT was a two-cylinder bike.) I had no idea if this rig had spare plugs or even a tool kit and confidently retrieved my own.

*"It's just a fouled plug,"* said the Kawasaki. *"Here's your big chance to ride home with a blond."*

Throughout this 50¢ show of male know-how, I kept up a running dialogue on the superiority of the two-stroke engine, the beauty of the Hudson River, and what a great day it was for a ride. She told me her name was Brandi; that she was 17-years-old; that she had been the captain of cheerleaders at a high school not ten miles away; and that she'd gotten the bike as a graduation gift two months before.

I had traced her tan lines in my mind at least twice by the time I got the oil-fouled plug out. Showing her the unburned "splooge" in the gap between the electrodes, I flashed my irresistible boyish grin, known today as the "battered baby seal" look. (It had been successfully resisted by every woman to date.)

*"Don't get cocky and don't make up any stupid nicknames for yourself,"* said the Kawasaki. *"Just ask questions about her and act impressed with every answer. At some point say, 'Wow, that was smart.'"*

She learned that my name was "Jack;" that friends called me "Blades;" that I was a sophomore in college; and that I was (or planned to be) a writer. (Only the part about my nickname being "Blades" was a false-hood.) Considering she was a cheerleader, and had been shaking her fantastic ass at football players, it was only natural that she asked me if I played anything. I almost said,"the French horn," but cheerleaders are not known for their appreciation of biting sarcasm. The truth would be damning enough: I was a varsity fencer on my college team. No cheerleader ever wagged her ass at a fencing meet. I hesitated to an-swer, as the complex nature of fencing is not easily conveyed in casual conversation.

*"Don't do it,"* yelled the Kawasaki. *"Don't tell her you're on the fencing team! Make up something that sounds cool. She is ten minutes away from wagging her ass in your face."*

"I got a letter for fencing last year," I said.

Her eyes glazed over and I thought she was going to ask me who the letter was from. Telling her I fenced had the same effect as stepping out of a closet with some guy's dick in my hand.

"So you prance around in a tights, yelling Toochey, Toochey?" Brandi asked.

I studied the oil-fouled plug for a second, wondering how surprised she'd be if I just threw it into the nearby Hudson River and left. My "battered baby seal" look melted into an expression that any serial killer would have easily recognized.

"That's foil fencing," I sighed. "There are thousands of moves in three separate disciplines of fencing. I fence saber. The only kind where it is ethical to deliver a full body chop with the blade of the weapon."

*"Why don't you tell her how the transmission on her bike works,"* said the Kawasaki. *"That's almost as interesting."*

"Do you still yell Toochey, Toochey?" Brandi asked.

I am always amazed how the Touché bit sticks in the minds of simple people.

"We don't say 'touché' when fencing saber. It's more like 'Fuck, yeah,' as a good hit leaves the other guy brain-dead."

The numbers on the Suzuki plug did not match the ones on my spares, and I had no idea what would happen if I tried to use another kind. So I made a display of cleaning the fouled one with the emery paper in my kit, then gapped it to the same specs as my own. I gapped it three times, stressing the importance of this. But it was too late. The fencing team gambit had broken the cadence of the conversation. All that remained for me to do was get her bike running and get back into the closet.

Her bike started right up, blowing blue smoke from the pipe exhausting the recently cleaned plug. I rolled my tools up in the vinyl sleeve, wiped my hands on my pants, and was about to ask if she'd like me to ride along with her, just to make sure I'd caught the problem — when a growl of different nature presented itself. A green TR6 convertible, the last decent-looking car Triumph ever made, pulled up behind us. Brandi looked at the driver and gave the kind of squeal I'd only heard in the captions beneath the cartoons in Playboy Magazine.

The guy got out of the car and she wrapped herself around him like a roll of adhesive. He was her boyfriend and the former captain of the football team. The guy stood about 5-foot-eight and when he spoke, the top of his head moved up and down like a piston, revealing a vocal chamber for a mouth. He reminded me of a master cylinder. It has always amazed me how clowns like this get their pick of the women.

"What's going on?" he asked, in a burst of reciprocal romantic recognition.

"My bike broke... Blades said it was my gap... And he cleaned it," said Brandi.

"Blades cleaned your gap?" asked the Human Master Cylinder, glancing down at the front of her jeans and giving me another look Charlie Manson would have recognized.

"Spark plug gap," I said. "Common thing on sophisticated Japanese bikes."

"I'm getting a Harley," said the Human Master Cylinder."

"Fuck, yeah," I said.

The HMC (Human Master Cylinder) nodded and grunted, demonstrating the communications skills that made him the logical choice for team captain. One more time, I was astounded. Here was an incredibly pretty woman running around with a Neanderthal sperm donor, while I was spinning my tires.

"How do these guys do it?" I thought.

*"They don't join the fencing team for starters,"* said the Kawasaki. *"And they have a perceived predatory value in the social food chain. You're under 'D' for 'douche' in the social food chain."*

I was about to straddle the H2 when the HMC grunted again. For a minute, I thought he was going to offer me a tip. "Do you work on a lot of engines?" he asked.

This was going to be one of those golden moments that occur so rarely in life. "As a hobby," I replied. "I only work on foreign stuff."

*"What?"* asked the Kawasaki.

"Ever work on a TR6?" asked the Human Master cylinder.

"I have one at home just like this," I lied.

"I think this car is making a funny noise?"

I nearly ruptured myself trying to keep a straight face.

The Triumph sounded fine to me. Then again, I'd never heard a Triumph engine running before. This was the first TR6 I'd ever seen with the "bonnet" up.

"Leave it running and come over here and listen..." I said to the HMC, who joined me by the open hood. "Listen... Hear that?"

He did.

"Did you buy this car used?" I asked.

He nodded.

"From a dealer or a private owner?"

"Private owner," he said.

"Get a good deal?"

He nodded glumly.

"I thought so," I replied. "The intake manifold assemblies and seals are shot. They are a common reason why these cars are sold at a seemingly low price."

The human master cylinder writhed like he was in agony. "My dad got me this car. I wanted a Jaguar XKE."

"Well, your dad got fucked," I winced. "Do not drive this car at speeds above 28 miles per hour, and do not shift it above third gear. If this was my car, I'd go right to an auto parts place and order a set of intake manifolds. Have a private shop put them in and insist on it. Hey, it'll be a great car when you get it sorted out."

"Thanks man," said the human master cylinder, giving me some sort of sports handshake.

Brandi kissed me, and since the HMC was looking at the motor of the TR6 (which was running perfectly as far as I could tell), I gave her ass a squeeze. I suspected it was not her first time.

I pulled away on the H2, holding the speed to 30 miles per hour, knowing that the human master cylinder would be crawling along with his flashers on.

*"That was cruel,"* said the Kawasaki. *"You're going straight to hell."*

"She was never going to wag her ass at me," I said. "And I hate jocks for the way they get over."

*"Technically speaking, you're a jock yourself,"* said the Kawasaki.

*"You're a varsity fencer."*

"I don't wear a jock when I fence. My Johnson is both bulletproof and prehensile."

*"As well as unused,"* said the Kawasaki. *"You know there are those who think fencing sabers are alleged penis substitutes."*

"There are those who believe motorcycles are mere penis extensions too," I countered. "You know what that makes you?"

*"It would give me great satisfaction to have people think the high RPM part of your Johnson was Japanese and green,"* said the Kawasaki. *"You'd have better luck too."*

Chapter 10

# "BLEACHED POETRY"

Cretin had disappeared and the voice of concern was murmuring. His disappearances were legendary but seldom spanned more than a week. He'd been missing for twice that long now. Calls and visits to his apartment went unanswered. His bike was not parked in the street. The signs of foul play were growing ominous, though the foul players had yet to be identified. The truth would blindside us all.

Cretin was in love.

Not "love" defined as the all-consuming reconciliation of heart and soul between two caring individuals seeking refuge in each other's arms. But "Luuuuuuuuuuuuuuuv," as Cretin said it. Shakespeare could have defined this level of passion had he written a romantic scene between two freight trains, pounding headlong toward each other.

The signs of true Cretin-like romantic affliction were evident from the moment he surfaced. He was dancing on the bar of the Bucket Of Blood to the strains of the Grateful Dead, with his pants down around his ankles. There wasn't six feet between the saloon's cheap suspended ceiling and the top of the bar, so Cretin was doing a kind of stooped shuffle, stepping around drinks, and kicking a few onto the floor. He was wearing camo boxers, which were years ahead of their time, and were probably authentic Marine Corps. issue (Vietnam era).

"Not again," I said to Spider, Cretin's wingman.

"Yup," said Spider.

"Some babe in here?"

"Nope," said Spider.

"Pretty?"

"Yup," said Spider.

"How pretty?"

Spider just raised his eyebrows and smiled.

"I know her?"

"Nope," said Spider.

"Complicated?"

"You have no idea," said Spider.

Cretin's women fell into two categories: starkly beautiful, street-smart hotties as sharp as freshly broken glass; or sexually-charged floozies who'd made being stupid their life's work. He treated them all like they were goddesses — in the beginning. Yet his Jekyll and Hyde personality burned through women's souls like acetylene. Cretin was a man of conflicts. He had the looks of Steve McQueen, scourged by acne. He had the logic of DesCartes, tempered by the reasoning of Attila the Hun. He had the compassion of Saint Francis and the instincts of a hammerhead shark. Cretin also had the hots for this new woman badly.

I noticed a woman at the bar I hadn't seen before. She appeared "average looking" to me, which translated to "nothing special." But average in those days was anything less than spectacular. She had a big smile, a smallish rack, and a round ass accented by a denim skirt. The hand of a local bar thug had staked claim to her ass simply by resting on it unchallenged.

Stepping up to the bar, I noted the claim and smiled at her anyway.

"You're the writer," she said.

"No," I replied. "I'm the douche with the green Kawasaki."

"All that too?"

The claim reasserted itself as the hand rose from her ass to a more visible position just under her breasts. She giggled and I turned away. I found it odd that she knew who I was, and surprising that her parting comment showed a bit of originality. Yet that was the moment that some other lovely reached up and tugged Cretin's shorts to his knees. Pandemonium reigned and I watched as the mob hurled napkins, spent bar fruit, cigarette butts, and whatever else was handy at the dancer. The bartender turned the soda spritzer on him, catching a dozen innocent bystanders in the crossfire.

Reep," said Cretin, re-pantsed with a drink in his hand. "I want you to meet somebody. She is fucking beautiful." I had never seen him so happy.

Four of us mounted our bikes and followed him into the urban murk just before last call. Spider was on Cretin's tail, trailed by two other Brit bikers who had a reputation for being tough. I brought up the rear. We rode in a loose formation that was closer to a spent war dance as opposed to a war party. Cretin handled his Norton with authority and the other guys were equally steady in their turns and stops. We passed cops, who raised nary an eyebrow as we roared by. (Today, we'd have all gotten the electric chair. I could never handle a bike now drinking like I did then, and three of the five riders out that night are deceased.)

We crossed an imaginary line and entered North Bergen. There was no visible difference between the city we'd just left and the one we entered. But it felt alien to me.

Fifteen minutes later, we pulled up in front of a gin mill that had already closed. The lights were dimmed and the place was empty. Cretin scanned the street and waved the other guys on, but indicated I should stay. I have never felt comfortable going into saloons in strange neighborhoods. Coming from Jersey City, places like Union City, North Bergen and West New York seemed like foreign countries. (Then there was Bayonne to the south, which was a foreign country.) I liked it less when we entered a darkened gin mill by a door on an alley, relying on the shadows to color our entrance. Yet this was Cretin's signature arrival.

"Hey Baby," I heard Cretin say to a woman behind the bar.

She was fucking beautiful.

Slender though well defined, this woman was different from any that I had ever seen with him. She was a brunette with subtle features etched on skin as flawless as porcelain. She had narrow lips and perfect teeth, which constituted one of the hottest smiles ever fired in my direction. I was riveted by her eyes. These were dark as coal and full of fire. She had a voice to match the rest of the package, and suddenly, he did too. Cretin became "Mister Ultra Smooth." Not a caricature of smooth, but a genuine homogenized version of himself. This was the genie from inside the bottle who made him so unbelievably dangerous. The physical contrast between this woman and man was astounding. He was as flawed as she was perfect. Yet the Cretin who was the master of the shadows had morphed into the Renaissance Sun King in a heartbeat.

I went from zero to insanely jealous in 3.5 seconds.

"Hey yourself," she said, kissing his neck.

"This is Reep," he said, gesturing to me like I was a naturally occurring atmospheric condition.

"Your writer friend?" she asked, extending her hand to me.

"The same."

"Hey Reep," she smiled.

I took her hand and made a noise like water gurgling in a pipe, amazed that my name had come up in a prior conversation.

Cretin's smile became a quiet laugh.

"You guys want a drink?"

"Rum and Coke?" he asked me.

I nodded and gurgled again.

"He doesn't talk much, does he?" she asked.

She was the bartender in this place. My eyes were glued to her movements as she poured the liquor, ran the Coke, and dropped a lime in the glass. Twice she turned to grab something behind her. The perfection of her form was emphasized by jeans which should have been a fashion industry standard. To say I was mesmerized would be understatement. Cretin was watching me watch this woman, and I exploded into a deep red blush when her fingers grazed mine, handing me the drink. He laughed again. It was a quiet, rich laugh, devoid of his venomous cynicism.

The two of them exchanged a look that defied my ability to describe it then or now. It wasn't quite a transfer of fire so much as the mutual recognition of heat. There are some women who have a thing for bad boys. Cretin was a different kind of a bad boy. And she was like finding "The Madonna" of the gin mill. They had barely said a word to each other, and I felt like I'd been eavesdropping for hours. I would have traded my soul to have a woman look at me like that.

Taking a sip of the drink, I said, "Adios."

"You haven't finished your cocktail," she said.

I gurgled a smile and stepped into the night.

I heard the lock turn in the door behind me and the last light in the bar was out by the time I got to the curb.

*"Not quite what you were expecting, huh?"* asked the Kawasaki. Though it sounded like a question, the bike was making a statement.

"She is exquisite. God, I am so jealous."

*"What did you like about her?"* asked the Kawasaki. *"It had to be the visual. You weren't in there long enough to notice anything else."*

"She's like living porcelain," I said. "Classically beautiful with the kind of face that age will only compliment. She had eyes and a smile free from the taint of guile. I can understand why he is in 'luuuuuuv.'"

*"Nothing is as you see it,"* said the Kawasaki. *"When you meet a woman who is free from guile, it is because she has sucked in 40-square miles of it, leaving no trace to lead back to her."*

"I wonder if she has a sister," I said.

*"The sister is usually the one with the mustache and the fat ass," said the Kawasaki.*

I sat on the bike for a bit, taking in my surroundings. This bar was on a back street in a neighborhood of flat roofs and houses separated by three-foot wide alleys. Aluminum siding was the decor of choice. It was the kind of place where somebody always saw something. I saw a cat move furtively into the shadows. A huge moth flirted with a streetlight high overhead. Heat lightning flared briefly. In the building behind me, a naked man and a woman were feeding each other in the muted light that filtered in from the street. It was then I felt my own hunger, and realized it was one more desperate summer night when the kitchen was closed.

*"Is there a reason why we are sitting here? You're not going to get invited back in,"* said the Kawasaki. *"It will look odd if you're still here when they come out."*

The bike started on the first kick. I had wedged the damned thing in between two parked cars and pulling out wasn't so simple. Cars had real bumpers in those days and kneecapping yourself was not impossible. I carefully angled the machine free and paused, before letting out the clutch. That's when I saw someone light a cigarette in a parked car on the other side of the street, about ten cars down.

Then I realized why the other guys had ridden up with us.

"Fuck me," I thought.

I switched the bike off, slid it back against the curb, and dismounted. I thought of going back to the bar. Then whoever was in the car would have us all in the bar. That wouldn't work.

The only muscle Cretin had now was his... And what passed for mine. I shoved my red bandana (snot rag and grease wipe) under the control cables on Cretin's Norton. This was the signal for "Watch your ass."

Whoever was in the parked car probably didn't want me. I fired up the bike again, angled it into the street, and calmly pulled away. No one followed, and for a brief moment, I wondered if I'd been wrong.

I went three quarters of the way around the block, shutting off my headlight and the engine before I got back to the cross street I'd started from. There was a cluster of trees at the corner, and I bounced up on the sidewalk, to sit in the shadows. I was now five car-lengths behind the parked car.

*"This is a stretch for you,"* said the Kawasaki. *"What are you going to do, turn into a bowling ball and charge like an enraged armadillo?"*

It was a valid question. The last time I had had a fight, the other guy beat the shit out of me with his breath. I thought I might be able to make a warning noise or something.

*"The kind of thudding sound a lifeless body makes when it hits the ground?"* asked the Kawasaki.

It was 4am when Cretin came out — alone — and mounted the Norton. He found the bandana, looked around, and switched on the ignition. The Norton caught on the first try. Cretin was a master of the fast getaway and was out of there in a second. The car, a 1970 Monte Carlo with blacked-out windows, lurched into gear at the same time I came off the sidewalk. I switched on my secret weapon — the high beam.

The Monte Carlo opted not to follow Cretin and disappeared down a street to the right. I wasn't sure if it was my high-beam that scared him, or the roof lights on the police car behind me. I pulled over in front of the bar that I had tried to leave an hour before, cognizant of the fact that I did not have a motorcycle driver's license and that I had spent the greater part of the evening drinking.

"Why were you sitting on the corner back there?" asked the cop.

"I was waiting to say good night to my girl," I replied.

"Yeah," said the cop, obviously taken with my sincerity. "What's her name?"

The only girl I knew in North Bergen was "Big Tits Babs." I couldn't think of her real name for the life of me. My hesitation nearly got me arrested.

"Linda," said Cretin's paramour, now standing in front of the saloon. "My name is Linda."

"You're his girl?" asked the cop. (She looked good to him too.)

She draped her arm over my shoulder, turned my helmeted face her way, and kissed me squarely on the lips. "He doesn't look like much because he's not," Linda said to the cop with a laugh.

The cop laughed back, and left.

"You're not going to make that gurgling noise again, are you?" asked Linda.

"Someone was sitting out here in a parked car," I said.

"Black Monte Carlo?"

"Yup."

"Hmmm," Linda replied. "Thanks. Cretin said you had balls."

I wanted to touch her face, and ask, "What would you like to know about my balls?" I didn't. I simply waited while she got in a car, and left. The taste of her lips had dried on mine in an instant. It was in that instant I understood why male wolves kill each other over a certain scent.

*"My, my,"* said the Kawasaki. *"What a night we're having!"*

"Shut the fuck up and let me enjoy this moment," I replied. There was the question of "complicated."

Spider filled in the details the next day. This cupcake-from-heaven was tending bar in a joint owned by her husband. He was currently away on "business," which was another way of saying he was gone until certain matters quieted down. Cretin was not directly related to these matters, but met this gentleman's wife as circumstances unfolded. He fell under her spell, pulling her over the edge as his free fall began. I knew of no married women at age 20, and none who were having affairs. Cheating girlfriends were to be expected (sooner or later), as every guy I knew screwed around with reckless abandon.

Most affairs burn like bonfires, with flames flaring one minute and burning down to embers the next. The trick is to keep a draft of intrigue and desire blowing over the inferno, and that's impossible. Eventually something happens to change the equation. I suspected the black Monte Carlo was that something. Her husband was apparently capable of retribution.

Cretin disappeared again the next day. I wasn't surprised. I would have done the same thing if I had a girlfriend like that.

Shortly thereafter, I met the average-looking woman at the bar again. She was average-looking in the sense that most people are ordinary looking, and make themselves stand out through a comment or a smile. (One of the most average-looking women I would ever meet could disappear in a crowd of five people... Until she said something. She was clever like Dorothy Parker was clever, and then she made everybody else disappear.)

This woman was a tad thicker than I liked, but not in way that you could put a finger on. Her hair was a slighter darker shade of something, but I can't remember what. Her voice carried the resonance of Hudson County, but not objectionably so. Her smile seemed genuine, though lacked magnetism. She was alone at the moment and I bought her a drink. I will buy a drink for anyone who refers to me as "the writer;" and at the time, I would have bought a drink for any woman with a pulse too.

We hit it off reasonably well, and I asked her if she wanted to join me for a ride the next day. I suggested we could go out in the country for a picnic. She accepted, and left the saloon with errands to run. Her name was Barbara Jean.

"It appears someone in this joint might throw me a pop this summer," I said to Vinnie. "Who is she?"

"That's B.J.," replied the bartender. "She comes in here from time to time. Sometimes she goes by the name of Annie. She's alright I guess, but you probably don't want her for a steady girlfriend." Every bar has myths, stories, and legends. In his kind way, the bartender had explained that I'd just met one. However, I'd missed the subtlety.

There is an art to putting together a great picnic. Lunch was a selection of Italian delicacies, which were the specialty of a deli in Hoboken. I got a rose at the florist across the street from the deli, with its stem in a plastic vial of water. I tucked away a container of lemonade, accompanied by a nearly full bottle of vodka. Included was an old quilt to spread on the ground, perfect for blunting the hardness of tree roots and stones.

*"Great expectations, eh,"* said the motorcycle, as I strapped the gear to the sissy bar.

"If you want to ask a question, then ask a question," I replied. "If you want to make a point, then make a point."

*"Sometimes you get exactly what you want,"* said the Kawasaki.

"I hope so," I replied.

*"Remember to act grateful."*

B.J. was wearing skin-tight jeans, heels, and a summer sun blouse, open in the back, when I pulled up to her house.

"You look nice," I said, really thinking, "you need a jacket, other shoes, and to lose ten pounds if you are going to wear those pants." I convinced her that the afternoon would become a more enjoyable thrill ride if she wore sneakers and a light jacket.

She complained that her feet were hot ten minutes into the run. This occurred about the same time I smelled burning rubber. Her feet were not on the pegs, but on the pipes. The once flawless (cheap) chrome now had burned rubber on it and her sneakers had furrows molded into their soles.

"Can I clean your pipes for you?" she asked.

I shrugged, smiling at the coquettish double entendre that just escaped her.

*"How long was your prior conversation with this one?"* asked the Kawasaki?

It was an hour-long ride to the secluded hill I had in mind and the bike ran well. Traffic was light, enabling me to jazz-ass around the curves and make some noise in the short straightaways. There was the sense

of weightlessness cresting hills and the feeling of the bike compress-
ing the shocks as we slowed. She gave all the perfunctory squeals, but
there was something too girlishly squeaky about the whole thing.

The Kawasaki was indifferently silent and that spoke volumes. I
stopped at the dirt road turnoff and told her to hold on tight, checking
to be sure her feet were on the pegs. She held on, with both hands in
close proximity to my lap. Technically speaking, the day was going
my way. We bounced over the last half mile of the run in first gear, as
the road was little more than tractor access. We were in upper Bergen
County, close to the state line.

Unpacking the picnic was the work of a few minutes, and I maintained
a running commentary as I got things to my liking. The was a view of
a nearby valley, a pastoral field, and lots of trees. We were absolutely
alone. She helped unfold the quilt in the shade, and marveled at the
detail of the picnic gear, right down to the pattern on the plates, matching napkins, and fluted (plastic) cups.

"Where are we?" BJ asked.

"Close to the New York border, about 50 miles from home."

"Is this part of a park or something?"

"It's land owned by a friend of mine," I replied.

"Do you come here often... To think about writing and stuff?" she asked.

"Yes," I lied. I had been there exactly twice, with a bunch of guys, to
drink and smoke cigars.

"Will I become part of your writing now?"

"Very likely," I said.

The bike ticked as the engine cooled, and I knew it was watching. It
was always watching.

She asked a few questions about me and started to talk about herself
as I served lunch. I can remember almost everything that happened
to me back then, but recall very little of her backstory. This is because

she bored me half to death. A person doesn't have to be beautiful to be attractive. Nor do they have to be well-read to be engaging. What they should be is interesting. She spoke about partying, getting drunk, and wild guys she knew. We seemed to be going through the motions of elaborate small talk superfluous to the purpose at hand. I had taken her for a ride on my motorcycle, with an elaborate picnic lunch that had set me back $30 bucks (in the days when $30 bucks would have bought a 12-inch line of coke). All I really wanted was a whiff of quiff. I was hoping that combining the raw excitement of being a biker (such as I was), with the panache of being an alleged writer, greased by a bottle of vodka, would persuade her to do something risqué.

All she wanted to do was blow me.

She was known in saloon society as "Blow Job Annie." She blew everybody. The effort I was putting into this picnic actually confused her. She would have honked my horn in the alley behind the bar for a couple of drinks, or even without the drinks. Now the gentle reader is undoubtedly wondering, "What the hell is the problem?" It is obviously a case of supply meeting demand, and opportunity shaking hands with the opportunist.

The problem was that I still had the taste of Cretin's woman on my lips and in my mind. I wanted what he had. Not so much in the looks of the woman, but in the looks he got from that woman. I wanted a sexual liaison that would burn this site into my mind as the epicenter of physical union. I wanted the particles of two souls, two minds, and two hearts to collide in a sexual fusion that would leave my senses concussed. I wanted the poetry, the thunder and the lightning. I wanted the seasons grinding to a halt. And I wanted some clue that there was something about me that made a woman wonder where I was and what I was doing when I wasn't with her.

I was about to get assembly line fellatio instead.

She took a deep swig of the vodka, followed by a quick gulp of lemonade. Then she sat next to me on the quilt. In ten minutes, she had two more drinks and I had yet to make a move. So she showed me her tits. One was slightly bigger than the other and I wondered if that one was the predominant breast... The "alpha" breast... The one that made all the decisions... The one with the nipple that got hard first. I had no desire to touch them. She placed my hand between her legs, and I noted that the greenhouse effect was certainly rampant there. But I had no desire to probe further. It was my turn to swig the vodka, and I didn't want any lemonade.

"Have you ever had a blow job?" she asked.

*"Answer the question,"* said the Kawasaki. *"Any answer is the right one."*

I waited my entire life to have this discussion with a woman. All I could think of was her blowing the guy with his hand on her ass, probably Vinnie, most likely Cretin, and half the other guys I knew. I was certain I wanted a bit more mystery surrounding my first trombone solo.

The wind came up from the valley rich with the aroma of ozone. The rumble of thunder accompanied a dark smudge on the horizon. The storm would most likely have passed us by, but I knew a good thing when I saw one.

*"Well, you did wish for thunder,"* said the Kawasaki.

"We gotta get outta here," I said. "Storms like these are very dangerous." She looked at me in total disbelief. So I added, "I don't want anything to happen to you." I covered the 50 miles back to her place in record time. We never saw a drop of rain.

She invited me in, and I declined, pulling away with a wave.

*"You never answered her question,"* said the Kawasaki. *"Then again, not answering a question is an answer in itself. Sometimes it's the only answer."*

The truth was that wrong person had asked the question. I wanted Cretin's girl to ask me that question. And the other truth was that I felt like an idiot. This was the second time something like this had happened to me... And the second time I had stalled. I had picked up a woman in bar, carried her off on my motorcycle, and got to the point where she was taking things off... Only to decide it wasn't the way I wanted things. What biker would turn down a guaranteed blow job on a summer afternoon. I spent $40 bucks to come home unblown!

*"So much of this biker mystique is pure bullshit,"* said the Kawasaki.

*"The first biker rule that can never be compromised is 'To thine own self be true.' You just might be a different kind of biker."*

"You would tell me anything to get out of being a douche's motorcycle," I said.

*"Oh you're still a douche,"* said the Kawasaki. *"And the only douche who ever turned down a trombone solo from Blow Job Annie."*

I went past the "Bucket of Blood" and noticed the row of bikes out front, sans Cretin's. Spider's Triumph was there and I went in to get a badly needed drink in familiar company. The great man himself was at the bar, however, with his face swollen and bruised. Someone had beaten Cretin to within an inch of his life. The atmosphere was somber, sullen, and simmering.

"What happened to you?" I asked Cretin.

"I fell off a barstool," he replied.

Spider gave me the look that said, "Next time," and I dropped it.

"Where'd you take BJ Annie," asked Cretin.

"To a yodeling contest."

"How'd she do?"

"I left her speechless and surprised," I replied.

"That's what I expected," said Cretin. "Did you kiss her?"

"From forty feet away." (Had I said, "Yes," he would have replied, "How'd my dick taste?")

Two days later, a bar brawl broke out in a neighboring town, resulting in thousands of dollars of damage to a saloon in North Bergen. One man had been assaulted with a car antenna and was hospitalized. Weeks later, I asked Cretin about the "luuuuuuve" of his life, and he replied, "Linda stayed with her husband. Just as well. She was a dead hump. But she sucked my dick in her husband's bar the night you met her."

The memory of that kiss faded instantly. It doesn't take much to tarnish a kiss.

# Chapter 11

# "BIKER BARS"

The Kawasaki went in for service and I remembered that strange feeling of being without wheels, especially two wheels. Any teenage male who has grown accustomed to mobility on demand feels odd when it is suddenly gone, even temporarily. That feeling is intensified when the daily ride is a motorcycle. I was prepared to sit in my apartment, lost in seclusion, until my bike was ready. This lasted two hours, when Cretin called, announcing he was on the way over to pick me up. I was to ride "bitch" on his Norton. I had never ridden pillion before and I was terrified, but damned if I'd admit it.

My ass was a fraction of its current size when I was 19, but even so, the seat on the Norton was chummy. I put my arms around Cretin's waist, at first, and that felt too strange. (He laughed.) There was a curved metal grab-rail behind the seat, but I could get no leverage hanging on in that position. The ride was brief enough and relatively smooth, so a tight grip was unnecessary.

Cretin took the most direct route to the saloon, which entailed the gentle, twisting, cliff-top curves of Boulevard East. The Norton's growl (so different from the Kawasaki's) had an intensely satisfying effect. Looking over his left shoulder, I anticipated each curve and leaned accordingly. There was almost no need to hang onto anything. The truce between gravity and centrifugal force planted me on the bike almost as if by tractor beam.

The magic of Boulevard East dissolved into the toxic knot of the Lincoln Tunnel's helix and the pavement turned to shit almost instantly. The Norton jolted on its suspension as we skirted badly patched potholes and raised manhole covers. It got worse crossing into industrial Hoboken. Cretin split lanes to get through traffic lights, oozing between trucks and buses. He shot up the 14th Street viaduct, banking into 90-degree left turn at the top, as the light went red in his face. This performance was repeated at two more intersections. The chances of getting creamed by tunnel-bound truck traffic had been excellent.

We closed the bar as usual, and were drunk as lords when we made the decision to go for breakfast. I had no hesitation getting on the pillion then, as I was numb from the eyebrows down. Six blocks from the bar, some asshole ran a "stop" sign and tore through an intersection. The car was doing about 40 miles per hour. I remember the screech of tortured tires, the sound of a motorcycle engine screaming, and a swerve that filled my entire field of vision with the ground. My arms went up to break my fall.

And that was it.

The car missed us and the bike remained upright. We pulled into the diner and Cretin never acknowledged what had just transpired. (If a tree nearly falls in the woods, does anyone really give a shit?) I liked this diner as the specialty of the house — sautéed chicken livers — was always available. Cretin and company decided to head into New York City, insisting I ride with them. Death can only be cheated so many times in an evening. I declined, and Cretin graciously offered to run me home.

I knew better. The Lincoln Tunnel was between the diner and home. It would be too easy to get Shanghaied. The guys roared out of the parking lot and I decided to hitch a ride covering the 39 blocks north to my place. Folks get generous or more openly strange at 2am. I threw out my thumb and a brand-new AMC Pacer pulled over.

"Get in," said the driver.

This canary-yellow Pacer was a strange bubble of a car. The passenger's door was wider than the one on the driver's side.

"Nice car," I said, automatically.

"I just got it," said the driver. Indeed he had — at knifepoint in Jersey City.

He drove carefully, making small talk as we got closer to where I lived.

I would have been out of the car in another minute or so, except for the two police cruisers pursuing us with a vengeance. The Pacer surprised me for its pep and took turns at 45 miles per hour relatively well. It exhibited a tendency to squat when cornering at 55 miles per hour. It wasn't until we turned at 65 miles per hour that the vehicle's limitations became obvious. We hit three parked cars.

I was briefly aware of a cutting tool going through metal around me, but didn't take an interest until I woke up handcuffed to a hospital gurney. My reaction to the handcuffs was to pull my hand through them, lacerating the skin against their ratcheting teeth. It was then that the cop standing next to me recuffed my wrist to the gurney's rails a lot tighter.

X-rays revealed I had a dislocated shoulder, a broken nose, and a mild concussion. I was given a nice soft bed, to which I was also handcuffed. The cop sat in a chair next to me, reading the Hudson Dispatch. My head was reeling, both for from the accident and the rum.

"What happens next?" I asked the cop.

The officer smiled. (I still remember this prick's name.) "You can sign yourself out and we'll go to the station, where you can give a statement," he said.

That made great sense to me. I'd be out of the hospital, free of the handcuffs, and I could get this whole thing straightened out. What I didn't realize was that the cop just wanted to get home on time and the best way for this to happen was for me to comply with his agenda. One of the nurses said, "I wouldn't do that if I was you."

Life changed for the prisoner Riepe once clear of the hospital. Both hands were cuffed behind me, which set my shoulder ringing. The cops transporting me didn't give a shit about my story.

The detective who interviewed me wrote down about a third of the details, took my fingerprints, and let me make a call. He didn't give a shit about my story either. I called a younger sibling and gave them the details. (I wouldn't dare wake up my parents.) The person I called went back to bed and promptly forgot about it. I was then remanded to a group cell.

The "group" included the driver of the Pacer, a suspected drug dealer, a drunk, and a young guy who had apparently walked out of a place with a candy bar, and got nailed for theft. This guy was crying his eyes out because the drunk told him he'd get a lobotomy. (The kid wasn't quite right to start with.) There was also some naked guy in an adjacent cell, yelling in Spanish, who was very proud of his dick, which was allegedly issuing telepathic messages.

The cell had been decorated by the folks who did the "Visitor's Center" at Devil's Island. There was a communal stainless steel bench/bunk. (I opted to stand.) Off to the side was an adorable enameled porcelain toilet, that had last been cleaned in anticipation of having John Wilkes Booth as a guest. (Toilet paper had been removed for fear that one of the inmates might weave it into a rope for a suicide attempt.) Several varieties of hard-shelled insects darted in the corners. (The drunk was now teaching one to talk, like a parrot.)

Four hours later, we were transported to the county jail to await arraignment by a judge. The ride to the county facility was one of the lowest points of my life. It was in a short, blue school-bus with bars on the windows. I put my head down in my restrained hands, thinking of how once prominent individuals would hide their faces when publicly arrested.

The county jail was the notorious "Pavonia Hilton," in Jersey City. The structure was modeled after the Bastille in Paris, though not nearly so well appointed. We were herded into this cathedral of the damned, the guilty, and the unlucky, to stand in long lines as the harvest from other municipal jails arrived at the same time. Cuffs were removed and we were matched with our paper work. It was here I learned I was charged with "assault with a deadly weapon" and "grand theft auto."

Part of our processing included turning over our clothing, letting a gentleman look up our asses, and stepping into some denim outfits that had only been worn by 700 other people. Of all the jobs in the world that should pay no less than $200,000 per hour, looking up men's ass-holes would top my list. Choosing bedding was my next favorite part of the day. We were sent into a storage room to pick out a foam mattress and a sheet. Thousands of stories are etched into the surfaces of county jail bedding. Each one is a romance.

It was then I witnessed social debate and resolution in the penal system. Lines of inmates going to breakfast were shuffling past when one kicked a loaded meal tray out of the hands of another. The second gentleman responded by smashing the first in the face. A guard, about 5-foot-two, pulled out a blackjack (a leather-covered piece of lead), and beat the shit out of the aggrieved party. I mean to say he beat the individual (with the spilled breakfast tray) to the floor, and then some. He then looked at me as if to say, "Next?"

I was inclined to compliment his side-swing but mutely stared at the floor instead.

My injuries were so severe that I was assigned to the jail's hospital floor. That was filled. So I was reassigned to the mental unit. This was a ward accommodating a dozen beds and 11 individuals. Six of these folks were the most muscular men that I have ever seen. They were playing cards, in silence. On one of the beds, a mutant was in the process of sweet-talking another guy (who had both eyes on the same side of his nose) into oral sex. The mutant advised me that he and "Bizarro" were a couple. I wished them happiness.

I sat with my ass in a corner and plotted escape.

"How do I get a call out of here?" I asked the council of card-players.

"What got you in here?" one of them asked.

"The pizza delivery guy ran off with my girl and I beat him to death," I replied.

"You beat a guy to death because your girl fucked him?"

"No," I replied. "I beat him to death because he brought her back without the pizza."

The card-players thought this was hysterical.

"The cops do that to you?" another card-player asked.

"Those muthafuckers..." was my response.

I had two black eyes, a bandage over my nose, and scrapes from broken glass all over my face. I looked cool.

103

Two hours later, one of the gayest men I have ever met, appeared at the window in the mental unit door. He had candy bars for the card players. "Who's the guy who needs to get a call to the outside?" he asked.

"I am not sucking anybody's dick nor taking it up the ass to get the hell out of here," I thought. Then I looked at the mutants writing another love story on yet another mattress and realized, "Well, maybe up the ass."

The guy at the window was the most considerate, compassionate, and informative person I met in my entire criminal career. He explained the process to me, detailed county jail protocols, and gave me some good advice (like retreating back to my corner). Shortly thereafter, a guard brought me to a phone. This time, I called my mother. There was no fucking around. I was out of there in 15 minutes.

The arraignment was two days later. My associates from the pit were brought in chained together. They had been held for 48 hours before they were charged and bail was either set or denied. The car thief stepped up to the plate and said I'd been hitchhiking. My story checked out and the charges were dropped shortly. It would be two weeks before I felt well enough to ride again.

*"Why do you save your best adventures for when I'm not around?"* asked the Kawasaki.

Chapter 12

# "MY EPIPHANY"

For want of a nail the shoe was lost.
For want of a shoe the horse was lost.
For want of a horse the rider was lost.
For want of a rider the message was lost...

I called in sick for my truck loading job because I had no clean underwear. I had no clean underwear because I hadn't done laundry for a week. I hadn't done laundry for a week because I'd been hungover a lot. I'd been hungover a lot because I was drinking more than usual. I was drinking more than usual because I'd almost gotten laid, until the woman discovered I wasn't wearing any underwear, and she thought that was gross. No matter how you looked at it, not getting laid got me fired from my truck-loading job in the last week of my first motorcycle summer.

No one should be loading trucks in the last week of their first motorcycle summer anyway.

I was tired of the direction this summer had taken. I kept waking up alone, smelling of cigarettes and stale beer, until the bed sheets carried the fragrance of the bar. It was time for a change, especially as school would be starting in 10 days. The first step entailed clean underwear. Not that I intended to do a load of wash, but I thought there was one last tatty clean pair jammed into a box of stuff at the bottom of a closet. I was wrong.

The box was filled with camping gear: my (two-man) canvas tent, my sleeping bag, a stove, a Primus lantern, a set of pots, and a collapsible 5 gallon water jug. I suddenly wanted to be alone for a weekend with the Kawasaki. Alone in the sense of not having to talk to anyone for two or three days. All of this gear fit nicely into a backpack, which looked cool bungeed to the sissy bar. The tent was in its own sleeve, which also lashed on without grief. I took two cheap frozen steaks (in plastic) from the freezer, and wrapped them in newspaper. Six eggs and bacon were stashed in the nesting pots. Three potatoes, two aging onions, and a handful of fresh carrots, plus a small jar of peanut butter and a loaf of bread filled the open spaces in the pack. The ball of paper towels coddling the eggs would serve as toilet paper. I was ready to go in less than 40 minutes.

The designated camping areas of Harriman State Park beckoned. I got on the bike and left.

*"No,"* said the Kawasaki. *"We always go there. We're not going there today."*

"Why not?"

*"I want to show you something,"* said the Kawasaki. *"Something you should have seen a long time ago."*

"Can we still head north?"

*"North it is,"* said the Kawasaki.

I was getting out of Dodge on a Friday, before the traffic mounted, and my riding style was aggressive but not excessive. I crossed into New York State an hour later and stopped for gas. These were the halcyon days when "service" was the key word in "service station." A kid in coveralls yelled, "Are you okay with the pump?" I answered with a nod and a smile. I spread a rag over the tank and carefully pumped in three gallons of regular gas, at a half-buck per gallon. That was when I discovered I had $9 to my name. I had no credit card and ATM's were far into the future. The minimum wage was $2 per hour and I had just gone through 45 minutes (from the four and a half hours) I had in my wallet.

"We gotta go back to the house," I said to the Kawasaki. "I left my cash in the bedroom. I've only got $7.50 for the weekend."

*"That's enough for 15 gallons of gas,"* replied the bike. *"What else do you need money for?"*

"But we have no cash for a campground or a contingency?"

*"We're not going to a campground and this whole weekend is a contingency,"* said the Kawasaki. *"If you go back to house, we'll never leave again. You'll end up in that fucking bar one more weekend."*

"Did you say something to me?" asked the kid with the coveralls.

I shook my head, and smiled, again in silence. The kid probably thought I was an asshole.

Fifteen minutes up the road, the turn for Harriman loomed and I signaled for a right.

*"No,"* said the Kawasaki. *"I'm not doing it and neither are you."*

"But I've never been down this road before," I said. "I have no idea where it goes."

*"Exactly,"* said the Kawasaki. *"You only ride the roads you know. Riding a motorcycle is supposed to be living on the edge... Not the edge of everything you know to be safe."*

"What if there is no place for us to stay?"

*"Suppose we find the best place? Suppose a lingerie model invites you into her trailer?"* asked the Kawasaki. *"Why do you always see the urinal as being half-empty?"*

The unfamiliar road passed through six or seven little towns, three of which looked like they'd been recently burning witches. A cop got behind me in one little burg and followed me right out the other side. I wondered just what kind of scooter trash had previously terrorized this community to the point where a Kawasaki H2 triggered the alarms.

*"He probably has a kind of radar that shows you're not wearing underwear,"* said the Kawasaki. *"His interest in you may have nothing to do with his job."*

There was a barbecue joint in one of these places and the aroma of sizzling pork made my mouth water. But there was no money for ribs nor chicken. I could smell pizza in the next community, but there was no stopping there either. I was now 80 miles farther north than I intended to go and the sun was transitioning from "high" to "merely buzzed." It was time to start thinking about where I'd pitch the tent.

A dirt road on state land led to a well-used campsite with stones piled round for a fire ring. A rusted grate that was once part of a supermarket shopping cart served as a grill. There was a rock-filled, burbling stream hosting a convention of mosquitos off in the trees. This campsite was more secluded than I anticipated. I had the tent pitched in 15 minutes. Dinner would be potatoes, carrots and one of the well-thawed chuck steaks. Then for the want of a spark that plan went to hell.

The book of paper matches packed with the stove had been there for a couple of years. The bright red tips had cracked and faded to pink smears on all but one. The stove would have to light on the first shot. While that was not impossible, I envisioned the unexpected puff of air and the sadness of watching the little flame evaporate into smoke. So my preference was for the lantern, as I had also forgotten to pack a flashlight.

Dinner the first night was a peanut butter sandwich and water. I spread the peanut butter on the bread with the flat wrench for adjusting the bike's shocks, as I had also forgotten utensils. Missing too were coffee, whiskey and cigars.

*"Such is the nature of escape,"* said the Kawasaki.

Gentle readers who have camped before might say, "Why not get the lantern lit first, then use a twig or something to light the stove from it?" This is a legitimate question. The Primus light used a fancy mantle on a porcelain collar to capture illumination in a little frosted globe. Once used, the mantle was little more than a dome of ash. It would dissolve in strong sneeze. The lantern would not work with a punctured mantle, and I only had one of those. The little boy in me believes that vampires are most likely to show up in dark forests and I wanted the option of uninterrupted light for most of the night. I was confident the lantern would light on one match. I felt less so about the stove.

The Primus light flared as darkness seeped out of the woods. This was one of the first micro lanterns, generating 75 watts of light from a little canister of butane. It sounded like a jet engine. The lantern was too dangerous to keep inside the tent, and I had it just within reach outside the zipped "no-see-um" screens. I lay naked on my sleeping bag laughing because I had also brought no clothes other than those that were on my back. I hadn't even grabbed a tooth brush. I was the epitome of the two-wheeled refugee.

I wrote for an hour, jotting down ideas in a notebook for a story that I would never finish. Then I turned the lantern down low and its roar became a muted hiss. The canvas tent was a lovely shade of dark blue-green in the subdued light. Dimmed, the lantern still attracted moths and little gnat-sized flying things. The smaller they were, the more erratically they flew. Some made the mistake of landing on the globe and turning into insect parchment, while giving off a puff of smoke and a bad smell. Larger moths would flutter close to the light, then soar on the lantern's thermals. These were the size of a nickel but cast much larger shadows on the tent.

Men will stare at a flickering campfire for hours. I didn't have a campfire, so I stared at the lantern. In time, a little toad appeared, and he stared at the light too. Then he began to eat the flying things within range of his tongue. Thoreau once described nature as a giant Ponzi scheme of reptilian opportunists. The toad may not have understood how the Primus light worked but he figured out the result soon enough.

I don't like camping by burbling creeks. After a couple of hours, the murmur of falling water becomes as penetrating as the sound of traffic. It eventually reminded me I had to take a leak. I grabbed my keys and crawled out into the dim light. My white naked flesh became a column of something brighter than the darkness around me and I could feel confused bugs crashing into my legs and back. I stepped around to the left side of the bike, inserted the key, and switched on the headlight. The trees and brush within 50 feet were bathed in harsh contrast. The Kawasaki was on the center stand and I could pivot the handlebars in a short arc.The light didn't show me anything that I didn't already know. But it was cool to flash it around.

There is something mildly defiant and genuinely satisfying about standing naked to the world and taking a leak — if you are a guy. The effect is the same whether in the woods or on the balcony of an exclusive hotel.

Switching off the headlight made the darkness tangible. Extinguishing the Primus light made the silence audible. I watched the stars duck in and out of the clouds, and I tried to imagine any of the bar beauties laying naked in this tent with me. The only one without a sharp edge to her was Blow Job Annie, and that was because her sharp edges were all turned inside.

I thought of the day's ride. I had stopped to look at six historic markers and to admire a handful of buildings. Even the cruddy little industrial towns had interesting structures that predated the Civil War. I camped in a spot that I commandeered and ate just enough for the moment. I'd found a huge ant hill with malevolent black ants swirling around the top. (Unfortunately for them, I was taking a piss at the time and they bore the brunt of it.) Aside from chatting with the Kawasaki, I didn't say six words all day. Not speaking has its benefits. I didn't offend anyone and I didn't have to apologize once.

Would I have done any of this with a pillion beauty? Could I have raced around miles from home, in the company of a steamy saloon goddess, on $7.50? It would have to have been a woman perfectly in tune with the experience. The smells in the confines of the tent were the slight mustiness of the sleeping bag, the pines from outside, a hint of gasoline, (from the Kawasaki), an errant coolness from the creek, the dried sweat on my body, the forest duff around the tent, and a faint trace of peanut butter. All would have been overpowered by the scent of a woman. I found these aromas strangely comforting. I still remember them after 35 years. There is no telling how you will remember a woman's scent.

"So what was I supposed to see on this ride?" I asked the bike. "Was it physical or philosophical?"

*"You're killing me,"* said the Kawasaki. *"Covering the same roads, ride after ride, defines your surroundings in a prison of your own making. You don't have to be absorbed and approved by everyone. You can visit a different monkey house without having shit thrown on you."*

The monkey house? Did the bike mean the bar? Or was the monkey house a metaphor for the whole biker mystique? I decided not to ask and fell asleep.

Nothing beats eggs and bacon for a camp breakfast. All I needed was a match. Another piece of bread smeared with peanut butter emphasized the importance of fire. I began to formulate a financial plan. Five gallons of gas would get me home. That would cost $2.50, leaving me the princely sum of $5 bucks to make the weekend better with a few modest purchases, like coffee. I thought of leaving the gear and making a run to the nearest town. With my luck, I'd never find this place again and lose the gear. I broke camp.

There is nothing complicated about spending "a fin" unless it happens to be your last five bucks. The first town I went through had a diner, with a breakfast special of eggs (any style) potatoes, toast, and coffee for $2.00. I swerved into the parking lot and dismounted. But that $2 was the price of an hour's labor at the minimum wage. Was any style of eggs, potatoes, toast, and coffee worth an hour of anyone's life?

There was a cigarette machine in the lobby of the diner. (There was a time when you could buy cigarettes in a vending machine.) These machines would dispense a book of matches with each pack. Not everyone took the matches. There were two books in the tray. I grabbed both, then put one back. There might be another rider through here who needed them.

There was a little market in town with three short aisles of stuff. Kraft Macaroni and Cheese was 37¢ a box, but that required butter and milk. In the end, I bought a small jar of instant coffee, a box of sugar, and a pint of milk. I also picked up the smallest box of Brillo pads they had. This left me with $1.37 (plus the $2.50 I had in reserve). This place sold sandwiches.There was a table with condiments and I stole the plastic spoon out of the mayonnaise.

I rode sparingly that day, visiting a local churchyard with headstones from the 1700s. Then I went through a state forest and witnessed bees acting out a nuclear holocaust. It was on a backroad that I met the first bee. It bounced off the cheap face shield on my helmet, leaving half its yellow and black ass smeared under my left eye. (The first dead bug or blot of bird shit on a face shield always lands in the rider's immediate field of vision. This is called Riepe's Second Principle of Moto Aggravation. The First Principle occurs when the bird shits or bug splats and the face shield is open.)

Seconds later, I ran into another bee, who seemed really pissed. Then I met a platoon of bees spoiling for a fight. One got in my jacket (but left when it discovered I was not wearing underwear). The bee issue resulted from a half-wit who was carrying one of those boxy commercial bee hives in the back of an open pickup. I don't know anything about bees that work for a living, but I suspect you have to lock them into the hive or something before moving them. The rusted hulk of a pickup had no tailgate and the hive had fallen out onto the road. The displaced occupants formed a buzzing mushroom cloud about 35 feet high. My trick was not to ride through it. The half-wit was running down the road with his own personal stinging entourage.

I waved as I accelerated past him at 80 miles per hour.

*"Didn't you want to help that guy?"* asked the Kawasaki.

"Fuck him."

*"You really are from New Jersey,"* said the Kawasaki.

I camped in the same spot again. The first time you see a semi-wild campsite it has an alien look to it. There is a potential spot for the tent, a likely place for the fire, and some sort of view or natural element (like the burbling creek). But when you come back to a particular spot, it is like returning to your first apartment. There are no surprises, but you check to make sure nothing scurries in the shadows. I put everything where it had been the day before. With a fresh book of matches in my hand, I lit the stove with reckless abandon, boiling potatoes and carrots together. The steaks had reached critical mass in their second day of defrosting, and I fried one with some bacon. My after-dinner cocktail was a little pot of coffee, sipped as the stars genially beamed.

The Kawasaki was quiet and I didn't want to get it started.

I was beginning to stink. It was the stink of honest moto-sweat, unfiltered by underwear and untainted by the saloon. (This didn't make it any better.) My aroma was occasionally reduced by the cool forest air. (This is pure bullshit. It was August and hotter than hell. The humidity during the early morning and night was a shade shy of fog.) I washed my face and hands with soap squeezed out of a wet Brillo, though I was not inclined to scrub with it. I rinsed my socks with soapy Brillo water and hung them to dry overnight on a branch. The moisture in the socks simply gravitated to the lowest point and the toes would be wet when I put them on in the morning.

My preparations for the evening began in the last hour of daylight. Water to drink, boots (bike keys and wallet inside the right one), pants and a shirt within easy reach. Matches where I could find them in the dark (inside the left boot), and the lantern just outside the tent. It made no sense to have a fire as the no-see-ums and the mosquitoes would be intolerable. The lantern lit with a "pop" as the last light of the day bled into darkness.

I fell asleep with the lantern on low. It was half-light outside when I woke up. The lantern was out. The gas canister was empty.

I had steak, eggs (my style) and bacon for breakfast, while looking at a map. There were two historic points indicated nearby, as well as a stretch of scenic road, all on the way home. I had four cups of coffee, to finish off the milk before it became butter. If I missed anything, it was not having a cigar. I broke camp with regret, vowing I'd return. (I never did.) The tank was a third full and I had 190 miles to ride. The $2.50 for gas would do just fine. The buck thirty-seven would buy cupcakes or something.

There was a battered gas station in town and that was my first stop. It was here I found a 1960 Triumph Bonneville rat bike, parked with a woman siting on the curb next to it. She must have been a real beauty in her day, but like the motorcycle, there were a lot of miles on the clock. Her complexion bore the blush of sun and windburn. Her jeans were ripped and smeared with old oil. Her boots were scuffed in a hundred places, but the upper of the right one was nearly worn through from the action of the shifter. Her reddish brown hair had been shaped by her helmet. Her demeanor was one of familiar resignation. She was old. About 32 was my guess. Nice ass for her age though.

The Triumph was faded black, like the ink in an old book of spells. By contrast, my Kawasaki was a disturbing shade of douche green. The woman was kind, however, and acted like my motorcycle's color had nothing to do with me being a probable douche.

She put a cigarette in her mouth and crumpled the empty pack. "Got a light?" she asked.

"Keep 'em," I said, flipping her the matches I got from the diner.

"I only need one," she said. "That was my last cigarette." She lit it and asked, "Where are you headed?"

"I'm on a personal quest," I replied, looking off toward the horizon.

"For what?"

"Underwear."

She laughed, and said. "I'm so glad you didn't say 'truth.' Are you looking for your underwear or someone else's?"

"Does it matter?"

"Not really."

"Where are you headed to?" I asked in return.

"Right here," she said. "I'm out of cigarettes, out of gas, out of money, and out of luck."

"Got underwear," I asked.

"Not on me," she laughed. I laughed too.

"Would you rather have gasoline or cigarettes?"

"I'd rather have the gas... I can always bum a cigarette."

"Here's $2 bucks for gas," I said. "Or an hour from some poor son of a bitch's life."

*"My, my,"* said the Kawasaki. *"We're living on the edge today."*

"Your bike always talk to you like that?" she asked.

"You can hear it?"

"Uh huh. I hear them all," she said. "You will too if you ride long enough."

"Hungry?" I asked.

"What have you got?"

"Peanut butter and bread," I replied

"Whole wheat or white?"

I was about to pump gas at that moment and glanced at her in amazement. She just started laughing.

"Got a knife for the peanut butter?" I asked.

She pulled a Buck knife out of her boot.

"Wait until you see what I've got for spreading peanut butter," I said.

I gently squeezed the trigger on the gas pump as $1.37-worth of regular topped off the tank. It wouldn't be the last time I headed for home with a half-a-buck for a safety net. I'd be on the reserve tank when I got there.

Her name was Amy. I gave her the bread, the peanut butter, the sugar, and the coffee. She asked me where I'd camped and I told her how to find the place. She asked if I'd be coming back that night, and for a fleeting moment, I thought about it. I could be home in a couple of hours, jump in the shower, grab some cash, pick up some groceries, and a bottle of whiskey. I'd get cigarettes too.

But she was 13 years older than me (or so I thought)... And here I was, scheming to come back as a source of gasoline, cigarettes, whiskey, and food. And for what? To wheedle my way into those tattered jeans? The idea was offensive even to me. Yet there was something about the way she looked at me... Like I really wasn't a douche on a green motorcycle. Or a kid wearing a helmet that made him look like a giant fly.

She was eating bread and peanut butter when I left.

*"See what happens when you follow a different road?"* asked the Kawasaki.

"Nothin' happened," I replied.

*"You got taken seriously. Now turn around and go back."*

I didn't. Forty years layer, I still think about that woman. Time hasn't softened my memories. It just puts the details in perspective.

# Chapter 13

# "THUNDER"

September's softer version of summer was reflected in the outfits worn by the women on the park-like grounds of the college I attended. Nearly all were in jeans with tops that ranged from subtly suggestive to openly revealing. I had forgotten just how beautiful college girls could be. Unlike the bar, where a handful of stunners comprised the dream-stock, there were hundreds of gorgeous women migrating between classes like butterflies.

College campuses have their own hierarchies. I spent my freshman year watching ball players assert their right of prima nocta while I scratched in the dirt. Technically speaking, I was an athlete, having earned a letter as a varsity fencer. Our fencing meets occasionally drew crowds as large as five, four of whom usually wandered in by mistake. But one doesn't fence to be viewed. One fences for the same reason one hunts rhino with a short pointed stick — to get in close and take a worthy opponent with meaningful elegance.

I arrived on the first day of the fall semester as a sophomore on a shiny Kawasaki H2, with (cased) fencing sabers bungeed to the sissy bar. Trading my army fatigue jacket for a brown corduroy sport coat, I ran a comb through dark hair that wasn't quite shoulder-length and set off across the campus. Carrying three books in my helmet with the swords over my back on a shoulder strap, I tried to convey purpose and promise. Presence is 60 percent of an impression. The other 40 percent is largely timing. Three women said, "Hello" in passing. They all looked good to me. It never occurred to me that I looked good to them.

I was starting an independent study and was thrust into classes intended for juniors and seniors. My focus was on the literature of the 'Twenties and 'Thirties. My overall impression of college had not been high, but my expectations of these classes were boundless. One professor, in his late 70's, was a survivor of the Dorothy Parker era, and had been on a first name basis with Hemingway, Fitzgerald, and Mencken. Another was a renown authority on Irish literature from the same period.

The class I found most exciting was an advanced writing course. Attending were published student-authors on a scale that vastly exceeded collegiate publications. One had been awarded a position with a prominent magazine and would go on to become a national columnist. Another was the Poet Laureate for a prestigious organization. I resolved to sit in the back and keep my mouth shut, hoping to pick up pointers from these writers. This resolution lasted two days.

One of the writers was an extraordinary blond who could detect bullshit in men at 600 yards. I thought about passing her a note from a distance just outside that. Next to her sat a brunette, whose long, straight hair was the color of deep space. Her skin bore the Tuscan tint of warm honey. She was wearing a form-fitting black blazer, a starched white blouse with a pearl collar pin, and beige jodhpurs. She was the poster child for the equestrian team and was competing immediately after class. For those unfamiliar with jodhpurs, they are riding pants designed to bring out every subtle line in a woman's ass. I memorized her subtle lines as if they were a soliloquy. She once rode a painted mare on campus, turning men to stone as she trotted by. I found myself wondering, "What would it be like to hold that woman in my arms, to brush a hair from her face, to get lost in her eyes, and to ask her to pass me the soap in the shower." From that moment on, there were no others.

Getting close to a woman of this caliber was a challenge. She was two years older than me and exuded an aura of pure sophistication. My first attempt stalled, and she called me an "asshole." I went to "Plan B." We had to read our work aloud in the creative writing class. Though I read for the class, I wrote for her. Others attempted to write profundity into the mundane. I wrote to make her laugh. (It helped that everyone else laughed too.) I staged a monthly comedy program on the campus television station. My thought was to be recognized as a source of refined humorous dialogue and a talking head on campus. Finally, she sat in the same place in the cafeteria each day, at the same time. I started holding court three tables away... Then two... And finally, at the far end of hers... Psychologists call this strategy "the glacier approach" as progress tends to be measured in centimeters per decade.

I can't recall the day she and I started having coffee together, but I think it was when I gave everyone else at the table $25 bucks to buy pot and get lost. I wanted to spend an afternoon with her away from the campus, but didn't know how to broach the subject. I didn't want future efforts tainted by early rejection, so I lied about scouting out a location for my campus TV show. I asked (without making eye-contact) if she'd like to come along.

"On your motorcycle?" she asked. "When will we be back? I have to meet my boyfriend, Josh, later on." Naturally, she was running around with the best-looking guy on campus. The way she said, "boyfriend" and "Josh," you'd have thought she was taking about a lesser god.

The brunette weighed all of 118 pounds and had the kind of tiny waist my belt would go around twice. Yet she put 1100-pound horses through jumps without hesitation. She swung her leg over the Kawasaki like it was an odd-colored green pony, and asked, "What do I do now?

She had never been on a motorcycle before.

"You can put your arms around me until you get used to the rhythm of the bike," I said. "But hang on tight if I tap your leg."

She hung on with her legs and held me for effect. I pulled away sans drama. It was a bright September day, and I noticed the shadow flying alongside the bike. There was I, astride a motorcycle, with the silhouette of a real beauty hanging on behind me. Anybody would see this guy, on a hot bike, with an even hotter woman, riding off to someplace cool. The best part though was that I could see it.

"Where are we going?" she yelled into my helmet.

"Not far," I replied. I didn't have a destination as I hadn't expected her to say, "Yes." It spoke volumes that she got on the bike without asking that question first. A road sign proclaimed a restored WWII submarine — the USS Ling — to be moored and open as a museum on the Hackensack River. I headed there. The profile of a Baloa-class submarine, anchored in the "Hackie" was amazing in itself. Viewing it could hardly be construed as a date.

Climbing ladders, snaking around equipment, and stepping over stacked torpedoes, she acted like it was the third submarine she'd seen that week. I brought up the rear, which allowed me to watch her reaction to everything. There isn't much space in a submarine and she smelled great.

She never mentioned the time and I took the long way back to campus. We threaded our way through ducks in a park, which made her laugh. I got the bike up to 85 miles per hour on the highway, which made her squeal. Then I found a twisty stretch that made her cling to me like plastic wrap. The Kawasaki never said a word, but seemed to run like a bike possessed. Then again, I was possessed. Despite the implied closeness, I couldn't bring myself to rest my hand on her leg, which was almost wrapped around me. I wanted to squeeze her thigh, and ask, "Having fun?" But I was afraid the spell would be broken. Still, it seemed like she was holding onto me in a much nicer way than she had when the ride began.

We roared into the campus parking lot to find "Josh" impatiently waiting by her car. His smile of welcome was tempered by a look of disbelief. Josh was 6-foot-1, blond, tanned, and lean. Pricks like this guy have been pushing me around my whole life. I had had enough. Besides, I had a steel and plastic penis extension that said "Kawasaki" on the gas tank. (His girlfriend was sitting on it.)

He gave her a 15-second kiss, and acknowledged the obvious by asking, "You went for a ride on a motorcycle?" Then he looked at me through narrowed eyes and added, "I'm Josh."

I smiled and obnoxiously replied, "So I hear."

What he meant to say was, "Get lost, asshole. This girl is mine."

And in my mind I said, "You are so fucking toast."

"Where did you go?" he asked her. "I've been waiting an hour."

"Jack took me on assignment to a submarine," the brunette said.

"Huh?" asked Josh.

*"This one is so stupid he can't even feel your foot in his balls,"* said the Kawasaki. *"Doesn't matter though. She is way out of your league."*

The horse show season had started and it would be two weeks before I saw her outside of class again. I got the campus TV station to assign me to equestrian events, where I'd pressed her into narrating dressage competitions. "Dressage" is a discipline where a horse demonstrates rigid riding techniques, like taking a dump while walking in a circle. The rider attempts to post, giving the impression he or she is in the final throes of rigor mortis, just like ninety percent of the audience. My editor at the TV station said dressage events were almost as boring as fencing meets, and unless I increased the jodhpur footage, there would be no point in running the stuff.

It was at one of these events I asked the brunette if she'd like to take a run out to the Delaware Water Gap, to videotape eagles. (I thought that sounded cool.) She declined, claiming she had to muck out her horse's stall.

"Can I help you with the stall?" I offered. "I love horses." (If lightning didn't strike me that day, it never will.) This is not the typical approach of a guy looking to knock off a piece. She was surprised and said, "Okay. What about the eagles?"

"They shit all over everything and eat their own young," I replied." I didn't know if there were any eagles at the Delaware Water Gap anyway.

She was wearing jeans that had a leather insert sewn over the derriere and stable work boots when I picked her up. She looked even hotter dressed down, with a western-style bandana hanging from a belt loop. The stable was 45-minutes away and had a name like "Ghost Ridge." It was just after 7am and I suggested we get a little breakfast. "My horse eats first today," was her response. The motorcycle ride was perfunctory, as she pointed out the turns over my shoulder.

*"What's that smell?"* demanded the Kawasaki, as we pulled into the stable.

"Shit," I replied.

"Shit what," asked the brunette.

"Shit, this place has a gravel driveway," I said.

"Problem?" she asked.

"No," I replied. "It looks firmer over by that manure pile. I'll park there."

*"You bastard,"* said the Kawasaki. *"I'll remember this."*

The average horse unloads 72 pounds of manure every 28 minutes. Manure attracts 15,000 flies per ounce. Her painted mare authored 17 tons of dung every week, attracting enough flies to give 2,000 of them to every person on earth. The fucking horse hated me on sight and started stamping like I was the antichrist. The brunette showed me a simple technique for reassuring the mare as I walked around it.

"Why does the horse have to be reassured?" I asked. "Doesn't it remember who you are?"

She stared at me and said, "I thought you loved horses!"

*"He said he loved whores not horses,"* yelled the Kawasaki from outside.

I busted out laughing, which caused her to ask, "Were you just handing me a line?"

*"He's been dying to hand you something for three weeks,"* yelled the Kawasaki.

I started shoveling. It was important that I appeared happy in my work so I tried singing. Opening my mouth let flies in, so I tried to whistle. In the end, I just wore a forced smile. While I hustled shit, she ran a hoof pick around the horse's shoes, removing traces of dung caught in the tiny openings. Then she cleaned out the animal's rectum. I now knew three reasons why the internal combustion engine was invented.

I hefted the manure into a wheelbarrow. When it was full, she'd take it over to a pile and dump it. She was out adding to the pile when Josh showed up and stood in the open stall doorway. Things had cooled between them and he was looking to make amends. My presence at the stable was an unpleasant shock for him.

"Cleaning this stall is as close as you'll ever get to her," Josh said. The way he emphasized the word "you'll" seemed to imply that I should take the next wheelbarrow to the manure pile.

There is a talent to getting a shovelful of horse shit airborne and I had mastered it. Josh caught it right in the kisser. He wanted to slug me but there was something about the way I hefted the shovel that made him think twice.

The next 15 minutes weren't pretty and he eventually left.

"You threw a shovel-full of horse shit in Josh's face?" She couldn't stop laughing.

"It was an accident," I said, giving every sign of being penitent.

I watched her exercise the horse on a lunge line and marveled at the bond between this woman and the mare. She offered to let me ride. The horse wore an English saddle the size of a tablespoon and I gave it the pass. With the stall cleaned, the horse fed, and Josh dismissed, I wondered how I could extend this day.

*"Help! Help me,"* yelled the Kawasaki. *"I'm drowning in shit."*

Josh's parting shot was to knock my bike into the manure pile. If someone is going to throw your bike over, I recommend it land in manure every time. Horse shit is soft, won't scratch the paint, and wipes off with a rag. My first thought was that Josh had put dung in the gas tank, which would have really screwed me. But that would have entailed picking up shit with his hands. Life's shit would never cross Josh's hands. The brunette climbed into the pile and helped pick up the bike.

"Gasoline's leaked into the cylinders and the exhaust system." I lied. "This is bad. I should really run the motor for a couple of hours to blow it out."

*"What are you talking about?"* asked the Kawasaki. *"There's no gas in the exhaust. That smell is from the spilled bowls in the carbs and from the gas cap."*

"I feel terrible about this," she said. "Where can we go looking and smelling like a stable?"

"I know a Harley bar where no one will notice."

"A bar?" she asked. "Really? It's only 11 o'clock."

"Not really," I said with a smile.

We skirted lakes and reservoirs on little back roads and rode by horse farms. I took her to lunch at a farmer's market and bakery, where we had hot coffee and warm pie. We had to eat outside because we carried the aroma of fresh horse apples. The owner of the bakery thought she was a doll and served us in a private grape arbor out back. I made no move throughout any of this, even when she touched my hand. I wanted nothing to jinx this.

The dark secret I held was jinx enough.

I avoided her all week, cutting classes so our paths didn't cross. Josh was undoubtedly making himself a pain in her ass and I wanted to leave room for contrast. I found her in the cafeteria on the following Thursday, writing a letter to her sister. She asked me if I would help her with the stable again. I begged off, claiming I had weekend plans.

"What plans?" she asked.

"I'm going camping. I ride off alone, into the woods, and think of stuff to write," I said.

There was a long pause, and she asked, "Can I come?"

I ordered every muscle in my face to remain frozen, and replied, "Okay."

Skyrockets went off in my heart and in my pants. Millions of butterflies were released in my stomach. Beethoven's Ode to Joy reverberated through my head. She gave me her phone number and her address.

"What do I need to bring?" she asked.

"A change of clothes and a toothbrush," I said. "I have everything else." I had 48 hours to prepare.

Chapter 14

# "LIGHTNING"

She was amazed that I was picking her up after 4pm, a late start for one night in the woods. Yet there was the bike loaded and ready to go. She'd gotten her stuff into a little leather satchel, which bungeed onto my pack. She slipped on the helmet, getting the "D" rings fastened right the first time. Despite having only been on the Kawasaki for a couple of rides, she grasped the routine and waited for me to start the bike, before dropping the pillion pegs and climbing on. (The kick starter on the H2 was clumsy to access with a rider on the back and the pegs down.)

I stalled it at the corner and she jumped off, to repeat the process. I stalled it again at the next light, and she asked, "Is everything okay?"

"Yeah," I replied. Then I stalled it again.

*"No,"* said the Kawasaki. *"He's not all right. He has a dark secret and he's stalling. He's on the verge of panic."*

Panic was not what I expected to be feeling, considering I'd made my plans carefully. I once read that careful planning is the foundation of something: confidence, success, or National Socialism. I forget which. I also forget who said this. It could have been Benjamin Franklin, Thomas Edison, or Joseph Goebbels. There was no unplanned aspect of this ride. I knew exactly where I was going, what was there, and how I would handle it. Nor would there be a question of missing gear. I'd gone through a checklist a dozen times. I knew what I had. I knew where it was packed. And knew I could find it in the dark. I could set up the tent blindfolded. Only the sleeping bags might be tricky because they were special too. Even knowing that I had covered all the bases, my mouth as dry as my palms were sweaty.

She was a natural pillion rider: anticipating turns, leaning with the bike, and avoiding any surprise moves. She knew when to put her feet down and when to hang on. She was always ready when the light changed. She'd comment from time to time, but knew better than to hold a conversation, nor to expect one. My riding was exemplary that late afternoon; even cautious.

*"For a guy who's been waiting 19 years for this moment, you sure are taking your time,"* said the Kawasaki. *"Afraid it will be a repeat of Boston?"*

I couldn't believe the Kawasaki knew about Boston. Then again, the bike seemed to know everything I knew. Why would my dark secret be any different? I found myself clenching the handlebars.

*"She didn't say she was going to throw you a pop tonight,"* said the Kawasaki. *"And you haven't gotten to first nor second base yet. In fact, you've gone out of your way not to make a move. What if she wants you to be that special asexual friend?"*

My palms became positively liquid. The butterflies in my stomach had turned into vampire bats. The thought of Boston hung over me like a shroud. My dark secret was devouring me.

*"Isn't it odd that a word like 'asexual' doesn't really mean anything sexual but connotes dickless?"* asked the Kawasaki.

The dark secret of Boston began to unfold in my mind.

Incredible women are wasted on adolescent boys. I'd met the archetype of the Riepe woman in high school, when I was 17. I went to an all-boys Jesuit Prep that maintained an alliance with four all-girls academies in neighboring communities. Our cheerleaders, female stars for school plays, and partners for school dances came from these places. I walked into a Prep student office one afternoon and found her sitting there. She was statuesque, with aquiline Celtic features, long burnt-sienna hair, full lips, and skin like expensive stationery. She glanced at me like I was an exhibit in a flea circus. She was an original jewel, brilliant, smart, and cutting; destined for drummers in rock bands and the cool guys, who were already making a name for themselves.

Our paths kept crossing and I became the exhibit who wouldn't quit.

There is an art to being cool, which some guys master early. (I was never one of them.) But cool guys end up competing against themselves, like human möbius strips (one-sided and non-orientable). I found something that ultimately trumps cool: funny. If you can make a woman laugh at the right time in her life, she'll remember your face. Make her laugh twice and she'll remember the color of your eyes.

I made this woman laugh a few times and we started hanging around together. She taught me how to use chop sticks. I taught her basic pillion technique. She wasn't quite sure what to do with me. Yet she invited me to her dorm, when she went to school in Boston. (In her bathroom, there was a sketch of a guy's jeans, with the zipper open. A rooster's head protruded from the gaping fly.) I was in so far over my head with this one that I didn't realize how much slack she was cutting me. The evening ended with me under a stunningly beautiful naked woman — unable to find the fucking starter.

She was expecting me to do so something and I was looking for the manual. Where the hell are the starter directions printed on a woman's body? Women should have birthmarks that read "You are here;" and "Kiss this for 20 minutes first."

They do not issue erogenous zone preparation manuals to boys in high school. I had four years of Latin in a Jesuit Prep school. What I really needed was four years of NBVS (Neck, Breast, and Vagina Study). I have since learned that no two women are wired the same way. What drives one woman crazy turns another into a psycho killer. (If a woman's body was a prescription drug, it would come with a 15-page disclaimer.)

The night was a disaster.

The hour-long return flight from Boston was the longest plane ride I'd ever had in my life. I was madly in love with a woman who never gave anyone a second shot. (And believe me, no one ever worked harder for a second shot than I did.) One of the most highly desirable woman I'd ever meet graced me with a naked vision, and I had revealed myself as a eunuch.

What if I was a eunuch? What if it happened again? What if happened tonight?

*"What if you lose it going into that turn around the lake? Suppose you hit a deer? Suppose a sniper fires from an undisclosed location and hits you in the dick?* asked the Kawasaki. *"Look at that fat asshole in the Chevy over there. Suppose he starts eating a hamburger and drifts left... You could be creamed corn."*

The fat asshole in the Chevy thrust a huge burger into his maw, squeezing the mayo-lubed all-beef patty out of the bun, causing him to grab for it. The Chevy swerved left, and I did too. Suddenly the world was sideways. I felt gravity asserting itself over centrifugal force and I responded with the throttle. Cranking the throttle on the H2 at 60 miles per hour unleashed an insidious demon. The bike shot forward as it exited the swerve. The engine screamed — not in rage, but in maniacal delight — as the Kawasaki straightened out like it was on tracks. That's when I felt the front wheel go light. I cut the power in half and we settled on the shocks. This burst of bike balls had thrust my rider into the pad on the sissy bar, and chopping the power slid her up against my back.

"Are you sure everything is okay?" she yelled. I gave an exaggerated nod and took a deep breath.

*"Don't blow this with your usual cheery outlook,"* said the Kawasaki. *"Can you pretend for one night you're not a gutless asshole?"*

My only thought was, "I hope this Japanese shit-rail is wrong about the sniper."

The first part of my plan called for dinner. I pulled into the parking lot of a little Chinese restaurant that made some of the best Szechuan cuisine outside of Manhattan. We had a table by a fountain in which tarnished koi surfaced and burped in the nature of carp elevated above their status. She'd never experienced Szechuan (spicy) before and let me order for the two of us. I insisted she use chop sticks, which entailed manipulating her hand with mine. We practiced on dim sum (dumplings) as they made slow-moving targets. I switched to a fork when she did.

We spoke about the literature we studied, specifically the complex nature of the characters and the various styles of the authors. I loved *The Sun Also Rises,* and saw myself as the Hemingway hero, stoically accepting reality. She deviated from the genre and cited Scarlet O'Hara in *Gone With The Wind*, as her role model. Building on the theme of wind, I also claimed I saw myself as the water rat in *The Wind In The Willows*.

"Nonsense," she said. "You're Toad," referring to the book's posturing windbag.

I gave her a wounded look, and out of nowhere, she said, "You have laughing blue eyes."

*"She fucking hates you,"* said the Kawasaki from outside. *"Just tell her you're a eunuch and drown yourself in that stupid fountain."*

It was dark when we left the restaurant. The headlamp flicked over the road like the luminescent tongue of a dragon. Riding a motorcycle in the dark is the closest thing to riding a beam of light. The universe becomes the rider, the passenger, and the bike itself. Anything outside the cone of light is non-existent.

The New Jersey traffic evaporated as we crossed into New York. Twenty minutes later, we banked into Harriman State Park, with the turn signal coloring everything bright orange in the dark. We didn't see another headlight for the rest of the ride. The high beam confirmed it was straight and slightly uphill for a couple of miles. The rising moon was flooding the woods with a soft light and I switched off the headlamp. I could feel my rider sigh through her arms around my waist.

*"Amazing,"* said the Kawasaki. *"The douche did something cool, and she's buying into it."*

There are limits to special effects and I switched on the headlight to take a small traffic circle. I was edgy about the damn deer as we had five miles to go in what amounted to a whitetail petting zoo. Five miles always seems to go by faster than it does and I wondered if I'd missed the target: a piece of reflective tape I'd stuck to a tree the day before. It gleamed back at me, and I turned left into a trail too small for any vehicle other than a motorcycle. I crawled ahead in first gear until I found the second strip of tape.

"We're here," I said, killing the motor, but leaving the lights burning. "Hop off."

She did and asked, "What do want me to do?"

*"You'd be amazed,"* said the Kawasaki. *"He has quite an imagination for a eunuch."*

"Close your eyes," I said. Then I switched off the bike and dismounted.

When she opened her eyes, we were bathed in silver-blue moonlight. The detail with which you could see everything was amazing. I plucked a leaf from a tree and showed her the veins in it. The night held the first autumn's coolness and she was chilly. I pulled the pack from the bike and propped it against a tree. Then I removed a sleeping bag and spread it against the packframe. "Climb in here," I said. I made her a cup of coffee on a butane stove, that lit instantly on one match and whose blue flame made little more than a whisper. A layer of thick whipping cream floated on the coffee.

Then I pitched the tent. I knew the tent stakes would penetrate the ground without challenge because I had set this tent up in this exact location the day before. I walked back down the trail and retrieved the two pieces of tape. While it was okay to camp here, it was not okay to bring a bike in off the road. Hence the need to arrive after dark. I spread the second sleeping bag in the tent. Her satchel and my stuff followed, including a water bottle filled from the tap at home.

"All warm and toasty?" I asked.

"Yeah."

"Want to see something?" I led her to a tiny brook that was straight out of Middle Earth. It gently flowed through the pines catching the light of the moon in a hundred different ways. Little frogs, disturbed by our arrival, jumped into the water. It was here that she kissed me, taking my face in her hands. Her lips gently enveloped mine with a soft, pensive touch that took me by surprise. It was the most natural thing in the world for her and it left me breathless.

*"One more sign of her growing contempt for you,"* hissed the Kawasaki.

The sleeping bags were a pain in the ass. I borrowed two state-of-the-art mummy bags that mated through an annoying zipper arrangement. I ended up just laying one over the other. I'd washed the sleeping bags twice and they carried the faint trace of fabric softener. She slipped into the tent first, as I jockeyed the motorcycle around, facing it down the trail, in case it was necessary to exit in a hurry.

*"Do you plan to leave her here so she can't tell everyone that you're a eunuch?"* said the Kawasaki.

I was incredibly nervous and resisted the fleeting urge to take a leak. The commentary from the bike was starting to get to me and I thought of taking a piss against the front tire.

*"You would so regret that,"* said the Kawasaki. *"If I shout, she might be able to hear me too."*

I grabbed a brown bag out of the pack and placed it by the tent door. Moving the stove to within easy reach, I took one last look around, and stepped out of my clothes. My brand new, white Fruit Of The Loom underwear glowed in the moonlight.

"Is that new underwear?" she asked, looking up at me. I just laughed.

"I bought new underwear too," she said. "Want to see?

"Yeah. I do."

She reached up and handed me a tiny pair of panties.

*"Unbelievable,"* said the Kawasaki. *"Against all odds...."*

"I'm keeping these."

"The hell you are," she said. "They were ten bucks."

Satin lavender panties have a soft glow all their own in the moonlight. It was hard for me to grasp that hers were in my hand. I crawled into the tent and got between the two sleeping bags with her. The moonlight poured in and ricocheted off her smile. I took a candle lantern from the bag by the door and lit it.

"There's more?" she asked.

I unwrapped two pony glasses from a dishtowel and lit the stove again.

Then I poured creme de cocoa into a little pot and heated it until the aroma of chocolate hung in the air. I half-filled the pony glasses with the liquor and floated heavy cream on top.

"What's camping without hot chocolate?" I asked.

That was my last trick. The moment of truth had arrived and I felt myself slipping. I doubted this woman, as perfect as she was, came with a manual either. I pulled another bottle out of the bag, and filled my glass with Jameson's Irish Whisky. I drank all of it and poured another. She took me in her arms and kissed me. Her mouth tasted of chocolate. Mine must have tasted like an Irish peat bog. The whiskey hit my gut like a sucker punch.

The scent of her perfume, Nina Ricci's L'Air du Temps, rose with her body heat and collected in a pocket under her hair, drawing my mouth to her neck and ear. I ran my hand along her stomach. It was flat and firm, but yielding to my fingertips. She was wearing a red football Jersey, which I tentatively started to raise, when she caught my hand.

"Here it comes," I thought. "The part where this isn't what she expected."

*"Dope,"* hissed the Kawasaki. *"Change places with me."*

She pulled the jersey over her head and held my hand between her breasts. The circuit breakers in my head started to pop one right after the other, and I began to shut down. This woman was beautiful like movie stars were beautiful. She had the soft lines of every model who ever posed for Art Deco statuary. She was as compelling as the inspiration for every romance poet from Shelley to Wordsworth. She was the northern lights captured in female form. And she was laying naked alongside me, attempting to read my eyes.

How had I talked myself into such deep water again?

*"You are the guy for whom she kept Mr. Perfect waiting in the parking lot,"* said the Kawasaki. *"You are the writer who makes her early for class. You are the douche who carries her off on a Kawasaki Widow Maker. You are here because she sees you without the bullshit you roll in. The music is playing for you tonight."*

I started to freeze. The master breaker was about to let go. My humiliation would be complete. In that second, the strains of the hottest motorcycle music ever written — Steppenwolf's *Magic Carpet Ride* — poured from the Kawasaki:

*"I like to dream... Yes, yes... Right between my sound machine.*
*"On a cloud of sound I drift in the night...*
*"Any place it goes is right.*
*"Goes far... Flies near...*
*"To the stars away from here..."*

I wrapped my hand around her hip and pulled her toward me. "I'm your ride tonight," I said. "Start me."

She did. I followed her lead. I leaned into the curves when she leaned. They were her curves. I clung to her kisses, rising and falling as they did. When she took me inside her, the sensation was not of triumph, nor of release, nor of relief. It was the abandonment of anything I thought it might be because it was better than anything I could have imagined. It was slow, and warm, and fulfilling. She looked at me in a way no woman had ever looked at me. And I wanted this woman to look at me in the same way at dawn... At noon... Forever.

She was soft, and elegant, and gentle, and insistent, and without realizing it, she met me halfway. She gripped me like a vice, and a current passed through her arms and went through me. And she bit her lip, and bit mine, and sighed, and kissed me through a smile. And when it was done, I was too.

She fell asleep on my shoulder not realizing I'd be awake for hours. The candle burned out, but not before I studied every detail in her sleeping face. The sleeping bags were too warm for early autumn and she'd wiggle out of the one we were using for a blanket, revealing a shoulder, a breast, or leg. It was like having the details of an artwork presented singly, outside of the frame. Then the night air would drive her under cover again.

I downed the remaining whiskey in the cup. The thing that I had wanted most had finally happened to me. Now I wanted it to happen again. Not at that moment, but soon. I wanted it to happen 483 times in the next two days. Not because of emotional and physical free fall, but because I wanted to study the free fall frame-by-frame. I wanted to remember all of this, from the feeling of her lips on my throat to the number of breaths she took as she slept. I wanted her to know that the scent of Nina Ricci's L'Air du Temps would forever be linked with the aroma of balsam, of coffee, of chocolate, and of anything else on this spot. I also wanted to be awake when she awoke. I wasn't. But I will never forget her first endearing words of the new day:

"How did you make coffee on this last night?" she asked, poking me with the stove. "Can you do it again?"

She sipped coffee as I broke camp. There was no new swagger in my step. I didn't carry myself like a samurai. Yet there was a new feeling of kinship when I straddled the motorcycle. My expectations of the ride were simpler and purer. I had been a rider for months, but now I was free to become my kind of rider. I was always free to do this. I just never understood that my kind of rider was as good as any other. It would be okay if I was the only rider of my kind too. This wasn't because I had gotten laid. It was because I had just learned that some things can be exactly as they should be. Exactly as I would instinctively know them to be. I would never share the details of this night in a bar. It would be more than 35 years before I even wrote them down. While some might argue that I'd ridden up here to get laid, the truth is that I was looking for something a lot deeper. That I'd found it was amazing.

*"Get enough sleep?"* asked the Kawasaki. For the first time, the machine addressed me like I was an equal.

"Some," I said, wiping condensation from the seat with a rag.

*"What do you want to do about breakfast?"*

"We gotta get out of here pronto," I said. "I thought I'd take her to that place on Route 17."

*"She'll like that."*

"That was a nice touch with the music last night."

*"My second choice was Light My Fire by The Doors,"* said the Kawasaki.

"Do you do requests?"

*"Depends."*

"Can you do *Under My Thumb* by the Stones?"

*"Don't get cocky. You're still a douche,"* said the Kawasaki. *"She'll figure that out soon enough."*

There was a stronger feeling of casual closeness when she got on the back, and a sense of possession in the way she held on to me. Not that she was mine. It was the other way around. I took it easy exiting the park. The morning was breezy and some of the trees had a golden tint to their leaves. The road curved around a number of lakes, and she pointed out clouds reflected in the water. Riding a motorcycle allows two people to speak through squeezes, hugs, taps, and the occasional punch. There are times when a touch, or the absence of one, says so much more than words. Sometimes not. I came to an easy stop as a buck crossed the road in front of us. She put her head against my shoulder and in a voice just louder than the idling motor, said, "Fucking deer."

We rode to the Red Apple Rest for breakfast. The place looked like a prop from a 1950s movie about the Catskills. (I loved this joint. My parents used to come here.) She ordered eggs over easy, then said to me, "You are the gentlest guy I have ever met. I thought you were going to apologize for kissing me last night."

I just smiled and looked down at my plate. A sense of presence is 60 percent of an impression. The other 40 percent is largely Steppenwolf.

## Chapter 15

# "THE EDGE"

**B**eing released from my own biker expectations was better than being let out of any jail (in my limited experience). No longer a prop nor a tool for sexual conquest, the bike acquired the status of a favorite pair of jeans. Our relationship became what everyone hopes for when they get a motorcycle. In the saddle, my feet and legs melded with the machine and it became an extension of my body. It was my only body part that smoked and was capable of killing me with a high-speed death wobble.

It carried my hot new brunette squeeze and me for thousands of miles. We rode to the beach, to the mountains, and to every point in between. We camped, stayed in hotels, and were guests at the homes of friends. I never once came close to dropping the bike when she was on the back. In all of those miles, my girlfriend never experienced a panic stop, a skid, or a near-miss with a car. We got caught in thunderstorms, fog, and high winds. All without consequence nor penalty. I had three dramatic crashes, but always when out by myself. Our adventures included an attack by a rogue snapping turtle during the endless quest for a bathroom, roadside romance, two slight breakdowns, and a vicious episode with a rattle snake. When I rode with her, there was no need nor desire for other company.

The Kawasaki loved her. Rare was the day when I'd throw a leg over the saddle and didn't hear a variation of, "Let's go get the squeeze." Once the Kawasaki asked me if I thought it had a face. I hadn't really considered it, but figured the headlight was the bike's "eye."

*"The pillion seat is my face,"* said the Kawasaki. The implication of that statement didn't fully hit me for a while.

The Equestrian was the love of my boyhood dreams. She was smart, sexy, charming, well-read, extremely easy on the eyes, and passionate. She was compassionate too, eventually figuring out I was new to bedroom stuff. Criticism and cynicism were not in her nature. I've heard it said that women are smarter or more equipped to deal with life than men and boys of a similar age. I think that might be true. She took me at face value. That is to say she envisioned me as a dynamic young writer, destined to create for television, the movies, or bookstores across America.

She didn't realize that I was a typical 20-year-old male and a certifiable horse's ass. And when I started to become a writer, the process was agonizingly slow and incredibly uncertain. She cheered me at every turn, and saved copies of everything I wrote. Even though the stuff never went anyplace. She helped me get my very first writing job, which I blew. I was more of a biker in the image I wanted, but had become a poser of a writer.

She used to go through my waste basket looking for poems and little vignettes that I had tossed, and which she thought were terrific — when she found a letter written to my Dark Secret. She never said a word to me until after we'd broken up for good, years later.

I still wanted the adolescence that I had largely missed. I craved the sex on the beach and the riotous parties. I lusted for the whiskey-soaked kisses freely given by half-naked women in the sizzle of tribal bonfires. I lived for weekend after weekend of racing the wind from one Visigothic experience to another. It never occurred to me that most of the riders I knew weren't getting any of this either. I just wanted my cut of the action. In hindsight, I just should have explained this hunger to her. I should have asked for a month of the biker's Kama Sutra, so I could try everything five or six times, under moonlight, starlight, headlight, and broad daylight. I think she'd have obliged me, if she thought I'd have been sane and rational coming out of the other end.

My Equestrian was above all this.

Then there was the whole drug thing. Most of my friends (now prominent businessmen and pillars of the community) smoked pot, popped mushrooms and mescaline, or snorted cocaine. I would never spend a dime on this stuff. My drug of choice was speed — the kind concocted by a green Kawasaki. If we couldn't go someplace on the bike, I didn't want to go at all. And if we were going to go on the bike, then I wanted to drink when we got there, prior to having great New Orlean's-style bordello sex. My appetites were as predictable as they were short-sighted. This is sort of living is hard on a genteel woman with a real agenda.

There is too great a social incongruity when you are the organ grinder's monkey and your lover is a princess. My girlfriend was coming out of Manhattan one day and I arranged to met her at the Bucket of Blood. I hadn't been there in weeks and I thought it would be cool to show the wolves what the guy on the smoking Japanese shit-rail had been up to. The plan was to get there about 40 minutes before she did, to be oblivious to the usual bar beauties, and have her walk in.

I was late and she was there a good hour before I arrived. The contrast in her demeanor with that of the local talent was staggering. It was like comparing *Girl With A Pearl Earring* with the paint-by-number stuff. The women were standoffish but not the guys.

"Your friends know the most amazing things about you," she said. "You never told me you had clap in grammar school." They'd been buying her drinks too. I looked at the faces gathered at the bar that day, and not everyone was delighted with my success. I remembered something Vinnie (the bartender) once said to me. "Carrying a pistol doesn't making you a gunslinger... But it can make you a target." There are some guys who look at a friend's lover and think, "Why him and not me?"

At school, the older guys (the jocks and big men on campus) would talk to her like I wasn't there. One asshole of a musician had spent a night stalking her and was stunned to watch her get on my bike at the end of his two-hour spiel. The look on his face was priceless when I asked, "Do you think you can play that guitar with a motorcycle sticking out of your ass?" He was mortified when she busted out laughing.

While the biker changes in me did not advance my DNA along the evolutionary scale, I became a different person nonetheless. My I-don't-give-a-fuck attitude was no longer simulated. Somehow image and attitude came together in a bizarre fusion that appealed to an eclectic group of women. Getting laid elsewhere was no longer the ultimate challenge. I pondered two questions: "How many other women find me attractive?" And "what are their vaginas like?" Poaching unicorns in the forbidden garden became a thrill akin to taking fast turns in the fog. This behavior pulls the pin from the hand grenade of relationship reality. I wore that pin as an earring for a year. Then the grenade went off.

I simply exhausted an incredible woman. The result was inevitable.

Chapter 16

# "THE OTHER BRUNETTE"

I t was the Fourth of July weekend and my riding buddies were going north to the Catskills for a weekend of outrageous partying. The only prerequisites were having a bike, booze, cash and your own flavor of pillion candy. I had qualified right up until the morning of departure, when my girlfriend of two years called to say she'd made other plans.

"Other plans?" I asked. "For this weekend?"

"And for the rest of my life too."

What followed was an indictment of my character based on a recap of certain indiscretions, the secret details of which could only have been provided by an insider now turned snake.

"I sincerely hope you're not sleeping with the guy who told you any of this bullshit," I said in a perfectly flat voice.

She sniffed in reply and I had my answer.

There is a warped satisfaction in cheating on your girlfriend when you are 20 years old, especially if you get away with it repeatedly. The sense of satisfaction increases if the side-sex is wild, impetuous, and entails the sort of things that would embarrass a farm animal. Guys routinely justify these escapades through adjusted logic. "Hey, she doesn't know about it." After a few times, it becomes entitlement.

I once had the age-old argument (with a lover) that a blow job isn't full-blown sex. That it's more like a handshake. She looked at me and asked, "Would you rather I shook some guy's hand or gave him a blow job?" Context is everything.

The foundation of my psyche eroded into rage as betrayal gave way to visions of my girl going down on one of my friends. I imagined her sharing that "special" look with some scumbag I undoubtedly introduced to her, and felt the capillaries bursting in my eyes. My first thought was of what I'd suddenly lost...What was taken from me...And how could I get it back. I was cold sober and ready to kill somebody.

*"Take it easy,"* said the Kawasaki. "Let's think about this."

I kicked the starter with a vengeance, with the choke on and the throttle half open. The motor fired in a scream of mechanical rage, while emitting clouds of blue smoke.

*"I didn't fuck her,"* said the Kawasaki. *"Take it easy or you'll bend something."*

I slammed the bike into gear, aimed for an impossible opening in traffic, and stalled it. Then it wouldn't start. The vapor of unburned gas was thick.

*"This day was a long time in coming,"* said the Kawasaki. *"Even if you hadn't fucked up, she's 22 years old. Did you really think you'd be the last guy who'd ever appeal to her?"*

I jumped on the starter two more times and got a dull cough from the pipes.

*"You painted this impossibly romantic pipe dream and she expected you to raise the bar. The only bar you showed her was that shit hole in Jersey City,"* said the Kawasaki. *"She's a beautiful woman with expectations. Your expectations are getting drunk and laid because you say you're a writer. What did you think was going to happen?"*

I held the throttle and choke wide open, and stomped the kicker again. The cylinders fired sporadically, started running, and seemed to catch. The machine and I were enveloped in a blue cloud of dense smoke.

Then the plugs fouled.

"You fucking piece of Japanese shit," I screamed.

*"At your service,"* said the bike.

The spares were dirty and fouled from a previous misadventure. By the time I'd cleaned a set, switched them, and ridden out to her place, my girl was already gone for the weekend. (She had probably gone out the door the second we hung up.) My holiday plans and my life were a shambles. The day was hotter than hell, and I was cold enough inside to start shaking.

The Fourth of July has held me in a mystical grasp from the time I was a little kid. My earliest memories of fireworks were at the Fireman's Fair, in Denville NJ, where a chintzy carnival would spring up like neon and canvas weeds on the edge of town. Most of the rides back then were powered by diesel or gas engines, and I vividly remember the smell of exhaust fumes competing with the aroma of french fries and fried dough balls (also known as zeppoles). The skyrockets mesmerized me, mushrooming into millions of streamers and falling sparkles. But it was the finale, the fusillade of explosions high above the crowd, that enthralled me. The mystical significance of the Fourth of July lingered in me year after year. It was almost as if having a great and riotous Fourth guaranteed the rest of the summer would be an equal success. Here I was, on the morning of July 3, 1976, enraged, alone, and suddenly without options. Then I remembered "Stitches."

Stitches was one of the few people I knew who had several motorcycles. They were never Harleys, but metric marques like Ducatis, Moto Guzzis, and Nortons. (Stiches owned a Ducati when most of the country thought spaghetti was ethnic.) At 19, his family gave him his own house on the far end of their country property (rural Pennsylvania, on the Delaware River) and he was getting away with murder. I jammed my gear into a ruck sack, along with a quart of rum, lashed it to my Kawasaki's sissy bar, and headed northwest.

There are times when a motorcycle fails to deliver its usual distraction. The ride up to the Delaware was roughly divided into two halves, the first of which was in New Jersey, and rivaled the Bataan Death March for sheer enjoyment. I don't remember any of it. I had fifty different conversations with my absent lover, none of which would have changed the morning's outcome. Then I thought about beating the living shit out of the other guy. His fate was a foregone conclusion, whether I got her back or not. I had flashbacks of moments this woman and I had together, the most intimate of which were now a part of my inner being. I thought of times we camped together, rode together, laughed together, and showered together. I thought of things she'd done for me in bed.

The thought of her doing those same things for someone else fried any rational thought.

The second half of the ride started at Hawks Nest, a breathtaking series of "S" curves, 400 feet above the Delaware River, the border between New York and Pennsylvania. I had to calm down. I'd had three close calls with the guardrail that afternoon and my luck wouldn't last forever. I pulled up for a cigar break at a place where the river ran close to the road.

*"Good move,"* said the Kawasaki. *"Get your bearings. You don't want to arrive at a holiday weekend like a basket case. You lost something you thought was yours forever. You'd have lost it, at least once, sooner or later. You're really just pissed that you're alone for the Fourth."*

The river was filled with canoeists and rafters celebrating Independence Day. Half of these folks were women in skimpy bathing suits, laughing and yelling in the gentle current. I watched a canoe grind ashore in a half-assed manner. The woman in the bow, a brunette in shorts and a tiny top, was attempting to paddle and hold a beer. She had a nice laugh, which got louder as the current continued to swing the stern downstream. The woman in the stern was blond, tanned, and wearing a black one-piece bathing suit. I can still remember the crunch of my boots in the gravel as I walked over, grabbed the bow, and pulled the canoe up on the shore.

"I'll steady it while you get out," I said, mouthing the words around the four-inch length of maduro cigar.

"Thanks," said the brunette in the bow. "She has to pee." This announcement drew a nod from the blond.

"Why didn't you just jump in the river?" I asked.

"She's afraid of eels," said the brunette.

"Only the electric kind are dangerous," I replied.

"Do they have those here?" asked the blond.

"Only in this stretch."

"Want a beer?" asked the brunette. I smiled and she tossed me a frigid can of suds from a cooler.

"You camping around here?" asked the brunette.

"Sort of. A buddy of mine's got a farmhouse close by," I said. "Where are you guys headed?"

She mentioned a commercial campground down by a bar – the Pine Cone – which I had passed some miles back.

"Do electric eels ever come out of the water?" asked the blond, from the shelter of some brush, where she was squatting to piss.

"Sometimes. They're attracted to blond squirrels. So am I," I said, turning to see if she had a blond squirrel.

"I guess I'm pretty safe then," said the brunette, turning my face back with her hand.

"Maybe," I replied. "Who knows what goes through an eel's mind?"

I drained the beer, tossed the empty can in the canoe, and straddled the Kawasaki. I had learned that it never hurts to leave a chance introduction with a warm smile and casual indifference.

"Do you ever go into the Pine Cone?" asked the brunette.

"Only on Friday nights," I said. "What night is tonight?"

"Friday."

I kicked the Kawasaki into life. It snarled like a Komodo dragon and shot me onto the road in a blaze of blue smoke. I crossed the river at Narrowsburg, NY, and took a right on a curve so blind the caution signs were in Braille. I was looking for a farmhouse with a porch overlooking the river.

Stitches never required much in the way of advance notice. He was usually home in the morning, and if not, you could just wait on the porch, taking a beer from the huge tub of ice. I found him working on a 1976 Ducati 860, a bike that would relentlessly bust his balls.

"I could hear that rice-burning piece of shit coming up the river ten minutes ago," said Stitches, with a laugh.

"Speaking of pieces of shit, what's wrong with that one?" I asked, nodding at the Ducati.

"Nothin'," he said. "They all do this."

Stitches flipped me a cold one and I sat on a porch step while he cursed his way through whatever the hell he was doing on the Ducati.

"I've had this bike for three months and it smokes like the shit-rail you're riding," he said. "How come you're alone?"

I didn't have the stomach to tell him that my steady girlfriend had disappeared with a snake charmer, so I simply said she'd been ripped apart by hyenas at a family reunion.

"Really," he said. "I thought she was screwing that other friend of yours."

"She's probably doing him right now," I said, wondering, "How the hell did he figure this one out?"

Stitches looked at me and said, "I saw them earlier today, drinking at a joint down in Port Jervis." He punctuated the conversation with the ratcheting of a socket wrench. "It happens."

We spent the afternoon shooting the shit on the porch, then headed out to a topless joint. Stitches knew a firecracker performing there with the unlikely stage name of "Smidgeon." He thought she could hook me up with another dancer for the weekend. Some guys were riding up from the city later that night with their girlfriends and my pal didn't want me to feel like the odd man out. The bar was a run-down joint with trailers out back where the dancers stayed during their summer tours.

Smidgeon was on stage, polishing a brass pole with her ass when we walked in. Her face lit up like a Christmas tree when she saw Stitches. She was wearing lederhosen and nothing but broad suspenders on top, which pressed flat against her nipples. She started gyrating in a way which bounced her flawless hooters upward, then began thrusting her hips in a kind of demand.

"Hey Smidge, show us whatcha got," yelled Stitches. And with that, she held the suspenders aside.

"Does she have a twin sister?" I asked.

I never understood the thrill Stitches got out of watching his girlfriend dance half-naked in a room full of guys. Smidgeon sat with us when her set was over. It took everything I had not to stare at her suspenders. I almost asked if she would prefer a belt.

"Do you have a friend for my friend here?" asked Stitches.

"There's Christie," said Smidgeon. "She's already done for the day."

"Christie" joined us in a sheer, see-through body suit, which was her signature act. Up close, her make-up looked like she'd applied it from a spackle bucket. She had a Jersey City accent that made me sound like James Bond. Neither one of these attributes was a deal-breaker in itself, but there was an innate hardness in her eyes that was tough to ignore. I bought her a couple of drinks, and she kissed me. Her lips had the taste of old cigarettes and fresh onions. I suspected her life story was written by Stephen King and I decided to skip it.

"That's my first kiss since I got out of the mental hospital," I whispered, through a return kiss on her ear. She left 30 seconds later.

"What did you say to her?" asked Stitches.

"I told her I used to be a better hump when I was a woman. I'll meet you back at the house."

I fired up the bike and headed south. It was the perfect summer night with a moon hanging in the sky, leaving a trail of silver in the river. The headlight danced in that jerky way common to bikes with primitive suspensions. During the day, you can see everything from a bike. Yet the rider only gets to see what the motorcycle wants to show him at night. There is a defiant freedom in the high-beam. It shows up as a glowing blue-dot on the cluster but splits the darkness into stark contrasts. There is nothing like finding the pockets of cool air in the shady spots along the road during the day, but riding at night is always cool. I felt cool, but empty.

The light and the noise of the Pine Cone were anticlimactic after the ride along the river. The saloon was jammed with people, and a band struggled to sound like Frampton, unaware that only Frampton could sound like Frampton. I bellied up to the bar and ordered a "Negroni," which caused the bartender – who was accustomed to slamming beers and mixing the usual rum and cokes – to do a double-take.

"Campari, gin, and sweet vermouth," I said. "Shaken with ice and served straight up."

(It should be noted that even shitty bars carried Campari and sweet vermouth in those days. Today, the average bartender is fourteen years old, has his/her head up his/her ass, and will automatically reach for a spiced rum when mixing a rum and Coke.) I tipped the guy five bucks. That was a fortune back then and young crowds were notoriously cheap. I did this because having an attentive bartender in a crowded joint is always an asset. "Remember this face," I said, tapping the portrait of Lincoln on the bill.

I sipped my drink, and surveyed the crowd. Finding a pretty girl I'd met during the afternoon would be hard. Finding a pretty girl by herself in a mob like this would be impossible. Still, I had nothing else to do and the Fourth of July weekend was getting away from me.

The two ladies were at the very end of the bar, surrounded by wall-to-wall sperm donors. There were three guys sniffing around the tanned blond, buying her drinks and laughing too hard at her stories. There was one guy hitting on the brunette, who,in my opinion, had much nicer eyes, and a much smaller endowment. I have always had a thing for little tits.

I maneuvered into a spot at the bar barely a foot away from her, took the last sip from my glass, and asked the bartender (in a very loud voice), "Can you make me an Electric Eel?"

Despite the mob clamoring for service, he reached for my glass first, compliments of Abe Lincoln. He looked at me quizzically, and I said, "Campari, gin, and vermouth."

"Right," he said. "An Electric Eel."

"Hey," said the brunette.

"Hey yourself," I said. "How's the canoe trip going?"

"We ran aground in this bar," she said. "I can't believe you're in here and drinking something called an "Electric Eel.""

"The world is full of eels."

"I know," she said, rolling her eyes at the guy over her shoulder. This poor dope had no idea what just happened, but suddenly the topic was electric eels. His name was Tony, and he was probably the world's nicest guy. I have no doubt he's a millionaire working for Halliburton today, but he didn't know shit about eels, on what could have been the most exciting night of his life.

"Is that a fruity-sort of drink?" Tony asked.

"Take a sip," I said to him, while pushing the drink toward the lady.

She grabbed it and swigged a gulp. The Negroni is not for amateurs. She gasped for air. Tony started to reach for it next, but I took it from her hand.

"Let me buy you one," I said with a smile. "I don't like the idea of a guy's mouth on my stuff."

Tony hesitated...I don't think he fancied the idea of having to drink a whole one, and he obviously disliked the idea of having to buy me a drink later. He declined.

"Is it okay if a woman puts her mouth on your stuff?" asked the brunette.

"I live for that moment."

After twenty minutes of beating a dead horse, Tony went to drain his lizard.

"Are you here on your motorcycle?" she asked.

I nodded.

"I've never ridden on a motorcycle," she said.

"Want to go to a party on the river?"

"Will you bring me back?"

"Sure," I said. "Why not?"

The light and noise of the bar leeched into the darkness of the parking lot, which was jammed with cars for the holiday weekend. The saloon adjoined a campground where the festivities were running rampant. It was the Bicentennial Year and the campgrounds had been taken over by college kids, who were celebrating as if they had just gone through the winter with George Washington. And against all odds, I was leaving the gin mill with a pretty young thing (just about my age).

*"That didn't take long,"* said the Kawasaki. *"I guess it's Independence Day all around."*

I pulled a beat-up fatigue jacket out of the ruck sack on the sissy bar. It had been worn by my dad in the Second World War. "Put this on," I said. "It'll be cool along the river tonight." Then I handed her the brain bucket. She slipped her head into the helmet without sniffing it. I regarded this as a really good sign. Women who start sniffing things around bikers are almost always going to be disappointed. But in this case, that helmet still carried the perfumed scent of the hair of the last pillion rider. The helmet's "D" rings threw her, as they do most first-time riders, and she tried to tie the webbed strap to the little metal rings.

"This isn't right, is it?" she asked.

"Allow me," I said. "The strap goes through both rings then passes back through the first one. Is that too tight?"

Her response was a smile and a half-shake of her head.

I kicked the bike into life and snapped down the passenger's pegs. She climbed onto the pillion and pushed back against the sissy bar.

"This is real easy," I explained. "Lean with the bike. Hang on tight if I tap your knee once, and ease up if I tap it twice."

I took it easy coming out of the parking lot and brought it up through the gears without threading the tach needle. Some guys think women are impressed by the sound of an engine in torment and death-defying maneuvers. Not me. I wanted her to experience the sensation of flight just above the ground, without a thought of sliding on the pavement. I wanted to immerse the lady in sight, sound, and smell – which makes riding a motorcycle one of life's great pleasures. On a motorcycle, foreplay starts with the ride. The woman leans forward, puts her arms around the rider's waist, and the action begins. My thought was always to prolong the action, to extend this sensation, and to have a woman associate holding onto me with her racing heartbeat.

There were no auxiliary riding lights for most bikes in 1975. My headlight pierced the darkness with a solitary beam that shuddered with each imperfection in the road, with every vibration, with every surge in amperage as the RPM climbed and fell. This high-speed luminescent flicker added to the illusion of speed that night, when I barely broke 50 miles per hour.

We were about to take a sweeping curve above the river at Narrowsburg, NY, and I reached down and tapped her knee. (This was far from the kind of turn that would require extra hanging-on, but she wouldn't know that, especially in the dark.) The response was a tightening of her arms around my waist as I leaned the bike into a long right turn. Then the road straightened out to parallel the river, which had been dyed silver by the moon.

I reached down and slowly tapped her leg three times.

There was a second's hesitation, and she yelled, "What does three taps mean?"

"It means I like your leg," I yelled back.

Her response was a brief tightening of her arms around my waist.

"Watch this," I yelled.

And in that instant, I switched off the headlight. (It had worked once before.)

It was utter darkness for a second, and then the full power of the moon became obvious. Every detail of the road, the trees alongside, and the banks of the river acquired a crystal clarity in soft white light. The road began to drop down to the level of the water, and that feeling of descending into the sudden coolness of the air coming off the river, coupled with the "thrumming" growl of the motor, all in the surrounding moonlight, was positively surreal. I was almost carried away myself. Yet I was the maestro, spinning all of these things into one setting for a great line. And if I played it right, no line would be necessary. The motorcycle was doing all the talking.

Flicking the light back on revealed the turnoff for the bridge to Damascus, PA. We crossed the river in a spider web of shadow, created by the bridge's ironwork in the moonlight. The first left brought us to a narrow road that flirted with the river in little curves and dips. It became a gentle roller coaster ride in not-quite-slow motion. As brilliant as the river was in the moonlight, this road was black as pitch due to the overhang of the trees and a steep ridge on the right. Yet there was a point with an open field on each side. We had no sooner hit this clear spot, then a skyrocket shot up over the trees and burst.

"That's our party," I said.

The driveway up to the house was semi-paved by large round stones pushed deep into the dirt. It was like an old Roman road, constructed on a day when the old Romans didn't give much of a damn.

There were three other bikes parked next to Stitches's Ducati, and there were the silhouettes of men and women by a campfire. They may have been talking, but if they were, their voices were drowned out by the strains of The Doors, pouring from two six-foot tall speakers. Another rocket shot straight up, leaving a trail of sparks, before bursting with a loud bang.

Stitches was firing off the rockets, and Smidgeon, (the exotic dancer from the bar earlier), was again dancing, and again wearing nothing but really tiny shorts and suspenders. Christie, whom I had decided was too hard-boiled for me, was paired up with another guy, who'd ridden in on a Norton. The other two ladies were genuine pillion candy. One was wearing chaps to protect her legs and a skimpy leather halter to corral her ample hooters. She was with a guy on a Triumph Trident. The remaining woman had her hair in two long braids. She was in jeans and wearing a leather vest that did little to conceal a huge rack. She was rolling a joint as big as my forefinger, while sitting in the lap of the remaining rider, who had a brand new Moto Guzzi.

I knew the other guys well enough to drink their liquor and expected them to finish mine. They were "Louie", "Weasel", and "Fast Freddie." (It was said that "Fast Freddie" could steal a mechanical heart without missing a beat.) The other two girls were "Peaches" and "Sindy."

I introduced my friend, who looked a bit like a Korean War orphan in the oversize army jacket. She had a much softer way about her than the other women, and a keen sense of humor.

"Do you want me to come back when I have bigger tits?" she whispered to me. She fit in easily with this crowd, without asking questions nor giving too much information. At one point, she did comment (to me), "So this is a biker party?"

"No," I said. This is a Fellini movie without a plot."

She eventually noticed a sinister undercurrent, and asked about my motorcycle. "All of these guys seem to be your friends, yet they feel your bike is a piece of shit. What makes yours different?"

"It is the wolf pack syndrome in reverse," I replied. "It is a case of the weakest minds attempting to overpower the alpha dog. I have the only Japanese bike here. And not only is it the fastest, but mine is the only one that will start in the morning without fifteen minutes of swearing. It emasculates them."

The guys were fairly free with the pot and after taking a few hits, my companion asked me if there was any coke thereabouts. "You want me to see if these guys have any blow," I said, registering mild surprise.

"No, just Coke...To mix with this," she answered, pulling a pint of rum from her purse. "I didn't want to put my mouth on the same bottle that Christie was passing around. Fast Freddie said he had to relieve himself and I think she got down and did it for him."

The last of the skyrockets had been shot off into space and the campfire had burned to embers by 1am. Christie and Fast Freddie were wrapped up in a blanket on the porch, while Stitches and Smidgeon had disappeared inside. The other two couples were headed up to a communal loft.

"Want me to take you back now?" I asked.

"Only if we have to share a room with these guys."

Stitches had a first come, first reserved policy, and I'd been there in the daylight. We had the only other bedroom on the first floor. The bed was a 60-year-old metal framed antique that guaranteed intimacy as it was slightly concave in the center. The sheets were clean and crisp, but the only light in the room was a blue lava lamp from the '60's.

"Where's the bathroom and can I use your toothbrush?" she asked.

It was at the end of the hall, and while the door was functional, it didn't lock. "I want you to hold it shut," she said. "From inside."

The house was originally built in the early 1800's and the bathroom was added to the inside sometime after World War I. It was about the size of a bathroom on a commercial jet. I only expected to watch the brunette to brush her teeth. First, she put her arms around my neck and kissed me, tracing my lower lip with her tongue. The she dropped her jeans and sat to pee. With her hands modestly folded in her bare lap, she leaned forward and said, "Guys get themselves all worked up over the first kiss, and whether or not they are going to see some snatch. This pretty much takes care of things, don't cha think?"

She stood and tugged a pair of pale blue panties up to her tee shirt, then stepped out of her jeans. She washed her face and hands, and brushed her teeth with my toothbrush. The late great poet, Richard Brautigan, once wrote that there was nothing quite like having a woman padding around in the kitchen, bare-assed, making you breakfast for the first time.

This was close.

When I brushed my teeth, it was like getting kissed again.

The bed sounded like an accordion of springs when we climbed into it. What followed was pleasantly anticlimactic. Instead of the frenetic coupling that was going on all over the place, we delighted in a deepening of kisses. Her mouth tasted of mint toothpaste and a trace of Baccardi. She was game, but I was beat, and put my hopes in the promise of a great morning.

I opened my eyes before dawn and found her sprawled across my shoulder. I could feel her breathing on my neck, while the last of the moonlight fell across her naked form. She had the body of a swimmer. Just a day before, I'd been miserable... Left by a woman who'd been screwing one of my riding buddies... Facing the best weekend of the summer without a place to go. Now I was having a great time... On my bike... Carousing with friends... In bed with a hot brunette... And there were still three full days left to this holiday weekend. I would have to pour whiskey on the tires of my bike to thank the motorcycle gods, who blessed me with this woman after cursing me with the last one. Maybe I'd pass it through my kidneys first.

Chapter 17

# "THE FUSE"

**M**ost of my hangovers start with a low buzzing in my head. On this day, the buzzing was actually lifting my hair. I realized it was the electric fan aimed at the bed. It was 6:45 on Saturday morning, July 4, 1976. The first full day of the July 4th weekend, and I had just spent the night with a brunette who knew a million snappy comebacks, who could discuss the Kama Sutra or quantum physics, and who was hot enough to get constant sidelong glances from my riding buddies.

And yet I was alone in bed again.

I knew she hadn't left as her jeans, hiking boots and purse were in a pile. And I knew no one carried her off as I hadn't been awakened by anyone cursing and swearing while trying to start one of the English or Italian bikes. But somewhere in that house, a sultry brunette was tip-toeing around without her pants and I found the idea very appealing. The antique knob on the bedroom door jiggled, prompting me to close my eyes, lest I do anything to yield my position in the bed.

I heard the door swing open, and close again, as the aroma of fresh coffee filled the room, accompanied by the scent of Lifebouy soap, like someone had just stepped out of the shower holding a cup of java. Then the box spring gave a metallic sigh as the mattress yielded to another presence.

"I know you're awake," she said. "You have a hard on."

There are times when continued posturing is pointless in the face of overwhelming evidence.

"I always have a hard-on," I replied, opening my eyes. "It was very embarrassing for my mother the day I was born."

"Why? Did some other kid have a bigger one?" she asked, leaning over to kiss me.

"Not for another 18 years, and he was black."

"Well the important thing is that you tried," she muttered, nuzzling my neck. The towel wrapped around her hair was bigger than the one wrapped around her body.

"And I have one word for you..."

"If it is the word I have in mind, you're hyphenating it." I said. "Otherwise, it's two."

"That word is shower. Go take one."

I sat upright and noticed the two chipped, mismatched coffee cups. One was your usual summer-house mug. The other was an oversized cup that was more like a small bowl with a handle on it. It bore the faded picture of a waterfall over the legend "Souvenir of Shohola Falls, PA."

"What made you pick that one?" I asked. It was the cup I always used whenever I spent the night here.

"Stitches had the coffee ready when I came out of the bathroom. It's really strong. He said to give the big one to Sunshine."

"Your cup has an ounce of Kahlua in it," I said. "This one has about three ounces in it. It's how coffee is made around here."

It would be like Stitches to get up first and have the coffee ready in the kitchen. It would be like him to pour it in my cup. If you look hard, you can find the thumbprints of your real friends everywhere.

"Stitches must have loved the towels."

"He did, and even offered to show me a trick with them."

"He's that kind of guy."

I got up to shower, grabbing her jeans and top under my arm.

"Where are you going with those?" she asked, with a quizzical smile.

"I'm taking these with me so you don't get too far ahead of the program."

Stitches had a weekend tradition: No sympathy for hangovers. It was barely 7am and the music began to throb. The speakers on the porch thundered Cream's *Sunshine Of Your Love*. It may have been a tribute to me.

She was poised on the end of the bed like an early nude photograph taken by Gordon Ball when I returned smelling of Lifebuoy myself. She'd brushed her dark hair back, yet it fell about my face like a damp curtain as she kissed my throat and mouth, working her way south. Her kisses had the sting of hot wax, as she led with her teeth, and then her tongue. I surrendered an inch at a time, like a fuse that had been smoldering for 20 years.

Our room was in the front of the house, with one window, with one thin screen, and one set of filmy curtains separating us from the porch. I let out a gasp, like I had been punched.

"What the hell is going on in there," yelled Louie.

"Nothin'," she yelled back. And in a much lower voice she said to me, "Now I have to wash my hair again."

I swaggered off to find another cup of coffee and was in the process of pouring it when the music suddenly cut out. A sheriff's officer was on the porch, speaking in low but earnest tones with Stitches, his patrol car running in the driveway.

It seems someone passing on the road reported a dead, naked body on the lawn. Stitches was no stranger to the cops and he wore the appropriate look of shock and surprise. He and the officer took a walking tour of the premises, where they found a stupored Weasel hosing off a topless but pantied "Peaches," behind the house.

"You can't see her from the road," said Stitches, "And she certainly isn't dead."

The cop agreed, tipped his hat and left.

"That asshole Fast Freddie got bombed out of his mind last night and rolled off the porch stark naked. He came to a stop in the center of the lawn," said Stitches. "Louie and I dragged him into the chicken coop. He has been bitten by every bug in this county — twice. We should play it smart and ride out to breakfast. That cop will be back in a bit to look us over again. He'll find nothing and then it will be no big deal."

I was not in favor of the group ride and just wanted to get lost with my new love interest. Then again it would be presumptuous on my part to make any plans without asking her. There were no cell phones in 1976, I was sure she wanted to check in with her friends.

The brunette stepped out in hiking boots, jeans, and a tee shirt. "Stitches had a clean tee laying around here that just happened to be a woman's small," she said, looking over at Smidgeon's cushy hooters.

"A friend of a friend left it here." Smiled Stitches. "Her loss."

"How do you feel about breakfast," I asked the brunette.

"I'm all for it unless it means sticking up a gas station, in which case we should wear masks."

The other guys and their pillion riders mounted, while I just sat on the steps and finished my coffee.

"Aren't we going for breakfast, too?" the brunette asked.

"We have time."

The Triumph Trident wouldn't start. Stitches searched out a can of starting ether, and they got it going about 15 minutes later. By that time, we were in the saddle with the engine running.

Chapter 18

# "THE EXPLOSION"

Y ou can tell who the dominant riders are in a line of bikes by the order in which they assemble. The leader is the strongest, astride the most powerful bike, thoroughly confident in the choice of route and destination. In the line of bikes before me was a pride of lions. Stitches (at the head on a new Ducati) would be the one to get the first taste of the kill, his choice of women, and his pick of the best spot in the shade in which to nap. That would make "Fast Freddie" (on the Norton) the second strongest, with the second most powerful bike, and the implied second smartest.

Personal knowledge of the four riders ahead of me shot that theory to hell.

Stitches was in front because he knew the best place for breakfast. Otherwise he neither led nor followed, firm in the belief that his life was his road alone. The other three guys followed, content to passively pursue the next stage of a good time on a three-day weekend. I was voluntarily last because the two-stroke engine on the Kawasaki H2 would occasionally lay down a smoke screen that overpowered the scent of new mown hay, flowers in bloom, and road-kill. And when the smoke wasn't in evidence, the stink of burned two-stroke oil left an invisible presence. This tended to prejudice other riders.

We rode to a general store on the other side of the river that served breakfast. This was a regular stop for Stitches as the place offered a decent breakfast, great coffee, and sometimes had a hot tamale of a waitress. We were barely twenty minutes from the house. (The "sixty miles before breakfast" motorcycle rule was invented by someone who lived sixty miles from a diner.)

While not quite as formal as the Japanese tea ceremony, a proper motorcycle breakfast has a number of unspoken rules and rituals. The rite begins with the selection of a table that allows each rider to survey the door. Like a dog circling to lay down, this is thought to be a throwback to the days when bikers were Ostrogoths, Visigoths, or savage Huns, and when watching the door was a matter of self-preservation. Most sociologists agree that this has evolved into a reflex to look over every woman entering or exiting a place, as an on-going comparison in which each rider can revise his wish list. The waitress must either be a seasoned plate jockey (Kirk Douglas in a wig), who would never approach the table without a pot of coffee attached to her arm, or a hot young thing wearing the kind of uniform that accents a tanned cleavage, a tight waist, or the subtle curves of a naturally sculpted ass. The coffee should never be more than 10 minutes old in the pot.

I alone among the men sat with my back to the door. All I wanted to do was look at the brunette who'd ridden on my pillion. She was wearing no make-up and no underwear, as I had liberated her panties and stashed them under the Kawasaki's seat. She twisted my DNA into a knot every time I caught her eye. Yet I didn't want to surrender so early in the game, so I took my time looking the waitress up and down. She was an all-American, farm-raised, buttermilk biscuit beauty of 18 years, who appeared like a magician's assistant, with a coffee pot in her right hand. This was her second summer season here, and like Stitches, I occasionally thought to see her naked.

"Do you have decaf?" asked Stitches.

"What's that?" the waitress asked in mock innocence. "Something they have in the big city?"

"Good answer," nodded Stitches, never taking his eyes off the menu.

The first part of the motorcycle breakfast ritual is total silence as each rider looks at the menu. The only permissible sound is a spoon quietly stirring cream and sugar into the coffee. Riders use the menu as a kind of eye chart, to determine how badly out of focus their vision is from the night before, as they will simply order whatever the hell it is they want like line items on a municipal budget anyway.

"I'll have two eggs over easy, toast, home fries, and two pancakes," said Stitches.

"That's Farmer Zed's Favorite Plowboy," said the waitress, raising an eyebrow.

"I want the scrambled crumble, with hot peppers, sausage and onions," said Louie.

"That's the Ballet Dancer's Tutu."

Weasel ordered steak and eggs, rare.

"Pink suede shoes," nodded the waitress.

"Bring me the Rahway State Prison Anal Sex Breakfast Special," smirked Fast Freddie.

"That's a western omelet... Coming right up," said the waitress, dead-pan and nonplussed.

"How do you know?" Freddie asked, laughing.

"You look the type," said the waitress with a smile.

The ladies had ordered first and managed to do so without the comic relief. But my brunette, had passed, being undecided when it was her turn. Gesturing at the menu, she looked at me, then at the waitress and said, "I don't see any of those names on here."

"I'm just making them up," said the waitress. "These guys do this to me all the time."

"Then I'll have what he usually has," said the brunette, tipping the menu in my direction.

"That would be a nose bucket of angst. I like that tee shirt." It would have fit the waitress like a glove.

"How are you, Lucille?" asked Stitches.

"Better than you," said the waitress, whose name was Lucille. "You're still running with these bums."

"With the prices you charge here I can't afford real friends."

"When are you going to take me for a long ride on that Ducati?" Lucille said, over her shoulder, on her way back to the kitchen.

"Yeah," hissed Smidgeon, making a face. "When are you going to take her for a long ride on that Ducati?"

"Ten minutes after I drop you off at the bar tonight," said Stitches, with the broad kind of smile that could have been genuine, had it been on an alligator.

Breakfast appeared in record time and Lucille filled us in on the local news. There had been a fire in a barn, an accident on Route 97, and the state cops were setting up a sobriety check-point in town, specifically to catch bikers... Right outside, in fact. But the cops on the Pennsylvania side had a report of a naked, dead body somewhere on the river road.

"That was him," said Stitches.

Fast Freddie simply smiled.

"You reported a body?" asked Lucille.

"I was the body."

"They should have buried you."

It was interesting to see the women together at breakfast. Smidgeon could have been your average coed at any university or college. A half dozen guys looked her over when she walked into the place, undressing her with their eyes. They could have seen most of everything by paying the $5 cover charge at the shithole where she danced. She was a sweet kid, who'd get worn out before her time, by guys whose idea of romance was two beers and a trombone solo.

Thin, angular, chemically blond and perpetually aggravated, Christie was an exotic dancer much farther along the road of male disillusionment. If you wanted to see her without a cigarette, you had to catch her on stage, or in the shower. I think she hated the kind of guys she always seemed to find – and hated herself for always finding them – but was terrified at the thought there was at least one level beneath that waiting for her. She was paired with Fast Freddie, who was less of a human and more of a virus.

"Sindy" aspired to be an exotic dancer but ended up tending bar instead. This was because the owner of the topless joint where she poured beers and splashed shots singled her out for himself. It's hard to say how that arrangement would have worked, as the last shot he had was between the eyes. She was about 5'6", had a dynamite body, and a cute face. Louie was the "gin and tonic" at the end of the bar, who asked her if she knew anything about English motorcycles. When she replied "No," he asked her "if she wanted to learn the hard way." They'd been together for a year.

"Peaches" – a.k.a. Linda M. – was drop-dead gorgeous in the classic biker chic-sense of the word. She was a real blond, with a real tan, and a real nice ass, which was framed in an open pair of black leather chaps over skin-tight jeans. She was warm, trusting, pleasant, and dumb as a post. She adored Weasel and for his 20th birthday, posed on his Moto Guzzi, wearing the chaps only. (Peaches would be unbelievably pissed if she knew Weasel had shown us the Polaroids.) I liked her a lot and once thought about moving on it (before she was with Weasel), when I realized any of my conversations would give her a headache. (She once asked me if I knew that NASA had faked the moon landings... She insisted it was true having read it in the newspaper while waiting to check out at the supermarket.)

And then there was the brunette: she stood 5'6", with shoulder-length dark hair, spilling over an olive complexion, framing the kind of face that made me want to write her things. She was uncommonly well-spoken. After prodding a huge plate of breakfast for a bit, she claimed her food appeared to be regenerating.

"Like mitosis," I suggested. She looked at me and replied, "What kind of biker uses the word mitosis in breakfast conversation?"

"Yeah," said Weasel. "The proper expression is 'fucking mitosis.' "

"Who would fuck anybody with mitosis?" asked Peaches.

"This is how public opinion gets started," sighed Stitches.

With the breakfast formalities observed, we got to the business at hand: discussing our plans for the rest of the day. Initially, the agenda called for shooting clay pigeons, then sampling some of the other weapons in Stitches' collection. Yet the early morning visit from the authorities questioned the wisdom of that idea. The guys decided to ride.

"Do I need to drop you at the campground," I said to the brunette, dreading the necessity to ask.

"I want to let my friends know where I am. And I need to get some clothes. Someone stole my panties this morning. Then I'm free for the rest of the day. It's after 9am now, and my blond friend is probably awake." The brunette was referring to the other woman who was in the canoe when I first met her, only the day before.

"Won't she be worried that you've been gone all night?"

"Nope," said the brunette. "I told her yesterday that I would go riding with you if you showed up in the bar." She then gave me the frankest look I have ever seen in a woman's eyes.

Women's eyes are the epitome of human evolution. Whether blue, brown, hazel, or the incredibly elusive green, they are stained glass portals to the soul, letting out a special light that permits a man to see in only one direction. And they can be switched on or off at whim. This one had eyes like miniature copies of the rose window from Notre Dame cathedral. I could feel them on me, like a rip-tide of blue, drawing me into the deep water.

We were savoring the coffee, when a Harley pulled up outside and choked. There was nothing significant in that, yet the voices that could be heard a few seconds later turned my blood to ice. I slid my chair around and stared at the door.

I had heard one of those voices on my pillow as the last thing at night and the first thing in the morning for two years. I'd heard it whispering in the dark and laughing in the sunshine. I'd heard it on the beach, in the mountains, and on New York City streets. I'd heard it in the shower. And I'd heard it in a million adolescent dreams.

In walked a guy I once knew as a friend, with my former girlfriend, who he'd been boning every night that I was out catting around. She saw me, paused, and started back out the door. But he stopped her, looked at me, and grinned.

It was the grin that did it.

Despite the fact that I had been having a great weekend... Despite the fact that I'd spent the night in the arms of a red hot brunette less than 24 hours after getting the good news about this bullshit... Despite the fact that the brunette was every bit as beautiful as this one standing in the doorway... I went from "Zero to Fuck You" in 2.5 seconds.

I had one thought in my head, and that was to put my fist through this ferret's face. But I wasn't good with my fists, so I grabbed my helmet. Nothing gets somebody's attention like getting whacked in the face with a motorcycle helmet. Some guys act first and think about it later. I was a different person in those days. I'd act and never think about it. I was on my feet and moving in one fluid motion.

So was Stitches. What he had seen and I had missed was the uniformed figure of a New York State Trooper behind the focus of my hatred. The cop was on a donut run from the 4th of July traffic safety check-point outside. My display of manhood would have been short-lived.

Stitches power-walked me straight out the back door. Louie was right behind us, asking, "What the fuck just happened? I thought we only had to hide Freddie from the cops?"

Weasel and Fast Freddie covered the retreat. They were right at home in flash disagreements. Neither had moved, and they didn't need to fill in the blanks. These two guys had the ethics of cockroaches, the reflexes of cobras, and the loyalty of cocker spaniels. Weasel got his nickname from his negotiating skills with regard to certain pharmaceutical transactions. Fast Freddie wasn't a big guy. But he could turn into a human Tasmanian devil and easily beat someone half to death.

The clock stopped with the douche and the stolen woman standing by the counter, with a cop ordering donuts and coffee, and two guys and five women sitting at a table in silence. The silence was broken when Fast Freddie tapped the table.

Weasel was the first to realize there was nothing to do here. He glanced at the check and put a pile of crumpled bills on the table. "Keep the change," he said to Lucille.

"You'd have to add another ten to that to get fifty cents change," she replied.

Weasel looked at Freddie, who added another twenty to the pile, with a shrug. Then they and the ladies slowly exited.

"The chick used to be Jack's squeeze," Peaches said to my brunette pillion candy.

"I didn't think she was his sister," the brunette replied.

"Yeah, but did you know she was his old girlfriend? He just found out about it."

"I felt like I was looking into a mirror," said the brunette.

My former squeeze was about the same height, the same weight, and the same build as the woman who'd been with me for the past night. They were both brunettes. They were both modestly endowed and they were both hot. At that moment, I was pretty hot myself.

Stitches was a pragmatist. "What is the matter with you? You replaced that bitch in one afternoon on a ride to a party. What does that say for your sense of enduring romance? You were gonna clock that cocksucker right in front of that cop. He'd have arrested you, setting Weasel and Freddie off like a couple of hand grenades. The street is crawling with cops. We'd have all ended up arrested. Pull your head out of your ass and think. Now lets get on the bikes and ride someplace."

The brunette came up behind me and pinched my ass. "Take me someplace where I've never been before, and show me something I've never seen."

"How about rational thought and common sense," said Stitches. "He's never seen them either."

"Do you have someplace in mind?" I asked the brunette.

"Shohola Falls."

"Shohola Falls? Like on the coffee cup?"

"Like on the coffee cup."

"Why?"

"Why not?"

"What about your stuff at the campgrounds?"

"We'll get it later," she said, pointing at the road. "Start it up and go."

Chapter 19

# "THE PUNCH LINE"

The town of Shohola Falls was less than 60 miles away on the Pennsylvania side of the river. This was a hopping place between 1879 and 1907, when a gravity-operated railroad conferred amusement park status on a community better suited for trout fisherman. It is my understanding that huge crowds from New York City and Scranton came here on excursion trains run by the long-defunct Erie Railroad, to dance, roller skate, drink, gamble, and run riot during the last years of Queen Victoria. A change in venues, several downward economic shifts, and a hurricane have pretty much reduced Shohola Falls to its pre-1879 status.

The "falls" part of Shohola Falls is on Shohola Creek not far from a dam and is not anywhere near as built up, nor as touristy, as Bushkill Falls, billed as the "Niagara of Pennsylvania." Located at the tip of Pennsylvania state game lands, Shohola Falls is a regular destination for hikers, kayakers, and photographers. It is either too buggy for skinny-dipping or too fast moving for easy access. The township is cute, sleepy, and pleasant to look at while maintaining 40 mph. I didn't see anyplace for an afternoon stop.

Pulled over by a trailhead, I leaned back and asked the brunette, "What did you want to see here?"

She shrugged, and replied, "I wanted to buy you a new souvenir cup from "Shohola Falls."

I laughed out loud.

Stitches laughed too. "That cup is 90 years old. You'd have to find an antique shop. These guys want a drink. Let's head back to Barryville."

Riding the back roads of Pennsylvania, near the Delaware, can be fun if you're not in a hurry, if you're with friends, and if the squeeze on the back is an unpredictable pisser. With her head over my left shoulder, the brunette watched the road, sensing when to hang tight and when to relax. When it got hot, she'd lean back against the sissy bar. And when I stopped, she had enough control to keep our helmets from banging together. I reached down and rubbed her leg three times, which drew a long squeeze and a laugh.

Riding becomes automatic after a bit, especially if the road isn't littered with curves and gravel. I found myself daydreaming. Suppose this summer day became a full day. And suppose the fall became winter. What would it be like to wake up with this beauty in my apartment on the cliffs of Guttenburg, NJ? Would there be a KZ900, and rides to the ocean? Had I listened, I would have heard the motorcycle gods laughing.

*"Weren't you thinking about doing the same thing with someone else two days ago?* Asked the Kawasaki. *"Not that this one isn't nice. Have you missed the real lesson here?"*

"What lesson?"

*"That the worst pain you ever felt is` softened by the potential for another equally crushing pain."*

"Do you talk to yourself?" asked the brunette, leaning forward.

"Sometimes I think out loud," I yelled over my shoulder.

"I suppose evidence of thought is a good sign," yelled the brunette back.

There was a sad, down-at-the-heels gin mill not far from Barryville, where we stopped and had little cold bottles of Rolling Rock. Fast Freddie and Louie played pinball on a game that was 20 years old. The girls threw darts.

The rest of that run can be typified as your average, hot, July day. Smidgeon and Christie were dancing that night, and wanted to spend a few hours off their feet and off the bikes. The other guys were ready to try some shooting, and I didn't mind being alone with the brunette. We were close to the campground where she had left her friend and the two of us headed over that way.

"Would you wait at the bar while I take care of a few things?" she asked.

"I'll run you right up to your tent. I'd like to see your blond friend again. I've already seen her taking a piss. We have a history."

"It's better this way. I won't be long."

*"It didn't seem like she had any baggage,"* said the Kawasaki. *"There is a difference between traveling light and bringing the baggage along later though."*

She took exactly 90 minutes, during which time I had 4 rum and Cokes and got to watch a bartender read the paper. I wasn't exactly half in the bag when the brunette returned, but I could see it in my future.

"Anyone sitting here," asked a familiar voice. The brunette slid onto the stool next to mine and took a long sip out of my drink. In fact, she finished it. She was wearing an Ivy League jersey (from Yale) and ratty jeans.

"Would you like one of your own?" I asked.

"Yeah, but not here."

"I can understand that," I said, glancing at the bartender.

"Is there rum back at the house?"

"Not more than a few gallons. Is it going to be a long night?"

She kissed my ear and dragged me out to the bike.

"Is this really a fast motorcycle?" she asked.

"It'll snap your neck in four gears."

"Show me." She wasn't kidding.

*"Shit."* Said the Kawasaki. *"She's got you thinking and drinking at the same time. This may not have a pleasant ending."*

Holiday weekend traffic was heavy on Route 97. Restaurants were doing great business as were the ice cream stands in each little hamlet. There were hundreds of people drifting on the river, in tubes, in canoes, and in large flooby rafts. These folks were headed for shore, and eventually the road. Pick-up trucks roared by towing trailers stacked with rental canoes. And the cops were out.

Still there are a couple of straight stretches along the river where visibility is good. I passed five cars at one spot, with that two-stroke engine screaming. The road was curving to the right when I felt the sinister wobble that gave the H2 its reputation as the "Widow Maker." The clock chimed 100 miles per hour. I hadn't had enough rum to get smashed but the few I'd swilled let my balls work the throttle. Naturally, I took a turn too fast.

"Hang on," I screamed, chopping the gas but resisting the urge to hit the brakes or downshift. The road went to the left at that point and I leaned gently in that direction, but nearly too late. We followed the curve on the extreme right edge of the pavement, on the lip of a rock-filled trench. The brunette was clinging to me like a rash. With the speedo again reading a sane 55 mph, I took a deep breath and straightened things out.

"That was cool," she yelled. "Was there something on the road back there?"

*"Two weeks in intensive care,"* said the Kawasaki.

We found the guys hustling dinner back at the house, while the ladies lounged in various poses. The guys were bare chested. Stitches was grilling steaks over embers in the fire pit. There had been some kind of bet; the girls won, and so the guys were cooking. Had the guys won, the ladies would have been cooking topless.

The porch was littered with the evidence of two hours of target shooting. A couple of shot guns, an AK47, and an AR15 leaned against the wall, cooling off. Apparently the ladies outshot the men when it came to the clay pigeons, hence they won the bet.

"Too bad I wasn't here," I said. "I'd have made the difference."

"No doubt," said the brunette. "May I?" she asked Stitches. She snapped open one of the over and unders, checked to see it was unloaded, and in one move, snapped it back, tracking an imaginary clay bird in flight. Her stance was perfect.

"I guess you learned that at Yale," said Stitches.

For the first time, she didn't have a clever retort.

Everyone was going to cheer Smidgeon and Christie that night. I found the thought of being alone with this brunette, in this little country house above the river, to be more intoxicating than the rum I'd been drinking. Yet when the bikes pulled away, the silence was overwhelming. I knew the taste of this woman's lips, the scent of her skin, and the feel of her mouth on my body; and yet, I knew damn little else about her. I thought of Humphrey Bogart in the same dilemma with Ingrid Bergman in *Casablanca*, and resorted to his lines.

"So who are you? What did you do? And who were you before?"

"What difference does it make? I met you and you intrigued me. Whatever happened to you in your entire life up until yesterday made me say, 'This guy is worth a couple of days.' "

"It's not really a day yet," I said. "I only met you last night."

"How is it going so far?"

"I'm having fun..."

"But..."

"I really like you. I want to know more about you," I said.

"If all you could ever know about me started from yesterday, would it be enough to make you hit a guy in the face with a helmet for me?"

I didn't have anything to say. Not because the obvious answer was "yes," but because I didn't see the point of this thought.

"What could some guy possibly say about you that would require me to break his face?"

"Who knows? You don't. Maybe there are things about me that you don't know or would rather not know," she said. "Maybe I thought you'd hit some guy in the face with a helmet over less than what transpired today. Maybe that's why I asked you to wait in the bar."

We were sitting on the porch steps and she leaned against me, with her head on my shoulder. The scent of her hair had been intensified by the heat of the helmet she'd worn all day, and I didn't want her to move. So I said nothing.

"Okay... If you could ask me just one question, what would that question be?"

I knew this was a test. The wrong question would define me as a shallow, average man. The law of averages wouldn't work for me here.

I have always called women by the first thing that came to mind after meeting them. One had been "Kitten" Others were "Princess, Lambkin, Tsunami, Texas," and "Swig." I had been calling this one "Cricket." This woman and I had shared a bike, a bed, a night and a morning – and I didn't even know her real name. But I also wanted to know her age and where she came from. I wanted to know about Yale. And now I wanted to know what I shouldn't know about.

I finally asked, "Would you like a rum and Coke?"

It took a second, but she slowly smiled and nodded. I had passed, for now.

We hardly spoke at all after that.

It got dark sooner than I expected. My only objection to the darkness was that it brought us closer to the return of the others. The moon eventually made its appearance, and again tinted the river silver.

"Want to go down and touch the moonlight?" I asked.

"Can we?"

"Easily."

Stitches's folks owned a half-mile of the shoreline, and I knew a path to the water they always kept mowed. I put two cans of Coke and a bottle of rum in the bag on the sissy bar.

"Hop on."

"No helmet?"

"Its real close."

We rode down the driveway and turned right on the road, looking for a little overgrown switchback on the left. This quickly became a grassy path that meandered to the water's edge.

"Hop off and steady the bike by the sissy bar," I said.

The soft ground was just firm enough to hold the Kawasaki on the center stand. There was a large rock at the water's edge, and we sat there, each holding a can of Coke to which a couple of ounces of rum had been added. In its natural state, water has a cool, clean scent that doesn't really smell like anything. This scent mixed with the aroma of the path's cut grass, and the drifting smoke from smoldering embers up by the house. The riverbank smelled like the height of summer.

The brunette put the Coke down and removed the Yale jersey. Then she kicked off her jeans and stood in the moonlight. Her silver body gleamed like a trophy.

"Coming?" she asked.

The water was warm in the shallows, and the rocky bottom, though smooth, was hard on the feet. Moonlight has an elusive quality; it is always just beyond reach, even in the stillest water. She swam toward it in every direction and tried to catch it with cupped hands. There was another large rock under the surface not far from shore. I could sit on it, and still be largely submerged. She climbed into my lap, and wrapped her legs round me. She put me inside her and started to gently move up and down, framing my face in her hands, covering my mouth with hers. I started to meet her half-way, pausing at the end of each thrust, until we were writhing and contracting like an alien muscle creature, emerging from the water. I tensed into a bellow that must have been heard in town, while she stifled a gasp by biting my shoulder.

Then we just held each other for a long time.

We stepped out of the water by the light of fireflies and embraced again by the bike. There was something special about this for both of us, that neither one would spoil by speaking.

"I didn't think to bring a towel," I said finally. You can use my shirt if you want."

"The sweaty shirt you've been wearing all day?" Then she picked it up and sniffed it. Then sniffed it again with a deeper breath. "Sweat, cigars, and angst," she said.

"I don't think anyone has ever done that with one of my shirts and lived."

"You mean to tell me you don't intend to sniff my stolen panties."

I opened the seat on the bike and pulled them from the tailpiece. "These will need recharging soon. They're all sniffed out."

Though cooler than the afternoon, the night was warm and we sat on the rock in the moonlight, passing the rum bottle back and forth. When we stood up again you could clearly see the outline of her perfect ass on the tone. I stepped into my jeans and unlaced boots, pulling the shirt over my head. It was sticking to my body.

She jammed her boots, jeans, and jersey, along with the rum, into the rucksack on the sissy bar. I laughed and started the bike. She climbed on and tapped my leg three times. I laughed again, and guided the bike up to the house. She dismounted, collected her stuff, and went inside. That was the first and only time a naked woman has ridden pillion on my bike. Ten minutes later, Stitches and crew returned.

They pulled in with all the élan of a four-car pile-up. It was then I noticed that the pillion behind Fast Freddie was empty. "What the hell happened to Christie?" I asked. "Did she fall off or just give Freddie the slip?"

This started the guys laughing.

"As you are aware, it is the custom of grateful patrons to slip a dollar into the g-string of exceptional dancers," said Stitches. "Well some drunk dropped twenty nickels in Christie's g-string."

Stitches was laughing so hard I thought he was going to choke.

"Let me guess... She yelled and Fast Freddie beat the shit out of the guy."

"Oh she yelled all right. And then she saw that Fast Freddie was chatting up another dancer and never looked up. She threw the change at Fast Freddie like shrapnel. And you know how they have that bucket of water on stage for the wet tee shirt number...She threw that next," explained Stitches.

"Christie threw a bucket of water on Fast Freddie in the bar?"

"Actually, the water was first and the bucket followed. It was pandemonium. It was the first time the bouncer had to restrain one of the dancers," said Stitches. "She is spending the night in the talent trailer."

"Freddie should have said something to the guy," said Smidgeon.

"Like what?" asked Stitches. "It wasn't like the guy dropped fifty cents in her 'G' string."

"How was your night, Jack?" asked Peaches.

"Quiet and nice."

"Really?" she replied. That's good. Stitches said you'd be pounding freshwater clam on the half-shell. Where is Cricket?"

"Stitches has no faith in mankind. She's inside."

Louie threw some wood on the embers and built up the fire, but this group called it an early night. I found the brunette in bed already asleep. I slid in next to her and ran my hand over her back. Sometime later, I woke up to find her on my pillow, facing me. Her deep, rhythmic breathing told me she was asleep.

It was barely 5:30am and the grey light of dawn was leaking in the window, when I opened my eyes and found myself alone again. This time her clothes and shoes were gone. The bedroom door was open and I could hear movement in the hall. She tiptoed in from the bathroom, sat on the edge of the bed, and kissed me.

"You have to take me back to the campground," she said. "Now. Please. Before anybody gets up."

"There's two more days left in this weekend," I said. "It's barely Sunday."

"My weekend is over today," she said. "Please take me back, or I'll have to ask one of the other guys to do it."

"They won't."

"Stitches will," she said.

And I knew he would.

"Why do you have to go back now? It's 5:30 in the morning."

"Because I should have stayed there last night," she said. "And I wanted to be with you."

"Tell me what the problem is and we can fix it."

"Nobody ever fixes anything. They just find easier ways to leave the wounded. I was awake when the guys rode in last night. Do you think Christie is hurting any less than you are today, just because she's used to it? Christie is only two years older than Smidgeon. Did anybody put nickels in Smidgeon's 'G' string?"

I had nothing to say to that. But I was thinking I'd run a credit card through Smidgeon's 'G' string, if I could hold it in my teeth.

"You met your reality at breakfast yesterday," she whispered. "I get to meet mine today. I got you through yesterday, and this weekend was what I needed to get through today. Besides, you're not done with your old girlfriend yet... Not by a long shot."

"How will I get in touch with you?"

Once again, she gave me the frankest look I'd ever received from a woman. Then she said, "Write your number down and give it to me on the bike."

She was by the bike when I stepped out and handed her the slip of paper. She put it in her pocket and said, "Can you start this thing quietly? I'm not up to saying good-bye to everybody, and I really had a good time."

I mounted the bike, turned it around, and held it on the sloping driveway with the front brake. "Get on," I said. When she was settled, I shifted into second gear, switched on the ignition and released the brake. The engine surged into life when I popped the clutch at the end of the driveway. Cranky, the H2 ran like total shit for a mile before firing on all three. I rode at the absolute speed limit, hoping something would occur to me before Barryville. Nothing did.

With less than a mile to go, the brunette tapped my leg three times. I held her arms around me with my left hand, and then we were there. All of her stuff was in her bag and she was off the bike in a flash. I got a big hug. She touched my face and said:

"I'm Donna."

Then she was gone.

My first thought was to wait a few minutes, and then to slowly ride through the campground, looking for anything that would enable me to turn the clock back another 24 hours. Then I thought to ride someplace, eat, and come back when the bar was open, so I could stake the place out, and stay in the game somehow. Yet doing anything but riding away would have failed the last test. And there was always a chance that she would call. Why do anything to blow that?

*"Ride away from this one,"* said the Kawasaki. *"She did what she had to do. But wherever she is at this second, she's watching. Make her proud. Make me proud, too."*

I rode back in utter anguish, cursing the motorcycle gods every inch of the way. I was tired of losing women I wanted to keep. This was the third one in three years, and the second in a week. Years later I would realize that at 20 years old you want to keep the last good-looking woman who screwed your brains out, without putting any real demands on you.

*"One of the things that had you crazy was the thought you'd never find a classic beauty again. You did. Now what has you crazy is the thought you can't keep one,"* said the Kawasaki. *"You'll never get to keep anything under 30 years old. The young ones turn into something else every six months."*

The only reasonable thing to do was to head back, at a ridiculously high speed, and replay the weekend in my mind.

*"Look at the weekend,"* said the Kawasaki. *"You got a classic beauty, on your terms, and had a biker weekend with her. What were the odds of that two days ago?"*

I was flying and missed the first bridge; and was tempted to miss the second one too. But I hooked the left at the last minute and realized the breakfast place was open. The situation called for breakfast for one. (Had I gone back to the house, I'd have been rip-roaring drunk in less than an hour.)

"Where's everybody else?" asked Lucille.

"Sleeping. I have a thing for riding at first light."

I ordered coffee and apple pie, then asked if there was a Sunday paper. There was one from Scranton (as if anybody would give a shit what happened in fucking Scranton). The breakfast action hadn't yet started, and Lucille sat down with coffee of her own.

"Were you really gonna smash that guy in the face with your helmet yesterday?" she asked.

"It occurred to me."

"It occurred to the cop too. He was going to talk to you about it. I told him that guy owed you a lot of money, that you lent it to him for food and clothes for his kids, and that he used it to buy a Harley."

"Did you really?" (I couldn't help but notice that Lucille had eyes like miniature stained glass windows too.)

"Yupper. I know you and Stitches are tight." (She said this looking out of the tops of her eyes, like a co-conspirator in a 1940's movie.) The cop asked me how I knew all this, and I told him you were a friend of my brother's. Well they ran that guy through the safety check, and found he was on the suspended list someplace. They took his Harley away on a tow truck. Then that guy got into a big fight with that woman and he left her here. She was drinking coffee at this very table all afternoon."

"What happened to the woman?"

"She asked about a bus out and there's only the one that left already. So she checked into the hotel in town. Old Pete ran her up there in his car."

"What time is the bus out of here today?"

"Not until late...Being a holiday and all."

"Can I get two of those apple turnovers and two regular coffees to go?"

"Sure."

"Lucille, would you like to take a long ride on a red hot Kawasaki some time?"

"You're cute, Jack, but I go riding with Stitches...A lot."

"That smug-faced son of a bitch," I thought. "He's already seen her naked." Donna had been wearing Lucille's tee shirt.

A piece of white paper fluttered to the floor when I pulled my wallet out of my back pocket. Lucille picked it up and looked at it. "Is this number important?" she asked.

It was mine. There would be no call from Cricket.

My ex-girlfriend of two days was surprised to find me at her hotel room door with hot apple turnovers and fresh coffee. I got a life and death hug, and a stream of hot tears on my neck. In that moment, I wanted her back more than anything. There are times when the warmth and familiarity of what you are used to are better than one more set of memories. And yet, nothing is as easy as it should be. There would be no going back to Stitches's place on this holiday weekend. It would be years before I realized that there is never any going back to a lot of things. And I spent years thinking about those two words whispered to me on Rt. 97, in Barryville, NY.

"I'm Donna."

Chapter 20

# "THE BLOND SQUIRREL"

Patching up a shattered romance requires understanding, patience, commitment, and sensitivity. I possessed none of these attributes when I was 20 years old. Consequently, when my friend Stitches suggested I ride up to his place for another Visigoth weekend, I claimed it was for an emergency construction project. So I once again lied to a woman who wanted to believe me and took off to cheat one more time. Sometimes you get what you want. Sometimes you get what you need. And sometimes you get exactly what you deserve.

It was the Sunday morning of the last vicious biker party in August 1976, at the country house of my friend Stitches. I had awakened with a bad case of "Coyote Ugly" for the second time in as many days. I regained consciousness next to a woman, who while not unattractive, was so primitive and coarse in her habits, that under different circumstances it would have been preferable to gnaw off my own arm rather than wake her. She appeared to be in a coma, except for an occasional snore that sounded like sandpaper moving over a rasp. I traced her navel with a fingertip, then tousled the blond nest of her mons, causing her to open one eye.

"You want a little?" she asked.

"I want to know what you want for breakfast."

"You're gonna make me breakfast?"

"Uh-huh. Whatever you want," I said.

"Would you take me out for breakfast?"

"Sure."

"Can we go to the little place in town?"

"Why not?" I said.

"Cause I can get steak tartare with a raw egg and onions there."

I had nothing to say to that one.

"Do you think we can get a beer there this early?" she asked.

"We'll bring some of our own," I suggested.

She had clear blue eyes, an unusual build, and breath like a goat; a goat that smoked a maduro robusto cigar at 2am that morning. A shock of dirty blond hair covered her pillow. Most people would describe "dirty blond" as a darker shade of blond. In her case, it was blond colored by woodsmoke, cigar smoke, and two-stroke exhaust. I don't think she owned a hairbrush.

This woman had been introduced to me the previous Friday as "Laura The Animal." I was halfway through a bottle of Jameson at the time, and thought, "Wow! This one has potential." Jameson's Irish Whiskey has that effect on a lot of things, especially since I had been shooting it with ice-cold beer. It's too bad you can't achieve the same result by just rubbing it on somebody.

I believe in giving everyone the benefit of the doubt. I gave her a big smile and asked if she wanted a drink, holding out the Jameson's and a little plastic cup. She took the bottle and drank from it liberally, allowing some of the whiskey to dribble down on her already stained tee shirt, highlighting a nipple in apparent "attack" mode.

She was dancing on the edge of the fire pit at the time, and went back to gyrating and swinging her ass, turning her back on me in the process. I stood my ground and watched. She had absolutely no rhythm and seemed to be moving to music that had to be playing in her head. The party had been raging for six hours when I got there, and a full assortment of pillion candy was already melting in the heat of the bonfire, shedding tops and undulating their tattoos in the firelight. I have never gotten use to the sight of women going around topless, especially if they are the girlfriends of guys I know. All of these women, but one, were hot in every sense of the word.

Had the blond been an Indian, her dancing might have brought drought instead of rain, or snakes as opposed to corn. But she eventually turned to see if I was still standing there. I was, offering the bottle again. This time I held it short, and got my left arm around her when she reached for the whiskey. She took another sloppy guzzle, as did I. But instead of swallowing, I bent down and put my mouth over the other nipple – rising under the tee shirt – and blew the Jameson into the cloth.

"I like a matching set," I said.

She pulled my mouth onto hers for a whiskey-soaked kiss, then bit my lower lip, hard enough so it stung. It took an effort not to flinch. But these were my whiskey days and I did a lot of things better when I was 20.

She looked me in the eye and said, "Who'da fucka you?" There would be no benefit of the doubt for either one of us.

I took another pull on the bottle, swallowed for effect, and said, "Reep."

Then it was my turn to walk away. She followed. She followed because for once in my life I managed to act like a Visigoth at the Hun's Ball. She followed because I genuinely appeared not to give a shit. And mostly, she followed because I was the only guy there without a woman.

There was no dialogue that night. She was an aggressive drunk, and got a little pushy, actually shoving me if I turned away. She tended to be contentious, and always louder than the music. My interested in this two-penny opera waned when the whiskey was gone. No one was more surprised than I when she followed me into the back room where I was spending the night. There was nothing romantic about this tiny room, which occasionally had a dismantled motorcycle parked in it. It didn't even have a proper door. There was a lumpy couch with pillows and a blanket, and a droplight that doubled as a lamp. (Such were the accommodations for the last man to arrive at the party.) I kicked off my boots and jeans and stretched out, pulling the blanket over me.

My head was already beginning to revolve in the famous Jameson's

Irish Whiskey "Death Spin," and I had no interest in watching her peel off her jeans and the sodden tee shirt. She was traveling commando style, with nothing on underneath, and in the harsh illumination of the drop light, I could see the "carpet matched the drapes." It was the first blond squirrel I had ever seen up close – and I didn't care.

She squeezed in next to me, in some pantomime of a snuggle, and said, "I don't give blow jobs."

"Neither do I," I mumbled. "Maybe we're twins."

What followed was the worst hump I have ever had. She kissed with steel-belted lips and thrashed around like an alligator with its head in a noose. I made a mental note to ask if she had been a guy six months earlier.

The following Saturday brought a grim reckoning when I realized I had a hangover like a runaway nuclear reactor, and she had a voice like an air raid siren. My head hurt too much to move, even in minute degrees, and I considered taking a piss through an open window from my prone position. I had a genuine case of the horrors, and had just managed to sit upright, when a voice exploded from the blanket next to me:

"You look like shit," she said. Then Laura laughed, impersonating a 1500-pound, saber-toothed hyena. I could feel my skull fracturing.

"Stop making noise," I whispered, lowering myself back to the pillow. "And get your blond ass off the couch. I need you to do something for me."

"What?"

"I need you to open the window and estimate the angle of trajectory," I said.

"The angle of what?"

"Never mind," I replied. "Just stop making noise."

"You don't want me to talk?"

"Nor breathe," I mumbled.

Laura hung onto me like a cheap suit for the rest of the day, demonstrating how her voice had one volume setting (loud) and how she had the grace of a bison. (She managed to knock over a guy's bike while dancing around the fire.) She was tall, but not heavy. She was very modestly proportioned (which I liked). But she had only remotely heard of books and had an opinion on everything. Stitches and I got into a discussion on science fiction authors (his library held 2,500 titles). He quoted Isaac Asimov. I quoted Frank Herbert. Laura quoted Disney. Not Walt, but Donald Duck. I felt badly because she liked me, and I'd slept with her, but she was like a guy. She spit like a guy. She swore like a guy. She drank whiskey right from the bottle like a guy. She could piss 20 feet standing up like a guy. (She insisted on showing me this.) And like most guys, she would say the first thing that popped into her head.

Cold sober, Laura was making an effort to appeal to me. But I was cold sober too, and in the grip of a headache that rendered me into a flesh-eating zombie. She made coffee for me that tasted like shit. (I found out she didn't drink coffee and had made it for the first time.) She brought me headache pills. (They were "speed" that one of the other guys had left on the table.) And she offered to show me a sure-fire head massage that would dissolve the pain. (It made it worse.) And throughout all of this, her voice boomed like a fog horn.

I decided I needed a break and tried to steal away into the woods. Stitches had a couple of two-wheel drive Rokon motorcycles, and offered to let me try one. I planned to ride to an old quarry his family owned to see what the Rokon could do, riding over fallen trees, stumps, and huge rocks.

"Can I come?" Laura bellowed. "I promise I won't talk."

"If you didn't talk, you'd fart yourself to death," I found myself saying almost as a reflex. It was like I had slapped her.

Then I thought of all the women I had chased through the wreckage of my adolescence, just trying to get a date, let alone a look at their tits. Most of them had some very clever things to say, which I remember to this day. And others merely delivered a look that had the impact of a bullet. And here was a gawky blonde, who'd been willing to take off her clothes and throw me a pop, obviously struggling to get on par with the rest of the pillion candy that weekend.

All she wanted was the magic of a little romance, the feeling of being pursued by a guy, and the excitement of being looked at in a special way. Given the opportunity to rise to the occasion, I opted to be clever instead. I revealed my inner self as a real asshole.

"Of course you can come," I said. "We'll make a picnic of it."

"Can I talk?"

"Don't push it," I replied.

The picnic was a flask of lemonade, some cheese, fruit and crackers. I thought of tossing a book to read aloud in the bag too, and asked Stitches for a recommendation.

"I have the perfect one you could show Laura," he said. "But there are no crayons to go with it."

"Fuck you too," I replied with a sad smile.

The Rokon was a strange and primitive motorcycle back in 1976, with full-time two-wheel drive. Its tires had the kind of treads you would find on a tractor. The wheels had hollow tanks in the center of each, which could be filled with either gasoline (for an extended trip) or water (for better traction). The engine was slightly bigger than what you'd find on a lawn mower (7 horsepower), but had the same sort of recoil starter. The seat was a block of sponge cell foam, covered in black vinyl. I do not recall if there was anything in the way of a suspension, but I do remember that both the outer edges of the front and back wheels were edged with the teeth of an evil sprocket; the largest sprocket I have ever seen on a motorcycle. The drive sprockets were tiny, and the one on the front was at the end of an ingenious Rube Goldberg-like mechanism.

This unusual motorcycle, which is still made today in New Hampshire, was not designed for two-up riding with Amazons, and Laura's long legs made even the short run I had in mind somewhat dangerous. So I only went about a half-mile into the deep woods, stopping in the first clearing.

I killed the engine, and leaned the bike slightly to the left, so she could get off. Laura dismounted like she was falling off a roof and pulled the bike over on top of us. Fortunately, the Rokon was made for this and no damage was done in the clearing's soft grass. This was the second bike she had knocked over in two days.

*"What the fuck?"* gasped the Rokon.

"Sorry," I said.

"I'm okay," Laura replied, not realizing she was out of this dialogue.

I spread the blanket so that it was partly in the shade and partly in the early afternoon sun. Then I unpacked the picnic stuff such as it was, and stretched out with the intent of purging my hangover in the sun's rays and the gentle breezes off the Upper Delaware River. I fully expected to nod off, catching an hour of uninterrupted forest noises. I am partial to the wind in the trees, the drumming of woodpeckers, and the calls of indigenous birds. I am less enthralled with the droning of insects but you can't have everything. The largest insect of them all was about to sound off.

"Why is the grass pounded flat in some places?" Laura asked.

Opening one eye with a minimal effort, I scanned the clearing and said, "Deer were bedded down here before we pulled up. They probably heard the engine on the bike and took off."

"Where did they go? To another little field?"

"Some will find another clearing. Others will go to a Motel 6. And a few will turn to a life of crime," I replied.

There was a pause.

"Are you ever serious about anything?"

"Serious is depressing. I let everybody else be serious."

There was another, slightly longer pause.

"Can I ask you a serious question? And you'll tell me the truth?"

"That's two questions," I said. And then I gave her that soft open look, the one that has no accompanying words, and which most women think implies "Go ahead," but really means, "I make no guarantees."

"Did you want to go out in the woods to get the fuck away from me?"

There comes a time in a man's life where he is required to tell the best lie that has ever been crafted because making a woman believe it will prevent her from ever wasting a single second thinking about the shittiest thing a guy may have ever told her. I paused, ordering my soul to leach more blue into my eyes, and said, "Don't be silly." (And that was neither "yes" nor "no.") And then I reached out and touched her hand.

Relieve swept over her face like a tide. She squeezed my hand, which made me feel very odd.

This was followed by a shorter pause.

"What were you thinking when we laid down on the blanket?" she asked.

That was a much harder question to address. I paused again, forcing my mind to focus on an intelligent answer.

"In 1863, the French artist Edouard Manet painted a work titled, 'Le DeJeuner Sur L'Herbe.' It means 'Luncheon On The Grass.' It depicts two gentlemen in fine clothes, having a picnic on a blanket, with a woman who is totally naked. I have often wondered what that would be like. That's what I was thinking."

"Really?" Laura asked.

I responded again with a half smile, which again, was neither "yes" nor "no."

And with that, she stood up, shed her blouse, and stepped out of her jeans.

The sunlight turned the color of her skin to cream, with two pink rosettes on breasts that were borderline small. There wasn't an ounce of fat on her, but she was tall...At least an inch taller than me and her body was proportional to her size. I never expected her to do anything like this, and as fascinated as I am by the naked female form, I didn't take my eyes off her face. There are times when a simple gesture trumps everything. To this day, I firmly believe there is no greater compliment a woman can pay a man than to take her clothes off.

Laura sat down next to me, Indian style, and I laid my head at the point where her legs crossed. I had never seen a blond squirrel up close before and I was totally captivated. I felt pretty much the same way when I'd seen a giant panda in the zoo. I was utterly content to just stare at it indefinitely. It would have been cool to see it in the context of a little lace-something, but it was soothing to see it in a green field, surrounded by a blue sky and stately trees. It was like the ultimate sunflower: a combination of a daisy and an orchid.

"You can touch it, you know," Laura said.

"I don't want to get bit," I replied.

"It doesn't have teeth," she said.

"They all do."

She started to say something else, and I just put my finger against her lips. As endearing as this scenario was, her voice was still booming across the river and down the valley. I was content to just lie there, in the late summer heat, with a naked woman, in my own version of "Le DeJeuner Sur L'Herbe." We napped like this for a bit, and then she slipped into her shirt again, though she left it open.

It had never occurred to Laura that silence can sometimes be louder than any word. This was because Laura was from Hudson County, my county, where silence is the least understood of nature's marvels. I think it was a shock to discover that taking off her clothes didn't result in sex either. What she had done, and what I could never tell her, was that she made me wish that I was sitting on this blanket with my real girlfriend... An exquisitely beautiful woman who understood silence, and who could make music play in my head. In that context, I had no interest in sharing a blanket with any other woman. And yet when a woman takes her clothes off and climbs onto a man's blanket, he is required to make that lady feel like she is the most beautiful of all living things.

I ran my hand across Laura's flat stomach and said, "I never imagined I would have my own Le DeJeuner Sur L'Herbe this weekend."

I should have kept my mouth shut as I was already thinking about heading home.

It was close to 4pm when we started back. The Rokon took about 7 pulls to get the engine running, but eventually fired with gusto. It's very odd riding a motorcycle that not only pushed with the back wheel, but pulled with the front. There is a sense of resistance to the steering and a greater urgency to twist the throttle to maintain headway and balance. Of course, Laura was like riding with a load of concrete but there was only a half-mile to go.

The aroma of grilled pork and venison roasts wafting through the air was an indication that the Huns were gearing up for another night of howling at the moon. My hangover, which had spared me from worshipping at the porcelain idol, was just about gone, when Stitches handed me a rum and Coke as big as my ass.

"Well maybe just one," I said.

"You're not thinking of leaving tonight, are you?" asked Stitches. "I realize this babe isn't like the last one."

"As a matter of fact, I thought I'd get out of here before it gets fully dark. And you had nothing to do with the last one."

"Please don't leave, he said. "Aren't things gong well? They could be much worse for us if you left. I'll fill the bathtub with rum if you stay."

And before I could answer, I heard him say, "What the hell?"

Laura was dancing in place next to the fire pit, shirt unbuttoned, and jeans open at the top. Every movement was something of a bizarre pictorial. One of the other ladies, who was wearing leather lingerie, said to her, "Is this a new look for you?"

"He likes me this way," she said, pointing at me with a nearly full bottle of Jim Beam. Odder still is that she'd said this in a low voice.

I stepped up to her and put my hands inside her shirt, holding her just under her arms. Then I kissed those Kevlar lips and said, "Button up. We'll have dinner in town." It was my intention to put the brakes on another potentially riotous night.

"Okay," she said in a voice that was nearly a whisper. My fucking goose was cooked.

I took her to a touristy German restaurant that catered to old farts, and dined her in an environment that was as sedate as I could find. The clientele were all candidates to be buried alive with the pharaoh. Laura liked the food – she had a thing for hocks and snouts – but wasn't happy about the atmosphere, claiming it made her sad to see all these old, saggy people. She explained they got saggy as the life in them deflated. And since she was such a reticent soul, she shared this sentiment in a voice that could be heard three towns away. The whispering effect was somehow reserved for me.

"I want to go to a bar that has music." She said. "Did you know a French artist named Jean LaFoote painted a picture of a blond dancing on a pool table in a bar full of naked guys? I want you to take me to that bar."

I took her to a joint that had a dark reputation but one that would be a short ride back to the house. The jukebox was filled with country and western music. The cloth on the pool table had buttonholes in it, and there was s sign that said, "Asses Cheerfully Kicked."

"Just a fast one," I said. "There's a party going on at the house."

"You can go to it," she said. "I like it here."

Six drinks later, she started dancing to the theme from "Rawhide," and bumped into a guy who was lining up the winning shot for a money game on the pool table. Then she knocked over a tray of drinks and had something to say to the guys who ordered them. That was when some unwashed son of a sow stepped into the saloon and said, "Who owns that piece of shit Kawasaki outside?"

Every eye in the place was on me.

"It's hers," I replied.

The guy was about my size and just spoiling for a fight. He'd pulled up on a Harley Knucklehead that bore the scars of a self-customizing project that had not gone well. The banana-style seat was actually duct-taped to the frame. I'm not one to make snap judgments, but it was apparent to me the better part of this guy was left as a smear on his mother's leg. He was ugly, dirty, and evil smelling. He also looked tough.

"My mother's brother died at Pearl Harbor," he said.

"You mean your Uncle?"

"Yeah...My uncle died at Pearl Harbor."

"Was he flying a Zero?" I asked, knowing what was about to happen.

I looked around to see if there was anything that I could use as a weapon. Specifically, I was hoping for a flamethrower. The guy's arm came back for the wind-up and I saw the closed fist that would constitute the pitch. I was about to curl up like an armadillo, when the most amazing thing happened. The "8" ball from the pool table flew through the air and clocked this guy dead center in the forehead. He went down like a sack of shit.

"I turned and saw Laura "The Animal" menacing the crowd with the "2" ball and the "4" ball. (She apparently had a thing for even numbered balls.)

"Time to go," I said, heading for the door. I knew she was close behind as I could feel her breath on the back of my neck.

"Start the bike," she yelled.

The Kawasaki fired on the first kick and I was already moving, when I noticed she was not yet on the pillion.

"C'mon, Laura," I yelled. "Let's get the fuck out of here."

She pulled the duct-taped seat from the Harley and kicked the bike over. With a war cry that could have shattered church windows, she was on the pillion grasping the seat like a trophy. And then we were out the driveway and gone. Laura tossed the seat into a ditch about a mile from the bar.

"It was 15 miles to the house on back roads. We covered it in 17 minutes. I flew up the driveway and parked the bike out back, with Laura war-whooping the entire time. I discovered she'd thrown her shirt into the fire pit as we went by. The events that had just transpired were so alien to me that I hardly knew how to tell the story. I did know that Laura had saved me from a beating. Then again, I would never have gone into that bar if she hadn't insisted. So she was both the cause of the problem and its solution.

Once again, the green whiskey bottle was passed around the fire, but only Laura was running around without her top. She followed me to the back room after it because apparent that this was going to be a more quiet night. She made love like she danced, without a feel for the rhythm, nor with a sense of her own gratification. That didn't mean she had a sense for mine though either. I like to think that pure, unadulterated love, complete with poetry and romance, has the potential to spring from two naked people in bed, if it is not the reason they are there in the first place. (I learned nothing from the Boston incident.) If anybody needed pure, unadulterated love, it was this woman. Regrettably, I was 20 years old, had my head in my ass, and could only offer adulterated love as I was again cheating on one of gentlest, sexiest, and smartest women I would ever know. But I just wanted to experience another Visigoth weekend, and my regular girlfriend would never be the type to dance topless around the fire.

Dawn came with the first line of the opening paragraph of this chapter. I felt I owed Laura a decent morning, a civilized breakfast, and a ride home from this remote place in Pennsylvania. She did, in fact, order steak tartare for breakfast at the top of her lungs. She did have her first beer before I had coffee. And she did whoop all 105 miles back to her front door.

"Wanna come in?" she asked, as we pulled up to her place.

"I gotta run," I said, letting the blue leech out of my eyes in prelude to a hard truth.

"Will you call me soon? Will you take me to see that painting?"

"Absolutely."

I never saw her again. It's just too easy to leave the wounded sometimes.

# Chapter 21

# "CURTAIN CALL"

The patch was barely holding on the relationship with my equestrian lover and she'd become justifiably suspicious of my occasional absences and my transparent writer mentality. I was sick of the saloon and disgusted by romance. My soul needed the diversion of a weekend ride. A ride that was more than camping but not anything near a gathering of the tribe. I wanted the conversation of like-thinking men, without the competitive edge of moto tribal pressure. I needed to be in touch with my thoughts for a couple of days, without the influence of my testicles. And I needed the finale of fall, because every living thing gets sick of summer.

Fall arrives in two stages, the first of which is a rumor and the second is a bone chilling bleakness that signals the end of easy riding. The rumor called for the first slashes of color in the foliage of North Jersey on this particular weekend, with temperatures conducive to hot apple pie and steamy cups of spiced cider in the late afternoon. Golden sunshine yields to the first really cool nights of a new season and it is hard to shed a blanket in the morning. All I needed was a destination.

I called Stitches. He was up at his country house, taking care of a few odds and ends before the winter.

"Come up," said Stitches. "There's not much going on and most of the places in these little towns have closed for the season. The Pine Cone is shuttered until next summer. The country and western joint burned down. The strip joint is still open but the local dancers are wearing cow bells so the manager knows when they're out grazing."

Stitches was a diplomat. In his own gentle way he was telling me that there would be nothing to find if I was searching for the summer's past glory at the scene of the crime. "I'm not alone this weekend, but you'll be. This one has a sister, but we didn't bring her."

"Who's the cupcake?" I asked.

"No one you know. Her name is Audencia. She just made a yellow rice and seafood dish called Paella. I don't like it but you'll want to roll in it like a dog. It'll be warm in the oven if you ride up tonight." Stitches lived down in Union City and a lot of his girlfriends were Cuban.

It was late in the day and the sun was already the color of mild cheddar, but I wanted to be on the road. "Yeah," I said. "I'm coming. You will be there if I arrive after dark though, right?" There was an edge to my question.

"Yes and no," said Stitches. "We planned to hit an early movie in Carbondale, and should be back by nine. You'd only be alone for an hour or so."

"I can get through an hour, I think."

"Maybe an hour or so," said Stitches, with a laugh.

There was an obvious gap in the conversation. Stitches as good as told me that I would alone in the farmhouse for an unspecified time after dark. The house was charming, inviting, warm and cozy. It had a nice view of the river. It was nestled on the edge of a deep forest. It was the most peaceful of fall settings. And it was as haunted as Dracula's castle.

"What were you doing up there today?" I asked, trying to keep the panic out of my voice.

"I replaced one of the lolly columns in the basement. You know what that means."

"Will you leave the lights on?"

"Leaving the lights on won't help," said Stitches, hanging up with a laugh.

I cleared the ridge of New Jersey's High Point State Park in the last glimmer of daylight, and started down the sweeping curves to the New

York State line behind the cone of my headlight. It was dusk at the top and night time in the valley. The temperature dropped ten degrees and I enjoyed my first mini-shiver, with the cool air rushing through my open jacket collar. While the summer is the season of Mongolian-scale moto-migrations, riders arrive everywhere smelling like musk ox, pickled in rank sweat. Riding in the fall means no sweat. It means clothing won't be glued to your body. It means your helmet won't smell like a muskrat died in it. It means dry hands on the grips or light gloves that don't ooze.

*"Doesn't this feel great,"* said the Kawasaki. *"Just me and you and 58 degrees. Do me a favor? Don't talk to strangers, especially if they have tits. Don't stop to smoke a cigar until we get to the house. You can smoke on the porch."*

The last 53 miles of this run were in the dark. Not summer dark, where the last light of day lingers until the moon is up. But the darkness that starts to get serious ten minutes after sunset. It was the beginning of the off season for this region and traffic was non-existent. The river was on my left in a great black void, defined by the occasional street light on the bridges I'd passed. It was fast moving and roiling in the darkness. I couldn't see the clearing where I'd started the weekend of a lifetime this past summer. The tourist bar was dark and shuttered. Only one of the little motels was open and it wasn't open by much. I kept the speed to 60 miles per hour, or so, and noted that a number of reflectors at the tree-line occasionally blinked or moved as I went past. These were fucking deer.

Fall also means carved pumpkins and cool ghost stories, like *The Legend of Sleepy Hollow*. As Washington Irving originally wrote that story, schoolmaster Ichabod Crane expressed an interest in the daughter of a wealthy Dutch landowner. A local stud ran him off using a carved pumpkin and a cape. The presence that haunted the country home of Stitches had no such easy explanation. I had witnessed its antics before, and while they seemed harmless enough, I prefer the deceased to remain low-key. With less than ten miles to go, I wondered if Stitches would actually be out. "He knows how I hate being alone in that house," I thought. "He'll be there."

*"I once heard of a troubled house where the evil presence lived in the toilet,"* said the Kawasaki. *"And when anyone sat on it, it grew teeth like a chainsaw and chewed their ass."*

I took the blind curve that begins the final stretch with false confidence. This road has more dips than an ice cream stand. There is a certain delight in the momentary weightlessness that comes from jazzing a motorcycle through abrupt changes in elevation. It's even more fun in the dark. Topping the crest of each rise, my body wanted to continue upward until pulled back down by the handlebars. The headlight alternately illuminated the tree tops or the bottoms of the paved gullies ahead as the bike angled up and down. I wondered how a primitive man, suddenly transported to this period in time, would have regarded the beam of my headlight cutting through the darkness in such an erratic way. Would he have worshipped me in wonder or cowered in fear?

*"He would have nocked a poisonous arrow in his bow and shot you through the heart,"* said the Kawasaki.

There was no moon nor stars that night. The sky had clouded over. The weekend would be mild, but with overtones of gray. There were other houses along the river, but not of them showed a light. (Rural Pennsylvania has a way of converting the bucolic into the macabre on dark nights. I remembered that George A. Romero's horror classic *Night of the Living Dead* took place in rural Pennsylvania. I wondered if the people in these houses had already been devoured by flesh-eating zombies.)

*"Why don't you stop in the center of the road and flash the headlight behind you,"* suggested the Kawasaki. *"It might be choked with staggering cadavers."*

I hadn't thought of that. Now it existed as a possibility in my mind. The last turn in this adventure loomed on the left. I angled into the driveway with a sinking heart when I saw a dark house, a sole light burning on the porch, and something odd about the front door. There was a knife sticking in it, pinning a scrap of brown paper to the wood. Written in red lipstick were two words: "Get Out."

"Why does Stitches bust my balls?" I thought.

*"Because they are an easy target,"* said the Kawasaki.

The first floor was a country kitchen, a small living room, two bedrooms, and the sole bathroom. Stitches's bedroom was the one off the kitchen. Mine was off the dimly lit hall. It was the same one in which

I'd spent an incredible weekend this past July. I poked my head into the living room, switching on the lights before actually stepping inside. I moved into the kitchen and flicked the lights on there as well. My hair stood on end with the apparition that greeted me. From the darkness there emerged a naked, one-eyed, disjointed apparition of a man. I would have screamed, yet when confronted with the options of yelling, running, or just evacuating my bowels, my body did nothing.

The apparition was "Ted," the mannequin we sometimes used for target practice. He'd been propped up against the far wall.

"That son of a bitch," I muttered. I could barely breathe. I had nearly pissed my pants.

*"Do you want me to come in there and kick its ass?"* yelled the Kawasaki from outside.

I moved "Ted" over to the door of Stitches's bedroom and pushed him in. Ted's head came off and rolled back into the kitchen. It came to rest against a chair leg, glaring up at me with his remaining eye.

*"Another omen,"* laughed the Kawasaki.

I kicked the head into the bedroom. Stitches has a first class sense of humor and will go to great lengths for a joke. He once sold me a used GMC Suburban that sported a hood ornament from a wrecked Jaguar. There was something about the leaping predator that seemed in tune with the boxy truck. He also kept a set of keys. When I came down for the morning's commute one day, the Jaguar had been replaced with a life-sized dove decoy, that had been filled with plaster. There was now a fucking pigeon sitting on the hood of the truck. It was attached in a way that defied easy removal. I rode around with it for a year.

Stitches claimed the house was "protected" by the spirit of the aged farmer who was its last tenant. He'd actually met the man while he was still among the living and was alleged to have gotten along with him just fine. However, the deceased took umbrage anytime structural changes were made to the house.

I first met the deceased on a weekend when we replaced floor joists. Stitches told me about the ghost and that we'd be in for a little demonstration. There were a bunch of us watching an instructional porn video in the living room, when a glass broke in the kitchen sink. We exchanged surprised looks, and Stitches said, "It'll happen again." Not two seconds later, another glass shattered. Sure enough, the shards of two glasses littered the sink.

"That's the show for tonight," said Stitches. "He's pissed we screwed with the house."

The show got better on another occasion. The kitchen was tight, and the refrigerator, a huge running monument to the round-cornered designs of the 1950's, had been idling before another door to the outside for more than 26 years. The woodwork in the kitchen was painted white, in oil-based, heavily leaded paint that was layers thick. The door had not been opened in two decades and was secured by a deadbolt that was also painted shut. Stitches and crew replaced a beam in the house that weekend. Once again, we were in the next room when the dialogue was interrupted by a banging noise. The door in the kitchen was opening and closing, about two inches, and hitting the back of the refrigerator. None of us could move the deadbolt nor budge that door the next day.

While many reserve judgment on the paranormal, or just openly doubt it, I have been in two "troubled" houses and only returned to this one (over subsequent years) as I have gotten laid in it on occasion. But I have taken great pains to never spend any time in it alone. And here I was, at night, alone in this damned house for the first time.

I switched on the dim light in the hall, ventured as far as the bathroom (where I hit the lights in there too), and peeked into the guest bedroom. The only light in there was a screwy "lava lamp" from the 1960's, that cast everything in a peculiar globular blue glow. I switched that on too. The better class of hotel softens exorbitant room rates by placing chocolates on the pillow. Stitches had left a bottle of Meyer's Dark Rum on my pillow, for which I was almost ready to forgive him for "Ted."

The whole house had the aroma of the seashore, provided the seashore one favors is off the coast of Valencia, in Spain. Stitches's hot new squeeze had whipped up Paella Valencia, an extraordinary combination of yellow rice, clams, mussels, shrimp, lobster, and fish. I found it in the still warm oven. I dished a healthy portion of it onto a plate, and made myself a "Planter's Punch" with an aging lime and a carton of orange juice I found in the fridge. In fact, I made a pitcher of these and decided to party with the deceased.

I sat at the table and tried to eat facing the sink and the refrigerator. This didn't work as I was afraid either would host movement. So I sat with my back to both and this was worse as I couldn't tell if I was about to be dragged into hell from behind. Also, I could see Ted's severed head on the floor of the next room and thought the eye winked at me.

I moved into the living room, placing my meal on the coffee table, and switched on the television. Stitches got two channels. One was from a public TV station in Scranton and featured a chess tournament in Croatia. The other was from Pittsburgh (I think) and was actually showing *The Night of the Living Dead*. In either case each channel featured zombies. I switched the television off, which then seemed to magnify every sound in the house. The huge stereo speakers beckoned but I remembered that they often overheated the amplifier, which blew the fuses. That would pitch the house in darkness, requiring someone to go into the basement to rectify the problem. "To hell with that," I thought.

So I hit the switch for the outside flood lights and ate on the open porch. The afternoon had been warm, heating the shallow Delaware River. As the night cooled, a mist came off the water and started to creep up the lawn.

*"Can you see someone walking around in that mist?"* asked the Kawaski.

"Shut up," I said. "Don't start that shit."

*"Quiet,"* hissed the bike. *"Did you hear that?"*

There was the sound of a low growl and the almost ghostly illumination of the mist. A Ducati buzzed out of the fog and climbed the driveway. Stitches and Audencia had arrived. I could hear him laughing as they dismounted.

"I knew you'd be out here on the porch," said Stitches. "Did Ted chase you out?"

"Fuck you," I laughed.

Audencia had a hard body, a soft smile, and eyes that one only finds on deer in animated Disney movies. She was exotic as the Ducati. I took her hand, introduced myself, and complimented her paella. We had a pleasant evening of gentle conversation, quiet laughs, and tropical rum drinks, calling it a night at the stroke of twelve.

I awakened to a knocking on the walls at 2am.

"That asshole, Stitches," I thought. But the knocking persisted for 10 minutes, and I finally opened the bedroom door. The hallway was dark. There was a nightlight on in the kitchen. I was the only one awake and the house was as quiet as a tomb. Something from beyond had been knocking at the door... And I let the fucking thing in.

Never use a lava lamp as primary illumination in a paranormal investigation. It's too dim to draw any real conclusions and the shadows it throws on the wall may confuse the issue. I got back into bed and pulled the covers over my head. The knocking started again ten minutes later. This time, from inside the room. (I wondered if ghosts are like dogs, always on the wrong side of a wall.) I opened the bedroom door and tucked my head into the darkened hall. At that moment, the doors on both of the hall closets opened and closed twice. My scream could be heard in three counties.

Stitches came flying out of the other bedroom with a loaded .357 magnum in one hand, and his squeeze in tow with the other. They were naked. I can't tell you what she looked like. I didn't care. My ensemble included the finest cotton briefs, barely unsoiled. My jeans, shirt, jacket, boots and helmet were in my arms as I made my way out to the porch. I got dressed outside.

"What happened?" asked Stitches.

I told him in 36 words or less. Nine of those words were "ghost." Fifteen more were the adjective "fucking."

"I had the heat on in the house earlier today," Stitches explained. "Maybe you heard the system cooling down."

"When the house gets hot does it fan itself with the closet doors?" I asked.

It was my intention to jump on the H2 and bail out of there in record time. Stitches muttered something to Audencia and she retreated to the bedroom, only to return 30 seconds later, wearing a short, silk robe, adorned with an Asian print. She looked more naked now than she did when she was naked.

"You can't just run out of here on sixteen drinks and no sleep," said Audencia. "Let me make coffee."

*"He's done it often enough before,"* said the Kawasaki. *"Man, does she have one hot ass or does she have one hot ass."*

"Did you just say something?" asked Stitches.

"Not me. What did you think I said?"

"Now you've got me all jumpy. I thought I heard a voice coming from the motorcycles," said Stitches.

*"I would like to have your girlfriend's hot ass across my handlebars on a bumpy road,"* hissed the Kawasaki.

Stitches was one of the few guys I know who could stand on a porch, stark naked, holding a .357 magnum, without compromising his dignity. "There! There it is again," he said. "Didn't you hear that?"

"You're nuts," I said. "Does your bike talk?"

"Hardly," Stitches shrugged.

*"Vaffanculo,"* said the Ducati. *"I have been telling him for months not to touch anything below the gas tank. Now I just tell him, "Vai in culo!"*

*"They can be difficult,"* said the Kawasaki.

A scream as paralyzing as that in any horror flick shattered the night. Stitches dashed into the kitchen, pistol at the ready. Audencia was on the floor, with one hand pressed over her mouth, suppressing yet another scream. With the coffee heating on the stove, she opened the refrigerator to get the milk, and found Ted's head leering out at her.

She got up from the floor and started beating the shit out of Stitches.

"You and your stupid jokes…"

Stitches rolled with her punches, looked at me, and laughed.

"I'm getting out of here with Jack," said Audencia.

*"Okay by me,"* said the Kawasaki.

"What say we all get under a blanket on the porch, sip Irish coffee, and watch the sun come up over the river?" suggested Stitches.

"I'll let you hold my hand," Audencia said to me.

*"Ask her if I can hold something too,"* said the Kawasaki.

I had no idea how far a presence can go from the house, nor how fast they can move, but the thought of meeting one on that dark road was very unappealing. "Okay," I said. "But I'd rather hold the AR-15."

The only thing I wasn't wearing under that blanket was my helmet.

Stitches made coffee at the crack of dawn and dragged Ted out to a shed. I had Audencia's paella again for breakfast. While she was in the shower, Stitches said to me, "Well you got me back pretty good last night. That was pretty funny… Putting Ted's head in fridge."

"I never put Ted's head in the refrigerator," I said. "I kicked it into your room."

Stitches looked at me for long second and said, "I am going to apologize to Audencia for scaring her last night. You are never to tell her anything different."

I didn't know it then, but that was the last great weekend I was to have with Stitches in that house. His family sold the property two years later.

*Author's note: I visited another troubled house, in the heart of the Adirondacks. Unlike the benign presence of a farmer haunting a picturesque little farmhouse on the Delaware, this other place was magnificent late Victorian-era mansion, in which several people had been driven mad and to early deaths through lead poisoning by primitive* plumbing. So violent and miserable had the apparitions become that the Catholic church had been brought in to purge the place. *The beautifully wainscoted room in which the epicenter of the house's evil lurked was sealed with gold crosses hammered into each ceiling corner. The ghost isn't Catholic, apparently, as the trouble is alleged to persist. This magnificent structure, once a residence, once a hotel, and once a bed and breakfast, sits perpetually empty.*

*Author's Note: I drove past that little farmhouse of my friend Stitches a couple of years ago. It sits pretty much as I remember it. The ghost of the farmer seemed more like an anecdote against the backdrop of the four women I took there, of the hundreds of rounds of ammunition expended out back, of the millions of gallons of rum I drank on the porch, and of the music that blared from two six-foot tall speakers Stitches had on the porch. It almost seemed like I was recalling someone else's life. And I wonder which is more haunted, that house or my mind. My mind is haunted by the sounds of motorcycle's starting, and the taste of women's kisses.*

# Chapter 22

# "EPILOGUE"

So ended the first four years of my life as a motorcycle rider. I wanted one thing from riding a motorcycle and I got it in spades. Yet it was far from the most noteworthy gift conferred by the Kawasaki. I learned what it was like to part the dawn mist by flying through it. I experienced life in a curve at 90 miles per hour. I was devoured by darkness and consumed by fog. I had moonlight pass through me like an x-ray. I learned the thrill of pitting centrifugal force against gravity, which is like swimming between two sharks. I encountered life as a projectile, capable of changing direction at will. I confronted my own mortality three times, and spit in Death's eye twice. I hung with some of the toughest, roughest and best guys I'd ever met. I got the shit beaten out of me once, by a woman. I had a barfly threaten to kill me. I had a woman tell me, "I love you," over the scream of an engine. I got lost in the sudden silence of desolate places. I found freedom. I was jailed. I can't say that I lived to ride…But I lived on a much higher plane · because I did ride.

I changed jobs three times in three years and finally got hired as a writer… Not by a newspaper and not by a public relations firm. Both thought I was too skeevie for consideration. I was hired to write press releases by a political organization that had no minimal employment requirements. If you think being shot out a canon on a motorcycle is cool, you should try the utter thrill of public service in a dominant political party that takes no prisoners.

A career in politics is like sitting in quicksand for the view. My colleagues were career ward heelers and black-op specialists for local campaigning. I remember one episode in which our campaign had run out of funds at a time when opposition money had peaked. The other candidate, a distinguished bag of dog shit, had put together a full-color campaign flyer that showed him kissing babies, healing the sick, and turning tax dollars into talking peacocks. The piece was quite good. One of our staffers, a gentleman known as "The Sultan," went down to the enemy print shop wearing an enemy tee shirt. He picked up the entire print run in a van — about 12 cases — and threw it into the Hudson River. (We won the election in a special runoff three months later.)

My relationship with the Equestrian had so many patches on it that it looked like an Amish quilt. But I really wanted it to work with her. She was my first real love and the kind of woman with whom a man could grow old. Unfortunately, she was aging seven years for every hour we were together. I thought she was perfect. And in the end, she thought I was a perfect bastard. She envisioned a life of the literati... Where we'd be surrounded by novelists, poets, and playwrights... With me eating cucumber sandwiches and quietly admiring the asses of other writers' wives. (The last part came true.)

She survived the motorcycle... But not the politics.

My political colleagues had names like "Squishy... Bennie The Glyp... Fingers Mulrooney... And Limpy." (They were not Republicans.) The Equestrian accompanied me to a political event one night and whispered, "This is like being backstage at a police lineup." She was right. She did point out a number of folks in expensive suits. "Are they Congressman and Senators?" she asked. I explained they were from the FBI.

The Equestrian read my press releases and quotes in the newspaper with mounting horror. "This is the kind of writer you want to become?" she asked.

I expressed shock and responded, "Do you think I could be swayed by absolute political power, easy money, and proximity to those who shape local, state, and federal policy?"

I never heard her answer. She was crying too hard. That was the night a brunette reporter with fire in her eyes and sway in her ass came up to me at a political event and said, "I knew you'd be here. There's blood in the water." My girlfriend was not nearly as impressed with this Dorothy Parker-esque exchange as I was.

I had been riding the motorcycle less and less, and finally not at all.

Those who engage in the business of politics are always working. Newspapers that wouldn't hire me were calling twice a day. My focus changed. I hung a picture of Boss Tweed on the wall. I stopped going to the bar. Actually, there was a different bar, now. The reporter who'd wagged her ass at me was wagging it with greater emphasis. Dark forces were at work.

My Equestrian found a buyer for the bike. She thought I could sell it and get new living room furniture. I was now 24 years old and she figured it was time my place no longer looked like a Third World bordello.

The bike was tatty now from being kept outside. The paint gave evidence to the miles that were on the clock. The cheap chrome on the mufflers had started to peel, encouraged by a splash of battery acid from a misrouted vent hose. The chain was droopy. The sprockets had beveled edges.The black vinyl seat had faded. The sissy bar and there padded backrest looked dated. But the bike still started on the first kick.

My last conversation with the Kawasaki occurred as I was selling the machine to a new rider. I'd had the bike five years and it carried the scars of a motorcycle that had never been indoors.

"Good bye, old friend," I said.

*"This isn't good-bye,"* said the Kawasaki. *"It's kiss my Japanese ass."*

Some posturing windbag bought the Kawasaki for his new wife, a 19-year-old sizzling redhead. She was a thong of a woman, with a smattering of freckles and potent green eyes. Anybody who marries a redhead who looks like this at 19 is a highly optimistic asshole. Anyone married to a 19-year-old redhead who looks like this, and who buys her a motorcycle (when he doesn't ride), might just as well leave the barn door open.

I started to explain the nuances of the two-stroke motor to this glowing rivet in jeans, when her husband blurted out his credentials as a chainsaw and lawnmower mechanic. "Fair enough," I said, "but what if she fouls the plugs 80 miles from 'Mr Wiggley's Chainsaw Hospital and Lawnmower Sanitarium?'" He hadn't thought she'd ride 80 miles away.

*"He's trying to figure out who's Mr. Wiggley,"* said the Kawasaki.

"She's only gonna ride it a few miles to college," said Mr. Wiggley.

Her eyes told me differently.

I showed her the tool kit, the manual, the spare plugs, and the spare fuses. I let her keep the flashlight. I kept the dipstick rag, which was a pair of panties belonging to another brunette I met one Fourth of July weekend on the Delaware River.

"Is there anything else I should know?" asked the redhead, whose name was Liz.

I smiled and said, "The fucking thing talks... And it's full of shit."

She looked at me and laughed.

"All engines talk in a variety of ways," chimed the human chainsaw meatball.

"This bike will never lie to you... But it will never tell the truth."

Her smile faded from the one used to mesmerize the average male of the species to one that suggested I had reached a higher level of evaluation.

"Saddle up and take it for a dance," I said.

She hadn't brought a helmet and used one of my "Human Fly" green ones. They looked really stupid now. Her trailing red hair and the green metallic helmet made her look like heaven's Christmas ornament.

Running the bike up and down the sidewalk a few times, I suddenly saw her jaw drop in amazement as she glanced around, looking to find the trick in something. The Kawasaki was talking to her already, in a whisper that only she could hear. They loaded the bike into a lawn-mower trailer and left.

The last I'd heard, Liz met a college professor who also rode a bike. They disappeared together during her first full summer as a rider.

Never take advice from a motorcycle.

Appendix One

# "AN OVERVIEW OF NEW JERSEY"

Nestled between the Empire State of New York and the Common-
wealth of Pennsylvania is the no man's land that is New Jersey, the
most misunderstood state in the Union. This cauldron of attitude, road
rage, and cynicism has come to represent a national punchline for millions of people, the staggering majority of whom have never visited the
"Garden State," let alone tried to live there. New Jersey is the original
"State Of Mind." It is where Satan learned to whisper to women. It is
the place where Machiavelli came to study politics. It's where big hair
was invented. It is the birthplace of sarcasm and the bitchslap. It is
where legions of people, driving home each night, commiserate with
one-finger gestures.

New Jersey is everything everybody has ever said about it, and still
most everybody gets it wrong. Going back to the earliest days of colo-
nization, New Jersey was one of the crown jewels of the New World.
People talk about quaint little New England villages, the Pennsylvania
Dutch, and the first families of Virginia royalty. They can all kiss New
Jersey's ass.

New Jersey began as a colonial paradise of trout-filled streams, rolling
hills, stands of hardwood, and stretches of beaches that would eventually sell for $6,000 a square inch. Today, you can buy waterfront prop-
erty in Weehawken, NJ for $150 a gram. The colony was populated by
pacifist Native Americans, who were already conquered by every other
tribe within 700 miles. Then the Dutch arrived and added robbery to
that humiliation. The colony had half of the best deep water harbor in
the world, and access to two incredible river systems (the mighty Hudson and the pretentious Delaware). Every crop that grew in Europe,
grew better in New Jersey. Even the cranberry was here long before
vodka. New Jersey had tidy little fishing villages without the dour faces of New England. It was a highly social state, in contrast to Quaker

Pennsylvania, where smiling would get you arrested. It had warm months accented by enough humidity to remind you of hell, without the alligators and snakes that infest the south.

New Jersey was claimed by the Dutch, a curious folk who as a nation prefer to live 22.5 feet below sea level. New Jersey threw them for a loop. You can actually look down at the ocean from a lot of places here. The Dutch wasted no time in applying certain business practices to the indigenous population that earned them the admiration of other usurious Europeans. In response, local tribes killed a lot of the "wooden-footed devils" and burned most of their homesteads in 1633. This became a kind of holiday tradition, repeated again in 1655, when New Jersey Indians killed 1000 Dutchman in an argument that started over the price of a single peach.

"I'd rather see this whole colony burned than give a single peach away," said Hans Van der Groote, a short-sighted burgher who ended up well-done. Peace was negotiated three years later, and the Indians began saluting their Dutch neighbors with the middle finger of their right hand.

In 1665, the British took over from the Dutch and gained control of New Jersey by its proximity to New York. This arrangement lasted approximately 110 years, when many New Jersey residents extended the native way of saluting Dutchmen to royal governors, tax collectors, and judges. British soldiers marching through New Jersey in 1776 were astounded by the unbelievably high standard of living in this colony. Farms were picturesque, productive, and profitable. All of the women were beautiful. Farmers were judged to be provincial clods. One British social wag observed, "These assholes would be dangerous if they ever learned to shoot."

The more dramatic parts of the American Revolution were fought in New Jersey by patriot real estate agents who prophesied that the 25-mile radius around Morristown would be home to 19 of the Fortune 500. George Washington slept in so many places around Morris County, NJ that people thought he was opening a hotel chain. The American Revolution may have started in Boston (with a dramatic but futile stand at Bunker Hill), but the first major ass-kicking of the British by the Continental Army occurred in Trenton, NJ, when 2400 provincial clods defeated elite Hessian mercenaries, the special forces of the 18th Century. The Continental Army attacked in freezing conditions and took 918 prisoners, plus their cannon, provisions, and military stores. Washington regrouped a week later and attacked Princeton, catching another British force with their pants down. It would not be until the War of 1812 that the British learned to march with their pants tightly cinched about their respective waists, and they still got their asses kicked.

The rest is history... But it is a history that few people know.

The motion picture industry was born in new Jersey as was the first commercially available electric light. (The world's first motion picture studio was in Jersey City.) The first chlorinated drinking water system — in the world — was switched on in Jersey City, in 1908. In 1928, Jersey City had the best drinking water in the US, and no cases of typhoid fever. Bubble wrap and modern air-conditioning were invented in New Jersey. What do transistors, condensed soup, and Band-Aids have in common? All invented in New Jersey. Princeton University, one of the leading educational institutions in the world, is in New Jersey. Pizza was not invented in New Jersey, but it was perfected in Tenafly, after being served with bacon, pineapple, and cornflakes to rubes in Chicago.

What does all of this mean? It means that due to its compact size, New Jersey has more smart people living in it than any other state in the Union. The actual count is 362 smart people per square inch. And herein lies the problem: they are nose to ass in a state where job-related angst, soul-crushing traffic, and oppressive taxes are entwined to create a day-to-day Valentine.

How crowded is it in New Jersey? In 2015, the Garden State was the most densely populated state in the Union, with 1,218 people per mile. Every mile. The state is roughly the size of a mall parking lot and is home to 8,958,013 people.

These statistics paint a picture that is hard to visualize, especially if you live in Wyoming, a place with 912 antelope (all with first names) per registered voter. Consider Guttenberg, NJ. It is 4 city blocks wide and 13 city blocks long. It is home to 11,176 people. (It is a pretty nice place to live, if you want to live in Hudson County.) Most of these people leave for work or school at the same time each day. (Just imagine what a tsunami of people looks like.) Yet Jersey City topped these figures in 2010, with 16,736 per square mile. Many of these people

have dogs that shit once each day, and do so on the sidewalk.
Is it any wonder that tempers flare? Jersey City is home to 117 languages, which can be heard at the same time each morning as thousands of people greet each other with, "I can't believe I stepped in dog shit again."

New Jersey ranks third, fifth, or seventh for taxes in the nation, depending on how they are computed. The state spends upward of $15k per year on each student and the money has to come from someplace. Blessed by God and nature with oil refineries and huge tank farms skirting Newark Bay and Linden, gas prices recently dipped below $2 bucks per gallon in the Garden State. People danced in the streets — naked. Just 4 years ago, gas prices were tickling $4 per gallon mark and people were walking to work in bare, bleeding feet. To celebrate the new era of cheap gas, New Jersey's governor signed into law a .23 cent gas tax increase and the state turned sullen. I listened to folks in grocery stores, in parks, on beaches, and even in church, curse the new tax, swearing revenge on the asshole(s) responsible. Cheap gas, and having an attendant to pump it, are two of the remaining benefits of life in New Jersey. Most New Jersey residents regard both as a constitutional right.

Yet it is the traffic that amazes visitors to the tranquil Garden State. The average New Jersey resident owns 9 cars and drives them all at the same time on Friday night — either headed to the shore or to what passes for lake country. It can take an hour to drive from Parsippany to Denville, NJ — two towns barely separated by a common attitude — at rush hour. On a historical tablet, somewhere on US-46 by the Jersey City reservoir, are the words, "If God wanted humanity to go from Parsippany to Denville in under an hour, he would have made them the same place."

One of my closest friends lives in Hackettstown, NJ, and now lists Interstate 80 as his home address.

"I spend 6 hours a day sitting in the car on this road, commuting 33 miles in each direction, so I decided to list it as my home address. I can now get a pizza delivered to my car as I sit on the Denville hill," said Stewie Effanucci. (Stewie is a traditional New Jersey first name.)

One brilliant New Jersey entrepreneur is applying the Amazon business model to the daily commute for thousands. His company is called

"Get Bent New Jersey" and he caters meals, pedicures, manicures, hair cuts, and companionship for Garden State drivers trapped in their cars going to and from work.

"By the time drivers arrive home, they've had something to eat... They've had their hair or their nails done... They've relaxed a little... And through a special service, they can even be bitched at so they feel like they've had quality time with a spouse," said Joey "Pyro" Laquatz, company founder. (Pyro is a traditional New Jersey middle name.)

Some commuters use this time to listen to audio books and to learn other languages. One Succasunna, NJ resident, Irving Grenwell, learned French, German, and Sanskrit in a single week.

In 2098, when all of the planned improvements and expansions are completed on the New Jersey Turnpike, the road will be 462 lanes wide, running from the Atlantic Ocean on the east while overhanging the Delaware River by 15 feet in the west. In 2042, the Garden State Parkway will be re-designated from a state toll road to a "temporary traffic sanctuary" in the Toms River area, where many children are born in cars and reach three years old before exiting in Seaside Heights.

Why am I so hard on New Jersey here, and throughout parts of this book?

Because it is my God-given right. I was born in New Jersey... Jersey City to be exact. I spent my childhood in Hudson County. Most of my adult life was spent in New Jersey. This book was written in New Jersey. Most of it's action happens in New Jersey. I knew New Jersey gangsters and politicians. I knew newspaper reporters in New Jersey. I knew cops. I knew the places that passed for rural in New Jersey and the urban alleys that provided refuge. I knew the state's roads of escape (metaphysical and otherwise). For the exception of two, every woman I have ever loved came from New Jersey. I knew that look of womanly empathy, when I was about to get laid, and that other look, when they were about to throw me from a moving car. I have stepped in acres of dog shit. I have earned the right to bitch about New Jersey.

It burns my ass when folks from states that have a third spigot on the kitchen sink — for vanilla ice cream — laugh at New Jersey. It gets me pissed when well-intentioned people, who grew up in the shadow of

Mayberry R.F.D., laugh at the pressures of day-to-day life in New Jersey. And I get riled when those, who come from states where trees can vote, cringe at New Jersey politics, the basic principles of which were honed in the Roman Colosseum. My grandfather, Michael Fitzpatrick, a dedicated Irish Democrat, once said, "Me politics is like me religion... Based on faith... Hard to prove... And motivated by the threat of vicious social recrimination." My sweet Irish grandmother, Bridie Murphy, who could throw a baked potato or a hand grenade the length of a boarding house, once said, "Start every day with a prayer and a smile... Then shoot one of the hostages." They came to New Jersey in the late 1890's for the interactive political atmosphere.

You have to live in New Jersey a full ten years before you can laugh at it. And you have to have been born in Jersey City before you can seriously criticize the place. Now I have bad news for New Jersey residents born in places like Newark, Camden, Metuchen, or Livingston: no one native to Jersey City really gives a shit about those places either.

New Jersey is a forge upon which souls are hammered or against which second-rate dreams are broken. The latest scientific calculations place the exact geological and cultural center of the earth at "Boulevard Drinks," in Journal Square, Jersey City. It is from here that all reason and logic descend. In his wisdom, God gave residents of Hudson County, NJ, an accent like broken glass fingernails against a chalkboard. This was so weaker people (everybody else) could mark them with suspicion. Otherwise, folks from Jersey City would conquer the earth. I once loved a woman from New England. She was flawless in every regard, and oozed sensuality from every pore. She was fascinated by my outlook, my insular sense of innocence, and by the way I wrote... But I lost ground every time I opened my mouth. After three weeks of perfect bliss, she tossed me. Her parting words were, "Your accent clashes with all of my outfits."

I was crushed. Then remembered where I was from. I replied with one of Shakespeare's lesser known lines: "Clash this," I said, gesturing to a part of my anatomy.

Frank Sinatra, originally from Hoboken, NJ, sang a song about New York City. The lyrics included the line, "If you can make it there, you can make anywhere..." New York City is where people from Jersey City go for practice.

Appendix Two

# "INDISPUTABLE NEW JERSEY FACTS"

**Fact #1**
How to get an instant kick in the balls from a New Jersey Resident...

When a person says they are from New Jersey, many residents of other states will reply, "What exit?" For some reason, people from Minnesota, Wisconsin, Utah, and Nevada think this is humor. It is not regarded as humor in New Jersey, as it bears no reference to fornication. This is actually secret code to all New Jersey residents. It means, "Please kick me in the balls as hard as possible." The joke is based on the fact that there are 250 boroughs, 52 cities, 15 towns, 245 townships and 3 villages, with more than 8 million people, all in a space the size of two large Texas ranches. Some of these designations overlap, but nearly all are served by one to four exits off a major highway.

I once saw some jerk pull this humorless gag on an elderly Catholic nun, from Convent Station, NJ. She kicked him in the balls faster than the speed of light.

**Fact #2**
If at first you don't succeed in getting kicked in the balls...

Upon hearing that a person is from the Garden State, many non-New Jersey residents will remark, "New Joisey?" No one from New Jersey ever said "Joisey." This is how people in far-off lands, like Queens (New York City), Brooklyn (New York City) and Flatbush (a subset of Brooklyn) were reputed to say "New Jersey." Saying "Joisey" to a person from "New Jersey" is a secret code meaning, "Please kick me in the balls as hard as possible."

• If you want to sound like a local, the state is pronounced "NU Jur-ZEEEE."

- Likewise, the largest city in New Jersey, Newark, is pronounced "Nork."
- Boonton, NJ, is pronounced "BOOtun."
- Once a thriving network of pig farms, Secaucus is pronounced "SEE-CAW-KUS" with equal emphasis on each syllable. Call it "Suh-CAW-kis" and you will be identified as a douche. Like Bayonne, Secaucus is regarded with suspicion and doubt by the true core of Hudson County.

**Fact #3**
Money is relative in New Jersey...

In 2006, the State of New Jersey paid an ad agency $250,000 to develop a state slogan that was never used — "We'll Win You Over." That's more than $80,000 per word. A local radio station heard of this ridiculous cost and came up with the alternative: "Our State Slogan Cost More Than Your House." I asked a dozen or so New Jersey residents if they knew the current state slogan. None did. That's because New Jersey doesn't have one. Some folks suggested:
- What The Hell Is That Smell!
- Honk If You've Been Indicted!
- We Don't Give A Shit!
- What The Fuck Are You Looking At?
- The Eat Shit And Die State!

The state legislature is moving to enact a law making the new state motto, "The Garden State." This is about what you would expect from a state legislature.

**Fact # 4**
Why is the most densely populated state in the union known as "The Garden Sate?"

There are two schools of thought about this one:
- Speaking on Jersey Day at the Centennial Exhibition in Philadelphia, August 24, 1876, Abraham Browning, of Camden, described New Jersey as a barrel filled with good things to eat, open at both ends, being emptied by New York City and Philadelphia. The name has since stuck.

- New Jersey was the original Garden of Eden. Eve, an incredibly beautiful woman was told not to eat of the "Beef Steak" tomatoes.

She did, and she got Adam to eat them too. They were subsequently banned from heaven. They didn't care. They lived in a place where clams, oysters, corn, tomatoes, blueberries, and peaches appeared year-after-year in abundance. Eve demanded a house from Adam. He had never seen one before. He built a wooden structure 20-feet-wide and two-miles long. He called it a boardwalk. Their two sons, Cain and Able, were conceived under the boardwalk, starting another New Jersey tradition. For their first anniversary, Adam gave Eve a ferris wheel. It all worked out.

**Fact #5**
New Jersey Produces World-Class Tomatoes...

The State of New Jersey produces the best tomatoes in the world. End of story. New Jersey tomatoes are so good that I will not buy tomatoes out of season, no matter how nice they look in any supermarket. It is just better to wait. I will only buy New Jersey farm-raised tomatoes from roadside stands. The classic New Jersey beefsteak tomato, which is getting hard to find even in New Jersey, routinely weighs a pound, is usually brownish red, and cracks from the accumulated juice inside. This is the best tomato in the world and it costs a fortune to grow, pack and ship. (There is a move to mass grow this tomato and it is a mistake.) New Jersey-raised heirloom tomatoes are the ugliest tomatoes in the world, and among the best tasting. Oddly shaped and peculiarly colored, one roadside stand had a sign over them that read, "These tomatoes are supposed to look like this. So fuck you."

Here is a recipe for an authentic Jersey tomato salad.
1) Cut the tomato into wedges; 2) add a pinch of salt; 3) eat.

Here is a recipe for an authentic New Jersey bacon, lettuce, and tomato sandwich: 1) Buy a loaf of craft-baked bread at a real bakery; 2) at a roadside stand, buy three Beef Steak tomatoes or heirloom tomatoes; 3) buy a head of fresh local lettuce; 4) at a butcher store, buy a pound of thick-cut, genuinely smoked bacon; 5) wash the bird shit off the tomatoes and the sand out of the lettuce; 6) cook the bacon until just crisp; 7) toast the bread; 8) slather the bread with Hellman's Real Mayonnaise; 9) use 1 crisp slice of lettuce that overhangs the bread; 10) use four quarter-inch slices of tomato; 11) use three slices of bacon (cut in half). Only drink ice cold tea or lemonade with this sandwich.
• Tip: Eat this while wearing a painters tarp.

**Fact #6**
The truth about New Jersey Corn...

Jersey corn is so good that it was used as local currency until 1964. An ear of corn was worth about 26¢, and was accepted as payment in candy stores, newsstands, post offices and hardware stores. As the corn season wound down, the value of a single ear would increase to $15.46. New Jersey women with birthdays in late July and throughout August prefer getting a bushel of corn to a dozen roses. In 1628, local Indians taught the incoming waves of Dutch slummers how to plant asparagus, but kept the virtues of yellow corn a secret from the "wooden-footed" bastards.

- How to cook Jersey Corn: 1) Bring a pot of water to boil; 2) drop four ears of shucked corn into the water; 3) when the water returns to a full boil, cook the corn for exactly two minutes.
- How to buy New Jersey Corn: Ask the person running the roadside stand when corn harvested within an hour is delivered to the stand. Buy that corn.
- Babies conceived during New Jersey's tomato and corn season are healthier, smarter, and better looking than children conceived on scrapple, fried green tomatoes, or cattle fodder sold as corn in other states.

**Fact #7**
New Jersey diners are the model for the rest of the world... Often copied. Never duplicated.

There are 525 diners in New Jersey and the worst of them is better than the best in any other state, for the possible exception of Auburn, Nebraska.

- In a New Jersey diner, you will be seated in 30 seconds or less.
- You will have coffee in 32 seconds or less.
- The coffee is always fresh.
- If you are a guy, the waitress will call you "Hon."
- You can get breakfast 24/7 in a New Jersey diner.
- Pea soup, the thickness of green magma, is served on Thursdays.
- The menu will have 364 items on it, from dolmades (stuffed grape leaves) to roast duck.
- Every diner has a display case of fancy baked goods in front. (Everything in this case with white frosting will taste like shit.)
- Never order a liverwurst sandwich in a diner!
- The most popular item in a New Jersey diner between 2am and 4am is a cheeseburger deluxe.

- If your cheeseburger is gray in the middle, the diner is a dive.
- There are 17 dive diners in New Jersey.
- The "Tick-Tock Diner" on Route 3 is a classic New Jersey diner.
- Mastori's in Bordentown, NJ is the best non-conventional diner in the state.
- Mastori's in Bordentown, NJ has the best baked goods of any diner in the state. All of their baked goods are wonderful.

## Fact #8
New Jersey seafood is without comparison on the east coast...

New Jersey has been enforcing clean water practices and advanced aquaculture for more than 50 years. As a result, New Jersey bays and coastal waters produce some of the best-tasting fish caught anywhere.
- The "Cape May Salt" is a local world-class oyster that is as good as anything flown in from Prince Edward island. Tangy, with a hint of natural salt, this oyster is typical of New Jersey shellfish. Try to limit yourself to 2 dozen at one sitting.
- New Jersey clams on the half-shell are sweet and delicious. More than a drop of Tabasco sauce or an equal amount of lemon juice is an insult.
- Lobster is caught of Belmar, NJ and is the equal in quality of what you will get in Maine. Fresher too, if you're in Ocean County.
- Water off the New Jersey coast is kept cold for lobster by throwing 15,000 mothers-in-law over the side each week. Sometimes the seawater freezes.

## Fact #9
New Jersey civil servants are assholes.

Absolutely not true. A paperwork challenge brought me to Trenton, NJ — the state capital. I dreaded this trip, imagining the indifference, the contempt, and the stupidity of the state employees I'd have to deal with. Here's what I discovered:
- While waiting for a state office to open, every employee who walked past me said, "good morning," with a smile, and asked if they could help me. I suspected a conspiracy.
- When the office was officially open, at the stroke of 9am, somebody walked me through the process and made calls to another office on my behalf.
- I was in and out of the other office, documents in hand, before my driver could park the car.

- The New Jersey Division of Motor Vehicles Office, in Hamilton, NJ, is one of the best run, most efficient, government offices I have been to a long time. Not only is it a paradigm for every motor vehicle facility in the state, it is model for service and politeness the world over.
- Whatever they are paying the staff and management of the New Jersey Division of Motor Vehicles in Hamilton, NJ, it is not enough.

**Fact #10**
Roughly one in every 15 New Jersey residents is a douche.

Out a population of 8.9 million New Jersey residents, approximately 533,333 are douches. This is well-within the 50-state douche average established by Congress. This last statement is questionable as Congress has also approved acceptable levels of lead in drinking water and bug shit in chocolate bars. To the casual traveler, New Jersey may seem to have an endless supply of douches. This is because the state is so densely populated... And the douches tend to band together, as they are shunned by everyone else. Also, drivers, pedestrians, pizza delivery guys, divorce attorneys, and religious leaders who flip you the bird are not automatic douches. (Many of these folks have alternate careers as life coaches and yoga instructors.)

- There are more douches in Washington, D.C. than in New Jersey, Los Angeles, and Disney World combined.
- There are two kinds of douches commonly found in New Jersey: the one who farts in a crowded elevator and the one who says, "That wasn't me."
- New Jersey made it illegal to "publicly call someone a douche in 1843." Not one person has tried to sue somebody in the state's history for allegedly being called a douche. No one wants to admit they have been called a douche.
- Look carefully at the people who sit in "Section D" at any ballpark.
- Remember that kid who used to shit in his pants in the third grade and tattle on everyone? He is now a Washington, D.C. insider and has season tickets to section "D" at the ballpark.
- In New Jersey social circles, it is possible to be a highly respected raging asshole, but not a douche.
- If you live in New Jersey and have 14 friends who are not douches, guess what?

Riepe's View Of New Jersey

* Map is not shown to scale

# "MY INTRODUCTION TO NEW JERSEY DOUCHES AND AN ACCUSATION"

Jersey City was where I saw my first urban rat running in the street on Boyd Avenue, below Mallory (on the westside). I was eight years old. I was more fascinated than afraid. The rat was utterly sinister. This was the abandoned barracks neighborhood in the early 1960s. Four years later, I found a black widow spider in a vacant lot. The spider was mesmerizing and terrifying at the same time. That summer, I learned there were girls who ran in the street with boys, and that there was something mesmerizing and terrifying about them too. One of these girls lived a few blocks away. Her name was Christina. I passed through her neighborhood a few times each week and felt encouraged to strike up a conversation, as she never spit nor cursed as I walked by.

I smiled and said "Hello."

Looking me up and down, Christina replied, "What are you? A douche?"

As vicious as this sounds, it was actually worse. She pronounced "douche" like it was spelled "doooooooosh." She said it loud enough to bring scores of people out on their "stoops." In Jersey City, where houses back right up to the sidewalk and space is at a premium, a simple flight of steps normally extends from the front door to the street. This is a called a "stoop," which is a Dutch word going back to the time when the area was part of the "New Netherlands" colony. Jersey City residents who sit out on the steps for hours on end are said to be in a "stooper."

In Christina's neighborhood, people sat on their stoops and waited for momentous things to happen, such as the arrival of the ice cream truck or having a car drive the wrong way on a one-way street. Identifying a stranger as a douche was like an announcement for the circus. On this occasion, hundreds of people — maybe more — pointed at me from their stoops and yelled "Douche! Douche!"

I fled.

This was the first time I had heard this word. It was ghastly enough coming from a pretty girl, and utterly mortifying shouted by a mob. Christina was one of these girls who got her breasts early, and who hung around with some of the toughest eggs ever hatched by Jersey City "Morlocks." (The Morlocks were a mutant species made famous by H.G. Wells in his epic novel: *The Time Machine*. The opposite of the Morlocks was the "Eloi.") I bore all the earmarks of a Catholic school seventh grader: clean-cut, able to use multi-syllabic words in conversation, and under the misimpression that applied education was the first level of attraction for women. This tainted me as an unmistakable Eloi douche to those in Morlock café society. Morlock social standards were based on the concept that whatever you wanted was yours, as long as you could beat the shit out of the person who currently held it. The guys in Christina's milieu could beat the shit out of just about anybody, and often did. She was one of the fast-developing women who appreciated this persuasive quality in a man.

Soon thereafter, I watched a neighborhood tough openly cop a cheap feel from her by simply saying, "Yo, 'Steena. Ca' mova heah." Her response was to slowly saunter over, swinging her hips, with a taunting smile. I was dumbfounded. The tough's forehead literally overhung his lower lip, nearly obscuring his forward vision. His head combined the most distinctive elements of a bass and a bison. But he had just beaten six other guys into powder sustaining his desirability as a romantic interest. I would later write an essay about this titled: *Love Among Young Morlocks And Why I am So Jealous*.

The word "douche" was burned in my mind. I knew that being called a "douche" was seriously bad, just like shitting in your pants was bad, though not as clearly defined. While the Jersey City caste system was apparently limited to three initial categories — eloi, morlock, and douche — the last of these was mob subjective. Technically, my career in public relations began here with "mob management." I was desperate to prove I was a not a douche, and twice as desperate to hide the fact that I might be, according to Christina. As critical as this issue was, I was also being pressured on the home front to win science fairs, get involved with Little League, and to prove myself academically. I regarded these three additional priorities as pointless distractions compared to the study of Morlock tits.

Jersey City was where I learned to write. My mother once said, "The only thing I regret in life is having taught my son Jack to talk." Realizing her error when I was still young, she resolved to teach me how to write. "Put everything down on paper," she said. "Because you sound like a horse's ass whenever you open your mouth." Having been born in New Jersey, mom was an advocate of getting the bad news out in front. My writing lessons began with an emphasis on reading. Mom said, "There are two kinds of people... Those who can read and those who walk on their knuckles."

I was tempted to ask, "Why is it the knuckle-walkers who get to cop the cheap feels," but I wasn't supposed to know what a cheap feel was in the seventh grade.

My mother explained that writing gave one an opportunity to think about something before committing it to paper, and to clear direction to thought, even if it meant writing it over and over again. "The trick," my mom said, "was to write something in such a way that the reader hears your voice in it, and wants to read it again." This philosophy was lost on a kid who regarded all forms of writing as "composition," and therefore as work. Since I couldn't grasp the significance of what my mom had just told me, she explained that all I had to do was believe it, or that she would kill me, and bury me in the yard. Once, she even showed me the shovel with which a shallow grave would be dug.

Despite this threat, I resisted.

A change in schools (one Catholic grammar school for a tougher Catholic grammar school) introduced me to summer book reports. It wasn't enough that the school year should be ruined, but the summer was now to be spoiled as well. My mother would scour the public library for books like, *Young Edison,* or *A Boy And His Dog,* or *Fighting Father Duffy.* She had to do this because I couldn't be trusted to pick out books. I would come home with *Paddington Bear,* or *The Wind In The Willows.* (I liked the character of Paddington and *The Wind In The Willows* is just a great book.) I also favored books on crime, like James F. Johnson's: *The Man who Sold The Eiffel Tower.* My mother eventually told the librarians not to let me check out books with talking frogs and otters, nor those that defined various felonies and prostitution as engaging lifestyles. (One librarian explained that I had told her those "other" books were for my invalid mother.)

I was twelve when I read *King Solomon's Mines*. "Can I do a book report on this?" I asked.

My mother was astounded that I had read a book, labelled "classic adventure," without having a gun held to my head.

"Sure," she replied.

I couldn't put it down. I read it twice. *King Solomon's Mines* was unbelievably exciting. It was the first time I realized that books could and would always be better than television. The book report wrote itself. These rudimentary literary reviews were based on a series of innocuous questions such as: when did the book take place; who were the principle characters; and what was the story about? For the first time ever, I was having fun recounting the details of a story I'd read. The report ran to two pages.

In answer to the question, what did you like about this book, I penned, "The wholesale slaughter of warring tribal factions sets the backdrop of raw adventure and insatiable greed, as yet another party of British freebooters attempt to loot the Dark Continent of a diamond legacy that predates the bible. The flawed characters in *King Solomon's Mines* transcend the predictable aspirations of douches like *Young Edison* and *Fighting Father Duffy*."

I read this to my mom.

When I got up off the floor, my mom tenderly asked, "Where did you hear this word douche? Are the girls who run with boys in the street calling you a douche?"

I nodded.

"This is why you must only hang around with your own kind," my mom replied. "It isn't easy being a member of the Eloi." (According to H.G. Wells, the Eloi were beautiful, sophisticated, and philosophical people. The Morlocks ate them. The time was coming when I'd dream of being eaten by a Morlock woman.)

"And this is another reason why you must join Little League. Everyone who plays baseball is cool," added my mom.

"But I hate baseball."

"Don't ever say that. Only douches say stuff like that. Do you want people to think you're a douche?" my mother asked. The question seemed moot considering Christina's perspective.

"Are there girls who are my kind?" I asked.

My mom hesitated and told me "yes." This was one of two falsehoods she ever told me. The second one was, "No one will ever hire someone to write incredible bullshit instead of the truth." Mom had never heard of public relations.

The Christina episode is how I came to learn that a society that favors the underdog and cheers when the runt of the litter comes out on top, instinctively gives the stink eye at the slightest suspicion that someone may be a douche. This troubled me. I had questions: what exactly was a douche; was there an official douche list; did anyone ever get off the douche list; and was there a 12-step program for douches? I couldn't trust my mother for this information. I already suspected that she thought Christina might be right.

# "THE CHARACTERISTICS OF DOUCHES"

The word "douche" is French, which to the minds of some Jersey City-born etymologists is suspect in itself. It means "a shower of water." In techno terms, it refers to the bag-like device once used to occasionally flush vaginas. The full and correct expression is "douchebag." Somehow, perhaps in the Dark Ages, vagina flushing got a bad rap. Knowing what I know now, I would have set up a vagina wash on the sidewalk when I was a kid instead of peddling Kool-Aid. The last version of the modern-day douchebag was a hot water bottle with 10 feet of hose attached to it. I have never known a woman to use one. I have never even seen one (a douchebag, not a woman). However, in my early motorcycle days, I was in a bar where women were as forward as men, and a lady, who'd ridden Harleys with General "Black Jack" Pershing in WWI, tried to join one of my weekend forays.

"I pack light," she cackled. "Two bottles of Scotch and a douchebag."

I thought about this for a second and replied, "Why the hell would you pack your husband?"

The streetwise meaning of the word douche is "a reprehensible man who drips meal worms from his mouth and who must breath an atmosphere of anal gas to live." While this definition seems to apply in most cases, it is more figurative than physically accurate. Outside of Congress, it is impossible to envision a society of fart-breathing individuals. Only men can be douches. Women have a category of their own.

Meeting real douches freed me from the fear that I could be one. For one thing, both of my eyes were not on the same side of my nose, which is a dead giveaway. Also, I would never scratch my ass in graduation and wedding pictures. I never met a public relations executive who was a douche. But I have met a few who were newspaper reporters. Years ago when I was in politics, a reporter once asked me, "So what did your boys steal this week?" I replied, "A brass placard that says 'Douche,' but they took it off your office door."

I asked more than a hundred people to define a "douche;" to list the qualities inherent to douches; and to describe douche-like behavior. Most of them stuttered and sputtered. It would seem that douches are not easily described. But when I asked these same people if they personally knew any douches, they rattled off names that went back to grammar school. I was stunned. Classmates of mine from high school had no problem naming several douches in scant seconds. Most of them named the same douches though they hadn't had any communication with each other, especially on this subject, in years. One former high school chum couldn't remember the last name of the biggest douche he met in freshman year. I guessed it right off. The two of us busted out laughing.

In an online poll I conducted, most respondents commonly used terms like arrogant, mean, narcissistic, and inconsiderate to describe the average douche. Most stated douches were incapable of empathy. Nearly all cited a substantial degree of innate stupidity as integral to the character of a douche, as well as falsehood as a reflex. Some folks found it easier to define douches by their actions. These included:

1) A real douche dumps a woman by text as opposed to doing it in person.
2) A huge douche fires somebody from a "volunteer" position via text, realizes that was a douche thing to do, so then cuts-and-pastes the exact wording into an email and sends it to an old email address. According to this survey respondent, "That douche lives as close to the center of New Jersey as is possible. Did you ever look at a map and notice that the state looks like it is bent over taking a dump? Well where that guy lives is right where the enema nozzle would go."
3) A true douche begs you to do them a favor... Then takes credit for that action to promote themselves while making you look bad.
4) Accomplished douches bathe in schadenfreude: pleasure derived from another's misfortune. Often they are the source of that person's misfortune.
5) A douche is one who sees life as his personal mirror.
6) One high school douche elected himself to that position for life by reminding the teacher that he had forgotten to assign algebra homework over a holiday weekend.

7) The douche is the guy who shows up for the annual ride with the motorcycle in bad repair. He invariably breaks down and delays the group while the experts struggle to get it running again. He laters reports he fixed it himself.
8) The boss who is an evil douche says, "Tell me when you have a great idea. I'll make sure you get the credit for it."
9) The boss who is a stupid douche fires you because you threaten his credibility, then hires other douches to guarantee he looks good.
10) A certified corporate douche places short-term shareholder satisfaction over long-term product excellence.

Speaking from experience, the acquaintance of mine who seduced my first lover was not a douche. He was a snake and true to his manly character. The guy who made sure everyone knew about it was a douche.

Classic douches tend to be both cheap and consummate snitches. One douche of my acquaintance would regularly find reasons to give waitresses a hard time, as an excuse not to tip. A friend of mine had a college roommate who was a first class douche. He'd use a marker to put his name on cans of tuna fish he'd bought, before stacking them in the communal refrigerator. (Anybody who stacks canned tuna in a refrigerator is an instant douche.) And a third douche, when confronted with a similar social misdemeanor not only denied it, but claimed he was ready to identify others douches guilty of identical crimes.

Some survey respondents described momentary behavior as being douche-worthy. These feats included: throwing lit cigarettes out a car window (onto a biker), foraging among the lunches in the workplace refrigerator, and cutting people off in traffic. In my experience, these activities are more in keeping with behavior attributed to assholes. An individual can become an asshole when they are aggravated, distracted, drunk, or plagued by deadly testosterone build-up. Their assholishness may pass. Also, women are fully capable of being assholes on occasion. But being a douche is 24/7 forever. If you are a douche in the boardroom, on the sales floor, or at the university lectern, then you are one in the bedroom and behind the wheel of your minivan too.

While the word "douche" is deeply rooted in New Jersey, you might go a week or a month without hearing it. But when you do hear it, it carries the wallop of a pistol shot. Here, the word is pronounced "doosh" (rhymes with whoosh). But there are apparent degrees of douche-dom that are expressed by the emphasis placed on the center of the word.

For example, lingering for an extra second or two on the "oosh" part implies an increased capacity for being a douche. The term "douchebag" may be clinically correct, but it is too cumbersome to flick like a poison dart. The words "doosh, doooosh," or the phrase, "you stoopid dooooosh" are infinitely more flickable. Use of the word "douchebag" may also identify the user as coming from west of Hudson County or from Canada, which could backfire.

Christina used an extended emphasis, saying "dooosh" to convey the idea that I had a serious character deficiency to assume I could merely introduce myself to one such as her. Basically, she was saying that not only was I a douche, but that I had the potential to be an extraordinary douche. Kids on the street grow in and out of idiomatic expressions on a yearly basis. I was surprised to discover that "douche" made it into the adult lexicon. Almost twenty years later, I worked for a rising star among local politicians. There was no Republican party in most of Hudson County at the time. Two Democrats, either "Row A" or "Row B" routinely ran against each other for positions like state senator, mayor, councilman or freeholder. The guy I worked for was smooth as silk. I never saw him in anything other than a perfectly tailored suit. He was precise in his movements and in his language. On this particular day, he had a meeting with a ranking citizen in opposition to just about everything: a meeting that had taken weeks to schedule. My boss cancelled it five minutes before zero hour.

"Why?" I asked.

"The guy is just an absolute douche," the politician replied.

I exploded into laughter. Not only was this candid answer hysterically funny, but to hear this cultured elected official lapse into saying "dooosh," was so thoroughly unpredictable. And yet as I approached the visiting citizen to cancel the meeting, all I could think of was, "This guy really does look like a douche." The trouble with identifying an individual as a douche is that you can never talk about this person again without thinking, "douche." Years later, a reporter asked if I knew "Billie So And So." I was looking for something on my desk and therefore distracted, when I replied, "The douche from the seventh ward?"

"That's the guy," the reporter replied.

The two of us busted out laughing.

# "A DARK DAY FOR NEW JERSEY"

Nothing offered greater cause for celebration than landfall on the New World shore in 1663... Unless you were attempting it in dense fog... In a water-logged craft... With a crew that had tried to abandon ship three times before. The ship wallowed in an incoming tide with barely a breeze to disturb the dripping sails. There was no horizon and the gray hue of death tinted the water and the sky. The muted boom of breakers, precursors of a wreck on unseen barrier islands, mocked the ship's bell, which tolled each time the vessel rolled.

This was the "Matilda," a worn-out, three-masted veteran of the guano Island trade route. Bird and bat guano was a highly sought-after fertilizer and the Matilda had been hauling it for 25 years, before being purchased for one last voyage: a one-way trip to the Americas. The ship's bottom was home to layers of bore worms and weeds, and the vessel could barely make 2 knots in a stiff breeze. Its hold appeared dry on initial inspection, but that was because powdered bat and bird shit filled every available crevice. The ship would be reeking and leaking on its second day at sea, but the die was cast for the crew, cargo, and passengers. No one realized that the brine of the ocean was reacting with the agents in the residual guano to dissolve the wood and fittings of the ship. This chemical reaction had a quarter-century head start on this dismal voyage.

The passengers, from four of Europe's most unusual families, huddled on deck against the masts, against the fog, and against each other, in sodden clothing dampened since the voyage began. Most had been drenched with sea water, puke, or piss since leaving port. Children clung to their mothers and the women clung to hope, while their men offered pointless opinions as to the handling of the ship. These were ignored by the captain and crew, who knew the significance of the breakers, and who were getting ready to swim for it. The ship threatened to broach before staggering through a narrow inlet into a sheltered bay. Experienced seamen said the landing was purely by chance, but those who believe in higher powers claimed the ship got through when destiny blinked.

The chop on the bay was nothing like the chaos of the ocean, and the ship seemed almost motionless. The fog was thick and right down to the water. This concealed the shape of the bay, which ran for miles to the north and south but which was only about a mile wide at this point. The Matilda ghosted west to within a hundred yards of the opposite shore and nosed aground in the soft sandy bottom. The anchor dropped into six feet of water.

The passengers raised an exhausted cheer. Women wept openly to be embraced by their husbands, as soon as the men could extract themselves from the ship's two open boats. (Fifty of these gentlemen had spent the last two days and nights crammed into these boats, expecting the ship to sink at a moment's notice.) Most of the men had no experience with the ocean nor ocean travel. Some were farmers. Others were weavers and cobblers. Two were blacksmiths. Several were ministers. Yet all had one thing in common: they were Douches. The first of the great European plagues had landed in the New World, in the place that would come to be known as New Jersey.

The Matilda had been purchased by "The Majority Of Ourselves," a loose confederation of four families: the Douchemoore's, the van der Douches, the Douchombres, and the Douchesacz for the purpose of transporting their entire genetic line to America. The scheme was to create for themselves — and for all Douches — a colony where they could all live in harmony, enjoying social freedoms as opposed to the suspicions, accusations, and recriminations generally extended to them. While they were not officially persecuted in England, Germany, France, nor anyplace else, those of the "Douche" line found themselves shunned. Shunned at the opera... Shunned at religious events... And shunned in nearly all aspects of social society. They were shunned by Kings and beggars; abbots and aldermen; and pimps and whores. The Douches dreamed of a change. They dreamed of a place where they would do all the shunning.

The move to the New World was part of a highly ambitious plan. First, the "Douche" families would consolidate their resources. Then they would become something of a political power, trading influence for a land grant. This would be followed by the voyage to America, and finally, the creation of the Douche colony.

There were problems from the beginning. Though the third of England's civil wars had been over for nine years, members of the Douchemoore family had been distrusted and hated by both sides of all three conflicts. It was said that the Douchemoores had turned their coats so often that they had revolving closets. This distrust extended to the van der Douches, who came from Amsterdam, and the Douchombres, who were Basques if you asked the French; or French, if you asked the Basques. The Douchesacz were Romanian Gypsies who were held in low esteem even by the other three "Douche" families. It is interesting that the "sacz" part of the "Douchesacz" name means "satchel" or "traveling bag." This is one of the first references to the term "douchebag." Technically speaking, there were douchebags long before the actual douchebag was invented.

Being natural born Douches, each of the four families tried to soak the other three for the lion's share of the trip costs. They had all planned for a quick departure, but the search for a suitable ship took longer than anticipated. It would take a year for the ship to rot sufficiently to meet the price these Douches were willing to pay. The Douches paid less for the Matilda than the repairs could legitimately cost to make her seaworthy. That amount also included the services of the captain and the crew, plus supplies for the trip. The crew was the scum of London's prisons and gutters. They were men whose sailing abilities were exaggerated by a desire to be as far away from the gallows as possible.

Missing was the land grant from King Charles II. His Majesty was a sport with a great sense of humor, an eye for pretty women, and a ruler who knew a good thing when he saw one.

"Is it my understanding that every Douche in the kingdom will be on this ship when it departs?" asked the King.

"Yes," your Majesty," replied Aleister Douchemoore, with a flourish.

"I'll sign," said the King.

The land grant gave the "Majority Of Ourselves" total ownership of a 18,000-acre tract, three days walk from any existing settlement or coast, to be governed by God and the principles of his church, provided none of the Douches returned to England for 100 years. But the Douches figured that the oldest among them could only walk 30 feet in three days, and they planned on settling close to the Dutch. So the ship's hold carried 1600 pairs of wooden shoes and 1600 chamber pots, some painted with windmills in the blue Delft fashion, and others with humorous sayings like "The donation Dutchmen willingly give."

The cheapest provisions the Douches could buy were plums that had been dried into prunes for the trip. There would be stewed prunes, stuffed prunes, roasted prunes, prune soup, and coarse prune cake for the trip. The voyage was supposed to run 65 days. It went 93. By day three, every Douche on the ship was walking around with one hand tightly held against their respective ass. (This led to a common New Jersey expression, "Don't hold your hand on your ass...") The last three weeks of the voyage were spent in storms so terrible that the crew openly spoke of abandoning the Douches. The Douche men countered this threat by sitting in the life boats 24 hours a day until the Matilda made landfall.

The Douches waded through the shallows and disembarked in the lower end of modern Barnegat Bay. In the European tradition, the religious leaders among them held a ceremony of praise and thanks. They staged this on the only quicksand in 30 square miles, however, and ten of them disappeared imploring divine help. It took 72 hours to offload the ship, which then dissolved like a huge Alka Seltzer tablet in the next high tide.

The New World's first douches had arrived to stay in what would soon be New Jersey.

These Douches were met by a tribe of indigenous native people who came to the area every year to eat clams, oysters, corn and tomatoes, while adding a much deeper tone to their strikingly handsome skin. These native people were lean, fit and laughed often in comparison to the European Douches, who were pallid, saggy, and burdened with opinions on everything. It was humid and hot during this time of year, and the native women collected clams in the ankle deep water wearing nothing but a tiny loin cloth, barely covering their asses, and an equally tiny top, that did more to enhance their savage beauty than to conceal it. This did not sit well with the Douche women, who according to the legends of the native peoples, had faces like the pooping end of a cat.

Like the true Douches they were, the new settlers insisted on converting the native people to a more civilized approach to life. This entailed wearing more clothes, smiling less, and obeying disagreeable folks who bore facial expressions like a cat's ass. The native people soon realized that the most respected among the Douches were the ones whose faces were permanently puckered with rules and a sense of social governability.

The native people had a truly remarkable sense of humor. They decided to inflict a neighboring tribe with the benefits of civilization and came up with a great way to get these Douches to move on. The chiefs shoved extra moccasins, shirts, bits of hides, and even small sticks into the front of their loin cloths, and strut around to the obvious delight of their indigenous women. The Douche men were fascinated. The chiefs then claimed that outrageously huge "man tomahawks" were the result of drinking the bitter juice of a little red berry that grew only in the ghastly swamps of the now fabled Pine Barrens.

The Douche men were not only prepared to drag their Douche women into the swamps, but they wanted to pay for the exclusive privilege for doing so. So on a blistering hot day in August, the Douches traded 800 pairs of wooden shoes and 800 chamber pots for a 30-mile tract of bog, swamp, snakes, and mosquitoes. They then walked 170 miles, less than 60 as the crow flies, led in circles by an unnamed native guide, to a cranberry bush. The guide then shook a few hands and disappeared. The male Douches busted out laughing and said, "Boy are these indigenous native people stupid." Then they stripped the cranberry bush bare, ate every berry, and stood around waiting for something to happen. Something did. It rained for a week.

The indigenous native people living in the swamp got the joke, but they also got the Douches. True to their nature, Douche men swore the cranberries made a huge difference in their personal profiles. They stayed. The local tribe even helped them build a fort, which spanned an area the size of modern football field. The Douches didn't think a fort was necessary, but the indigenous people told horrible tales of a devil that roamed the pines at night, taking souls through puckered faces. The fort was built of pine, pegged together, and was almost as tight as a barrel. There was also no gate, and the native people ran off, leaving the Douches trapped inside. The Douches remained in captivity for two or three years, until they realized they could easy climb over the six-foot walls.

One by one, the Douches would slip over the wall and attempt to disappear in colonial New Jersey society. Douches played a prominent part in developing British rule in the New Jersey colony, advocating a tax on tea and on stamps. Before long, the Douches were on the short end of the stick. George Washington mentioned this select group pf people during the dreadful winter of the Jockey Hollow encampment. The Continental Army was starving while New Jersey barns were filled with a record harvest and locked by their Douche owners. Washington was alleged to have said, "What is it with these Loyalist New Jersey Douches?"

The Douches never had their own colony. They never became a political movement. They never became a special interest group. And yet, everybody knows at least one. Douches became widespread enough to become a household word, but no longer rate as a proper noun. Yet they are still a social anomaly. Corporate America is riddled with douches. Washington D.C. has an 87 percent douche rate. Many douches have had careers as college professors, traffic cops, and authors of twelve-step guides. Douches gravitate toward occupations that allow them to tell everybody else what to do.

New Jersey has one defense against any potential douche take-over. In New Jersey, when anyone tries to tell anybody else what to do, the reflex response is "Kiss my ass."

As for the Douche settlement New Jersey? The pines reclaimed it. It's exact location is lost. New Jersey recovered. The state has not one more nor one less douche than any other place in the U.S. New Jersey residents are just more vocal in identifying them. New Jersey children as young as three years old can identify other kids and adults who are douches. In New Jersey, dogs are trained to bark at douches. Pigeons shit on them. Motorists blow their horns at them.

Douches have endured the crucible of history... Though being identified as one still instills doubt.